SEARCHING FOR AUGUSTA

The Forgotten Angel of Bastogne

MARTIN KING

LYONS
PRESS

Guilford, Connecticut

An imprint of The Rowman & Littlefield Publishing Group, Inc.
4501 Forbes Blvd., Ste. 200
Lanham, MD 20706
www.rowman.com

Distributed by NATIONAL BOOK NETWORK

Copyright © 2017 by Martin King
This Lyons Press edition 2020

Maps by Melissa Baker

Jacket photo credits: Portrait of Augusta on front and street scene on front flap by unknown photographer (author's personal archive); soldier photos on front and back by unknown photographer (public domain); author photo on back flap by Ashley Rae King

British Library Cataloguing in Publication Information available

Library of Congress Cataloging-in-Publication Data

Names: King, Martin, 1959- author.
Title: Searching for Augusta : the forgotten angel of Bastogne / Martin King.
Description: Guilford, Connecticut : Lyons Press, 2017. | Includes bibliographical references.
Identifiers: LCCN 2017038114| ISBN 9781493029075 (hardcover : alk. paper) | ISBN 9781493029082 (e-book) | ISBN 9781493049424 (paper : alk. paper)
Subjects: LCSH: Chiwy, Augusta. | Ardennes, Battle of the, 1944-1945. | World War, 1939-1945—Medical care—Belgium—Bastogne. | Nurses—Belgium—Bastogne—Biography. | Nurses—Congo (Democratic Republic)—Biography. | Bastogne (Belgium)—Biography.
Classification: LCC D756.5.A7 K539 2017 | DDC 940.54/219348—dc23
LC record available at https://lccn.loc.gov/2017038114

♾™ The paper used in this publication meets the minimum requirements of American National Standard for Information Sciences—Permanence of Paper for Printed Library Materials, ANSI/NISO Z39.48-1992.

To Ambassador Denise Campbell Bauer,
for her wonderful support and encouragement

CONTENTS

Acknowledgments

MANY THANKS TO MY WIFE FREYA FOR HER CONTINUED SUPPORT FOR this work. Posthumous thanks to my late grandfather, Private 4829 Joseph Henry Pumford, who fought at Passchendaele in World War I and provided invaluable inspiration for all of my early interest in military history. He was promoted to corporal but then demoted for punching out a sergeant. He was unique in managing to terrify both sides in that particular conflict. Also, not forgetting offspring Allycia and Ashley Rae, brother Graham, sisters Sandra and Debbie, brother-in-law Mark, nephews Ben and Jake, and niece Rachel.

Special thanks to my dear friends, Mike Edwards, Lt. Col. Jason Nulton (retired), Comm. Jeffrey Barta (retired), Dan and Judy Goo, Gen. Graham Hollands, Elizabeth Thienpont-Dugaillez (Augusta's best friend, who assisted with translation), for their wonderful support and encouragement. Grateful thanks to my friend Roland Gaul at the National Museum of Military History, Diekirch, and Helen Patton.

Thank you also to Mrs. Carol Fish and the staff at the United States Military Academy at West Point, and to Rudy Beckers and Greg Hanlon at Fort Dix for their ongoing support.

Thank you also to Eric Lemoine, Bruno, Serge, Michel, Olivier, and Joel, the fantastic team at the Heintz Barracks "Nuts Cave" in Bastogne, for allowing me unique access to everything I needed there.

Many thanks to my dear friend Mike Collins, who organized the photographs, Rick Rinehart, Lynn Zelem, Evan Helmlinger, Sara Givens, and everyone who worked on this, including my agent Roger S Williams, and not forgetting Brian Dick.

—Martin King, 2017

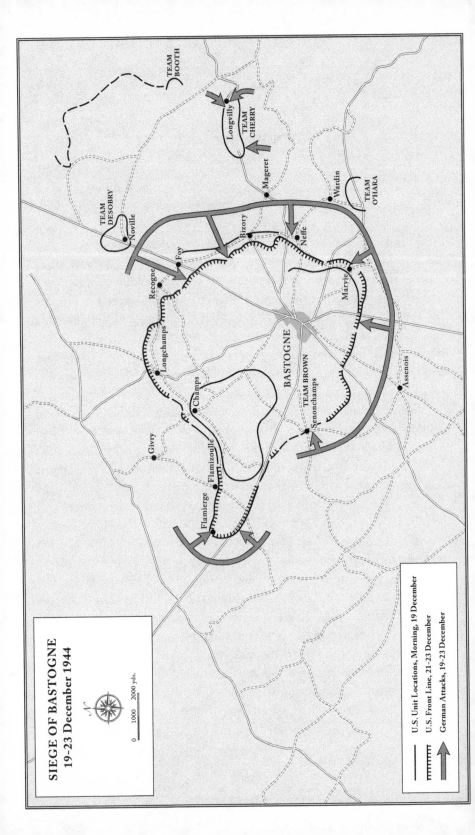

SIEGE OF BASTOGNE
19-23 December 1944

N

0   1000   2000 yds.

TEAM BOOTH

TEAM CHERRY

Longvilly

Mageret

Wardin

TEAM O'HARA

TEAM DESOBRY

Noville

Bizory

Neffe

Foy

Recogne

Marvie

Longchamps

BASTOGNE

Assenois

Champs

TEAM BROWN

Senonchamps

Givry

Flamizoulle

Flamierge

U.S. Unit Locations, Morning, 19 December

U.S. Front Line, 21-23 December

German Attacks, 19-23 December

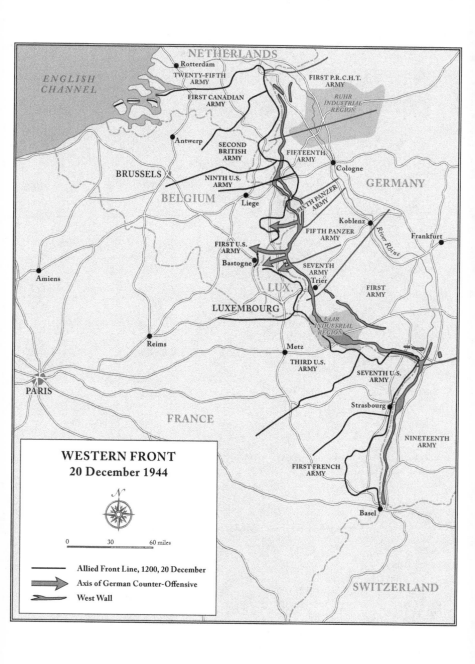

ENGLISH
CHANNEL

NETHERLANDS
● Rotterdam

TWENTY–FIFTH
ARMY

FIRST P.R.CH.T.
ARMY

RUHR
INDUSTRIAL
REGION

FIRST CANADIAN
ARMY

● Antwerp

SECOND
BRITISH
ARMY

FIFTEENTH
ARMY

● Cologne

GERMANY

BRUSSELS

BELGIUM

NINTH U.S.
ARMY

● Liege

SIXTH PANZER
ARMY

● Koblenz

FIFTH PANZER
ARMY

● Frankfurt

River Rhine

● Amiens

FIRST U.S.
ARMY

Bastogne ●

LUX.

SEVENTH
ARMY
● Trier

FIRST
ARMY

LUXEMBOURG

SAAR
INDUSTRIAL
REGION

● Reims

● Metz

THIRD U.S.
ARMY

SEVENTH U.S.
ARMY

PARIS

FRANCE

● Strasbourg

NINETEENTH
ARMY

FIRST FRENCH
ARMY

WESTERN FRONT
20 December 1944

N

0   30   60 miles

——————— Allied Front Line, 1200, 20 December

⟹ Axis of German Counter-Offensive

⟹ West Wall

● Basel

SWITZERLAND

Preface: The Setting

You embody what is best and most kind in all of us.
—Col. J. P. McGee, former commander,
Bastogne Brigade, 101st Airborne Division

This story is set in the small Ardennes town of Bastogne, Belgium. The first mention of Bastogne dates to 634 CE, and, like the rest of what is now Belgium, it changed hands many times over the centuries. It had been part of the Roman Empire and would later fall under Spanish and French rule. When Belgium gained its independence from the Netherlands in the nineteenth century, Bastogne became a prosperous market town known for its cattle and farm produce.

Today Bastogne is a town of around fifteen thousand. One can walk from one end to the other in about fifteen minutes. It heaves with visitors most summer weekends, during which the parking lot on McAuliffe Square quickly fills and the cafes and snack bars in the vicinity do a roaring trade. In a corner of the square there's a Sherman tank that was taken out by a German 88mm gun during the Battle of the Bulge. Everywhere there are reminders of what occurred during the fateful winter of 1944–1945.

About forty-nine yards from the main square on rue de Neufchâteau stands a Chinese restaurant with a series of pillars at its front. On one of the pillars is a plaque that bears an inscription in both French and English that can give a reader pause.

The plaque identifies this as the site of a World War II military aid station of the US 20th Armored Infantry Battalion. The building was struck by a German bomb on Christmas Eve 1944. More than thirty

Bastogne before the war. CREDIT: UNKNOWN

wounded US soldiers being cared for inside were killed. One civilian also died: Belgian nurse Renée Lemaire, remembered today as "The Angel of Bastogne." What the plaque doesn't say is that the bomb that scored a direct hit on the aid station was dropped by the German Luftwaffe early in one of the bloodiest and most decisive clashes of World War II. The plaque also fails to mention a second nurse who could have just as easily been killed in the bombing. That nurse was Augusta Chiwy.

The Stars and Stripes hanging outside the town hall (the *hôtel de ville*) and various other establishments serve as a reminder of the debt of gratitude felt by local residents. Most of Bastogne's visitors aren't on a nostalgic World War II pilgrimage. They're there to do a bit of shopping and enjoy some Ardennes specialties washed down with a glass of good beer. There are enough monuments and memorabilia to keep the discerning war tourist occupied, though, and it's worth going off the beaten track to find them.

There's an unambiguous atmosphere of real history pervading the streets and buildings, and one doesn't need to be a historian to absorb Bastogne's unique ambience. Some of the town's elderly remember the days and long nights when Americans lived with them through a terrible struggle, but they're in no hurry to talk about it. Soon, like the veterans who were there, they will all be gone.

Although decades have passed since the last world war, visible scars remain. Near McAuliffe Square there's a dilapidated house on the rue du Docteur Chiwy. Paint is peeling off the door and graffiti covers the triplex-boarded windows. On closer inspection it's possible to see exposed, scorched bricks and timbers awaiting refurbishment or replacement, silent testaments to another time. There's no plaque, but in any other country this house would be a national monument. This is the house where nurse Augusta Chiwy lived.

Introduction: The Spark

ONE NIGHT SOME YEARS AGO I WAS WATCHING THE "BASTOGNE" EPI-sode of *Band of Brothers*, the series based on the best-selling book by Stephen Ambrose. The character of nurse Renée Lemaire was featured in this episode. I knew her story well—or at least I thought I did. In one shot, a black nurse is working on a wounded soldier behind Renée. The character playing 101st Airborne medic "Doc" Roe asks Renée, "Who's the black nurse?" "Oh that's Anna, from the Congo," replies Renée dismissively. That is it. That is all we see. Where did Ambrose get that, I wondered?

I hunted frantically for the remote and eventually found it under the grumpy dog. Remote extricated, all fingers fortunately preserved, I pressed rewind, then pause, and shouted for my Belgian wife to come take a look. She doesn't normally watch this kind of thing, but there have been exceptions. These have often involved coercion and duress, but that's the price we pay for marrying nurses.

"Look at the nurse behind Renée," I said, pointing.

"Yes, what about her?" my Belgian wife retorted.

"Well, she isn't mentioned in any history book in *my* collection. Who was she, and what was she doing there?"

"Why don't you get off your backside and find out?"

While those weren't her exact words, over the years she's developed a remarkable capacity for using my vernacular, and you get the gist.

When I first began asking around about this black nurse, absolutely nobody knew who she was. Moreover, Stephen Ambrose had taken some serious liberties with the story of Renée Lemaire. Renée was in the same town, but she never worked for the famed 101st Airborne. She was on the other side of town, working for the 20th Armored Infantry Battalion, attached to the 10th Armored Division of Patton's Third Army. There were one or two vague references, but nobody could provide any concrete answers.

My mother was a nurse, and my wife and sister are both nurses. At the time of this writing, my daughter is also training to be a nurse. I've been around nurses all my life. I think if there's any group of people in public service who deserve our respect and admiration, it's nurses. So when I learned about a nurse who'd basically been ignored by history, of course I was going to zero in on her. I wanted—*needed*—to know more about this woman. I had no idea what I was getting myself into, or the story I was about to uncover.

Here was a person who deserved credit and had gotten none for what she'd done in 1944–1945. I would discover the circuitous route that led this woman from her birth in 1921, in what was then the Belgian Congo, to Bastogne and the Battle of the Bulge twenty-three years later. I discovered sometime later that the nurse's name wasn't "Anna." It was Augusta Chiwy.

Who was this African nurse?

In December 1944 she was visiting her father and adoptive mother in Bastogne. She had come home for Christmas from Louvain, where she worked as a nurse, unaware that Bastogne would soon become a city under siege. In a last-ditch effort to win the war he knew he was losing, Adolf Hitler had ordered his armies to launch a massive assault on the Allies' front line in Belgium. Bastogne was right in the crosshairs. It was defended by poorly equipped and badly outnumbered American troops who would soon be tested in one of the bloodiest confrontations in US military history. Augusta Chiwy would selflessly volunteer to help US medic Dr. Jack Prior for nearly a month of sleepless nights, numbing cold, and relentless bombing in a place of abject terror, where anyone could be killed at any time.

This story is not only one of remarkable courage and compassion in the face of appalling inhumanity. It's also the story of a black Belgian nurse, a white army doctor, and the circumstances that drew them together and pulled them apart. It takes a lot to melt the heart of an irascible historian, but mine melted when I discovered their histories. I needed to know more. What had happened to Augusta?

It wasn't easy to uncover the stories of two "ordinary" individuals during the Battle of Bastogne; that's the writer's tale, and you can read it at the end. But everything described here happened. I interviewed dozens of people and read hundreds of pages of primary source material, including letters and diaries. While the characters in this story may not have said every word as recorded here, where I have filled in dialogue, it is psychologically and historically true to the record.

I'll confess that a sort of ménage à trois evolved. I'm much more comfortable talking about military events than emotional ones, but I fell in love with these people. I'm very protective of Augusta in particular, but she deserves to have you know her story. It starts in the Belgian Congo in 1921.

CHAPTER ONE

Who Were These People?

THE NURSE

AUGUSTA CHIWY'S LIFE WAS NOT DESTINED TO BE EASY. SHE CAME INTO the world on June 4, 1921, in Mubavu, a village near the Rwandan border in an area known then as the Belgian Congo. Her father, Henri Chiwy, was a corpulent, mustachioed veterinarian employed there under a standard renewable three-year contract. Her mother was a Congolese woman about whom virtually nothing is known. Augusta was named after an uncle she never met, Dr. Auguste Chiwy, who lived in the Congo during World War I. After that war he lived and worked in Bastogne, where he died in 1924, three years after Augusta was born. She was named for him, and Bastogne's rue du Docteur Chiwy commemorates him.

"The Belgian Congo" was the term for Belgian-colonized central Africa from 1908 to 1960, although it had its roots in King Leopold II's annexation of the area in the 1880s. Despite the great wealth the Congo generated, the relationship between its indigenous people and their Belgian colonizers was never happy. When Joseph Conrad wrote *Heart of Darkness*, many believed he exaggerated, but in fact the novel barely scratched the horrific truth: An estimated ten million or more deaths have been attributed to Leopold II's despotic regime. When he turned over the administration of the Congo to the Belgian people in 1908, he said, "I will give them my Congo, but they do not have the right to know what I've done." As a result, Belgium's turbulent colonial past is rarely taught in Belgian schools.

Belgium's Congo administration was regarded by other Europeans as a drowsy, unsupervised, coercive machine that ruled by intimidation and corruption. Official records state there were so many illegitimate children born during the Belgian occupation that the government had to devise a plan to deal with the situation. The ubiquitous practice of (often nonconsensual, sometimes economically driven) sexual intimacy between Belgians and the ethnic population forced the colonial administration and the Belgian Parliament to formally debate what they termed the *problème des métis*. *Métis*, or *mulatto*, was the term used for biracial children. The father was usually white, the mother black, but there were a few rare exceptions.

The most pressing issue at the time was whether the partly Caucasian biracial children should have the same status as other Congolese, or should be considered an intermediate group—superior to the indigenous people, but inferior to white Europeans. Numerous attempts to resolve the predicament produced a series of contradictory policies, resulting in considerable ambiguity. This equivocality heavily impacted the lives of biracial children like Augusta. Children's status depended largely on the degree of recognition and acknowledgment of parenthood by their fathers. Many abandoned children ended up living in Catholic and Protestant missionary boarding schools created for this purpose.

Ostracized by the indigenous community because of her light skin, at the age of three Augusta was placed in a government-funded mission school in what is now Burundi. Due to her father's status, Augusta would have been an almost-permanent resident at the school, which was run by zealous Belgian missionaries advocating God's love, but rarely applying it. Augusta would eventually become part of an active government-sponsored program for mulatto children that forcefully transferred hundreds of them to Belgium. The stated purpose was to relocate as many of these children as possible on the premise of offering them a new life in a civilized country, but often they became subject to even greater discrimination and exclusion.

In 1931 nine-year-old Augusta was brought to Belgium by her father along with her younger brother, Charles, who was born on September 9, 1922, at Mugomera, Ngozi, in Burundi. Since no mother is named on

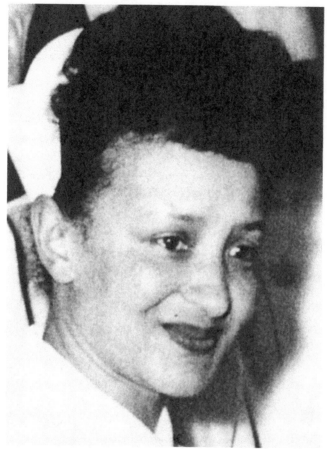

Augusta's wedding day photo. CREDIT: AUTHOR'S PERSONAL ARCHIVE

either birth certificate, Charles and Augusta likely had different biological mothers.

It was a misty April morning in Matadi when Henri bundled his two children on board the SS *Léopoldville* and prepared to bring them to his hometown of Bastogne. The journey usually took three to four weeks depending on weather conditions. Thirteen years later the same ship that brought Augusta and Charles to Belgium was hastily loaded with 2,223 soldiers of the US 66th Infantry Division en route to take part in the Battle of the Bulge, the same battle that would someday touch Augusta.

The SS *Léopoldville* was roughly five miles off of the coast of Cherbourg when one of two torpedoes fired from a German U-boat struck the starboard side aft and exploded immediately, killing three hundred men. American soldiers didn't understand the Captain's "abandon ship" orders.

Flemish speaking Belgian Captain Charles Limbor, who had assumed command of the vessel in 1942, didn't speak a word of English. Chaos ensued as American soldiers and the ship's Belgian crew, which included ninety-three Africans from the Congo, scrambled to the deck. The British destroyer HMS *Brilliant* drew up on the port side of the *Léopoldville* and attempted to rescue survivors, some of whom were making for the scrambling nets, but it was an extremely difficult job having to negotiate the eight- to twenty-one foot channel swells. Consequently, in their haste some soldiers and crew took their lives in their hands and jumped from the deck rails located about forty feet above sea level. Some were crushed to death between the two ships while others broke limbs as their bodies impacted the tumultuous sea. Captain Limbor and 515 US soldiers went down with the ship. Another 248 died from injuries, drowning, or hypothermia. GI's were ordered not to mention the sinking to the press and official documents about it remained classified until 1996.

It was a very different situation during the journey from Congo in 1931. White Belgian passengers on the upper decks passed their time living the good life, eating carefully prepared cuisine and playing card games. The ship's bartender wrote in his log that during the course of the journey the passengers consumed:

4,000 bottles of Saint-Emilion 1892

1,200 bottles of Château Roques 1897

A few thousand "cheap" red Bordeaux and Burgundy

2,500 bottles of white wine (Moselle, Rhine, Sauternes)

3,000 bottles of F. Secondé house champagne

300 bottles Fine (Cognac)

200 bottles Hasselt Old Gin (genever)

Several hundred bottles aperitifs

1,000 bottles of old Porto (cru 1847 and 1865)

Thousands of bottles of Belgian beer

The *Léopoldville* eventually docked in Antwerp on May 5, 1931. At the time many of these passenger ships docked at night in order to avoid upsetting local residents who lived near Antwerp harbor. Some of the children who survived these journeys were inevitably scarred for life.

On his return to Belgium Henri Chiwy had Augusta and her brother Charles legally adopted by his sister-in-law, Caroline (the widow of Henri's brother, Auguste), who became known to them as "Mama Caroline." In fact, they referred to Henri and Caroline as their parents, even though she was their aunt.

Caroline was a teacher by profession. She was a portly, middle-aged woman known to be self-righteous, deeply religious, and on occasion a little sanctimonious. There is no mother's maiden name on the adoption certificate, which reads only "Marie Caroline X." Henri never married.

In Bastogne, Henri continued to practice veterinary medicine. The rich agricultural land that surrounded the city provided no shortage of clients. Henri's family moved into a large detached house just off the main square in Bastogne once occupied by Dr. Auguste Chiwy. Belgium's African colonialism had made it affluent, having amassed more gold reserves than Switzerland. Life was good in the small, European country, and Augusta would have been well provided for in the middle-class Chiwy household.

Belgium had long been a battleground among European powers. The area had always lacked homogeneity, and when Augusta arrived it resembled three countries in one: Dutch-speaking in the north, French-speaking in the south, and a German-speaking section added in 1919 as part of the flawed Treaty of Versailles. All of these populations, though, were Caucasian.

The order of the Sisters of Notre Dame was founded in Amiens in 1804, but in 1816 it relocated to Namur, fifty miles north of Bastogne in the French-speaking Walloon region. These devoutly religious nuns were and are dedicated to providing education to the poor. Today the Sisters have foundations on five continents in twenty countries. Although their school in Bastogne was predominantly a boarding school, Augusta and her brother lived only a few hundred yards away. They were both day students who returned home after lessons. While there was strict segregation between the genders in other schools run by this order, records indicate this was not always the case in Bastogne.

In 1938 Anna Coventry (née Vanherle), who at the time of this writing lives in Texas, was a childhood friend of Augusta's and attended the same school in Bastogne. Anna had been a resident at the Sisters of Notre Dame boarding school for some years, whereas Augusta was a day student. Anna remembers that Augusta and her brother lived with their father and aunt not far from the school, and although Anna was a few years younger than Augusta, they were the only ones enrolled in an extracurricular business course there. According to Anna, Augusta was the only black girl in the school, yet the two became firm friends. She also recalls that their English teacher, Sister Ursula, was British, and that while the students had an option to learn German, Augusta preferred to learn English. Her proficiency in the language would serve her well later on.

Sister Ursula was their favorite teacher because she gave them English storybooks such as *Goldilocks and the Three Bears* and *Snow White* to read. Although Sister Ursula had a warm smile and a kindly manner, to incur her displeasure was a huge mistake. Anna describes her as being small in stature but quite robust and capable of physical punishment when she thought it appropriate. She could be extremely curt, but this was probably due to her poor command of French. Anna recalls how she would have to try really hard to suppress giggles when Augusta cheekily impersonated Sister Ursula's mannerisms (only when her back was turned). The nun wore steel-rimmed bifocals that may originally have belonged to another nun; they didn't fit her very well, and constantly slid down the bridge of her small nose when she was animated. When it appeared that the Germans were preparing to invade, Sister Ursula made the brave decision to remain in Belgium and risk arrest as an enemy alien.

When the threat of war became imminent, Anna returned north to her hometown of Tienen/Tirlemont. Augusta stayed in touch with her for a while, and once met her at a bus stop while she was at nursing school in Leuven/Louvain. (Most major Belgian cities have a Dutch name and a French name. In some cases, like Liège, they have an additional German name. Liège is Luik to Dutch speakers and Luttich to German speakers.) "I remember that she still wore that cheeky smile, and still referred to the nuns as 'penguins,'" Anna remembers. "She always made me laugh."

According to Anna, Augusta had often told her that she wanted to become a teacher like Mama Caroline. Unfortunately, Belgian regulations prohibited biracial or black people from working in the education system. This was just one of many racially motivated policies aimed at marginalizing mixed-race and ethnic immigrants. While German occupation would impose additional controls over cross-racial interaction, the Belgian policy had nothing to do with the German presence.

Augusta went from one group of devout Catholic nuns to another. Denied a career as a teacher, if that was indeed her hope, in 1941 Augusta enrolled in nursing school in accordance with her father's wishes. She attended the nursing college attached to the Catholic University of Louvain and the St. Elizabeth Hospital.

This nursing program had been formally inaugurated by the Augustine Congregation Sisters of Louvain in 1908, and was staffed by the same order. In 1928 they established the St. Elizabeth Institute and Labor Clinic, which had its own midwifery school. By the 1930s it had become a general hospital and had expanded its activities to include a children's ward. When Augusta studied and worked there it was regarded as one of the most important hospitals in Belgium.

Augusta's enrollment and program assessments indicate her exceptional abilities and character. According to her records she was a dedicated and capable student who quickly made friends and communicated well with patients. Once again she was the only African-Belgian in her year. Augusta applied herself heart and soul to become a dedicated professional.

Augusta alongside other nurses from the St. Elizabeth Hospital. CREDIT: UNKNOWN

After qualifying as a registered nurse in 1943, Augusta began work at St. Elizabeth Hospital.

THE DOCTOR

John Thompson Prior, the man who would later play an integral part in Augusta's life, was born in St. Albans, Vermont, a small town close to the shores of Lake Champlain and not far from the Canadian border. Today it is home to only a few thousand people, about the same number who lived there in 1917 when Thomas and Pauline Prior had the first of their four sons. They named him John Thompson, but he would become known to family and friends as Jack.

Jack's father was honest, hardworking, and conscientious, but his wife was the family decision-maker. In the Prior home, angering the matriarch could affect everything from nutritional requirements to personal hygiene. She would refuse to cook, launder, or clean for the offender until a satisfactory agreement had been reached. Pauline Prior could be overbearing and even tyrannical at times, but she loved her son. She decided early on that Jack was going to be a doctor.

As a boy Jack was considered a reasonably good student, but not especially athletic. In high school, he enrolled in the Citizens' Military Training Camp. Created by the National Defense Act of 1920, the program operated summer camps where young men could develop physical prowess and receive military training. He was deeply affected by his experience at camp and returned in peak physical condition. He'd become interested in boxing and although he never thought to actively pursue his pugilistic ambitions, at well over six feet he was a force to be reckoned with.

After high school, Jack enrolled in the University of Vermont, where he went out for football. Even though he'd never played in high school, he made the freshman team. He also was an enthusiastic participant in the school's ROTC program and received the university's highest ROTC honors. When he graduated in 1938, he was qualified to join the army as a second lieutenant. It was an opportunity he found very appeal-

ing. Jack may have forgotten his mother's plan for him to become a doctor, but she hadn't, and Pauline Prior was not a woman to be argued with.

Jack let his mother know that he had been accepted to medical school, but he was really thinking of making a career out of the military. She told him that if that was his choice then he was no longer welcome in her home. Under extreme maternal coercion Jack began his studies at the University of Vermont medical school and went on to become a doctor. In 1943 he earned high

2nd Lt. John Prior. CREDIT: US ARMY

honors, graduated, and did his internship in New York State. Jack had acquiesced to his mother's wishes but couldn't repress his burning ambition to join the army.

At this time the United States was already at war and all able-bodied men were needed, so Jack was inducted into the army as a medical officer. During his internship in New York, Jack had become engaged to a beautiful young nurse named Marion Golden; however, marriage and future plans were put on hold, as 2nd Lt. Jack Prior was about to report for duty.

In December 1944, due to a confluence of fate, the names of Jack Prior and Augusta Chiwy would become inextricably linked. They would be drawn together and their experience would leave an indelible stain on their hearts, one that would resonate for decades after World War II.

The Intersection

In May 1940 Adolf Hitler ordered a multipronged strike on Holland and Belgium by around 140 divisions. It was a gloriously sunny day when World War II reached Belgium. The Germans obtained complete tactical surprise, taking two bridges over the Albert Canal and destroying Fort Eben-Emael. As one of a line of defensive fortifications east of Liège, Eben-Emael was extremely important. It dominated the whole region and protected all the bridges there. The elite German pioneers (combat engineer troops) succeeded in landing at the fort, and in a matter of minutes they had destroyed most of the guns. The Belgian population would add a terrifying new word to their vocabulary—*blitzkrieg*—and discover all that it implied.

In the north, many Dutch-speaking Flemish nationalists had welcomed the German invaders. In the south, extreme-right-wing parties such as "Rex" had openly supported German fascists throughout the 1930s. Many had even adopted Nazi racial policies into their own agenda. Just before the outbreak of World War II in the province of Luxembourg, where Bastogne is located, Rex had secured 30 percent of the popular vote. Not everyone readily accepted oppressive Nazi rule in Belgium. There were many organized resistance groups. Courageous men and women dissenters provided invaluable intelligence to the Allies for the duration.

Hitler's plan worked like a dream—or a nightmare, depending on which side you were on. Within a week Germany had captured most of Belgium, and within a few months the British Expeditionary Force and the French army were beating a retreat toward the fateful port of Dunkirk. After the evacuation there it would be four long years before the Allies returned to those shores.

The Nazi racial policy implemented after the invasion dictated that African Belgians were to be excluded from military activity because of their non-Aryan status. As a rule the Nazis despised black culture and considered it vastly inferior. They even sought to prohibit "traditionally black" musical genres like jazz because they regarded it as "corrupt Negro music." Despite this, no official laws were ever enacted against black populations, or even against the children of mixed parentage, as they were not considered a serious threat in occupied territories.

After the capitulation of Belgium in May 1940 Hitler installed a military administration there. Initially there were no clear directives from Berlin regarding the governance of the country, but it soon became apparent that Hitler could implement control by replacing all former civilian municipal and national authorities with a chosen controlling body that would oversee and regulate all civilian activities.

The German occupiers were aware that in addition to the Belgian authorities, the Catholic Church was a powerful player on the sociopolitical field. The extensive and antiquated organizational powers regarding congregations and Catholic education were the primary sources of this power, and the German authorities were wary of them. Their policies in Belgium were inevitably influenced by the Vatican because of Italy's allegiance with the Nazis. These factors prevented the military administration from implementing uniform German cultural policy at an educational level. Consequently, Augusta had been allowed to continue her strict Catholic education relatively undisturbed.

Normally Augusta would work six straight days or nights at St. Elizabeth's and then have a day off, but during 1944 she'd regularly pull seven consecutive shifts without a break. This was largely due to a lack of qualified staff during the German occupation. Whereas some nurses eagerly volunteered to work for the Nazis, many were forced to assist their war effort, which inevitably left Belgian medical staffs shorthanded. Overtime was compulsory, often exceeding the allocated time parameters, and it wasn't unusual for nurses to pull double or even triple shifts. Augusta avoided being specifically requisitioned for the Nazi war effort because she was biracial and regarded as "unworthy" by the authorities.

Augusta would have been made aware of her ethnic identity by other Belgians, but this didn't make her deferential or shy in her approach to people. She was extremely proud of being from the Congo, and no shrinking violet by any stretch of the imagination. One reason for her social aptitude may have been her experience as a nurse who worked in a general hospital. She would claim that it was the only profession where a black woman could berate a white man with impunity.

By September of 1944 the Allies had liberated Belgium. British, Canadian, and Polish forces had fought through the Dutch-speaking areas in the north, while US forces had liberated the French-speaking south and were now enjoying a well-earned rest in anticipation of Christmas. Once a city or village was liberated from the Germans, reprisals against collaborators began in earnest. The consequences of the punitive German "purge" in Belgium would still be obvious through the end of the twenty-first century.

At roughly the same time, the man who would play such a major part in Augusta's life, Capt. John Prior—battalion surgeon in the 80th Armored Medical Battalion, attached to the 20th Armored Infantry Battalion—was serving with the 10th Armored Division. The fighting in nearby Metz had been a lot tougher than anyone had anticipated. Even a pep talk from General Patton hadn't raised morale much. All the soldiers knew that Patton had given the same speech with minor variations to every division in his Third Army.

In late November to early December the 10th Armored were at the division rest area in Reméling, northern France. Since disembarking with his division in Normandy some months earlier, Jack Prior had become familiar with the noise of battle. He'd been in the army for just over a year, but in that time he'd experienced combat and all it entailed.

After training in Georgia, his division was sent overseas, arriving in France in September 1944. The 10th Armored Division first saw action while attacking the outer fortifications of Metz on November 15. Jack's assignment had been to help operate a clearing station, preparing patients for transit to the nearest evacuation hospital. Since then some of the division had taken their furlough in Paris, and he'd occupied himself treating various forms of venereal disease and the ubiquitous "trench foot," a medical condition caused by prolonged exposure of the feet to damp, unsanitary, and cold conditions.

The original St. Elizabeth Hospital building dated to medieval times, and if Augusta had believed in ghosts, as some other nurses apparently did, this would have been a perfect setting for a haunting. On the top landing, the residential part of the building, the dim light and wide, dark, wood-paneled corridors would have been enough to test anyone's resilience, but it didn't seem to have bothered Augusta. That building was demolished in 1990, but late on December 15, 1944, when nurse Augusta Chiwy left the ward where she had been working, she scurried away to the large marble stairwell that led to the nurses' quarters.

Augusta had just finished her week on the wards. The circumstances that were to draw her and Jack Prior into each other's unlikely company began on December 16, the following morning. On that day three German armies launched a massive counteroffensive that would become known as the Battle of the Bulge.

Augusta's life would never be the same again.

CHAPTER TWO

Going Home for Christmas

DECEMBER 16, 1944

It was early morning, a Saturday, when Augusta buttoned up her cumbersome nurse's gabardine and wrapped a bulky hand-knitted black scarf around her neck. Her father had invited her to Bastogne for Christmas, and she was looking forward to returning to what she considered her hometown, about ninety miles south of Louvain.

Augusta's eagerness to go home could have been enhanced by the prospect of a good feed. The monasteries and convents in the Bastogne area cultivated their own vegetables and kept their own livestock, and would occasionally have needed Henri Chiwy's services. Consequently, her father was never short of meat thanks to his veterinary activities. Apparently the only vegetable that wasn't available in abundance, however, was potatoes.

Among the planted pine forests and rolling hills, no one would have noticed a solitary figure pedaling along the route de Clervaux from Bastogne on a rickety old bike the previous evening, on the night of December 15. As the evening mist settled in, Henri Chiwy did his best to stay balanced on the icy and uneven cobblestone road, avoiding dips and drops on a surface that was originally intended for horses and carts. The haze made it hard to see, and poor visibility was compounded by approaching dusk. Henri often worked long hours around that time of year, but that night he was on a foraging mission for potatoes.

Finding meat hadn't been a problem; the local veterinarian had real advantages when it came to acquiring meat. People would usually take

Troops and vehicles in Bastogne before the siege. COURTESY OF MIKE COLLINS

such a qualified man at his word, and when he said with gravitas, "That lamb looks ill and needs to be isolated from the rest of the flock; let me take it home for examination," nobody blinked. Who would dare to contradict a qualified veterinarian? He could later lament about how the poor beast had died under anesthetic, or while trying to escape, or whatever the reason. He had a solid reputation, and in most cases the locals would have believed him.

As he reached the junction just before the village of Marvie, he applied the hand brakes. When they didn't perform quickly enough, he took his feet off the pedals and scraped the cobblestones, creating a shower of sparks with his steel-toe boots until he managed to fall off and tumble into a plowed field.

Before leaving home that evening Henri had indulged in a large glass of calvados. It would have comfortably immunized him against the biting cold as he lay there between the frozen furrows. Like most residents of Bastogne, he wasn't against the occasional alcoholic libation. Under normal circumstances these people were *bon viveurs* who enjoyed life to the full, and there was never a shortage of good beer and spirits in the Ardennes. Moreover, they didn't need much of an excuse to indulge to the max. Henri was no exception. He actually found some abandoned potatoes in the field, even though he had almost broken his arm.

Oblivious to her father's nocturnal foraging, that Saturday morning Augusta stood in the aisle of a packed tram ambling lethargically to Brussels's southern station. The dim light inside the tram was subject to regulation "blackout" lighting which left the interior barely illuminated. Under the circumstances this wasn't necessarily bad, as most of the trams hadn't been cleaned since 1940.

On arrival at her first destination, Augusta left the tram and stepped into the cavernous Gare du Midi station echoing with commuters going about their daily routines with the accompaniment of rancid tobacco smoke, cold air, and a resounding cacophony of lively human and mechanical noise. Above the commotion the overhead public address system was relaying information about trains, platforms, and destinations in an almost unintelligible high-nasal monotone.

Augusta would have seen a hive of activity typical for a Saturday morning at the station, as crowds of passengers eager to enjoy the weekend thronged the platforms and waited expectantly for their trains. One of the announcements in French and Dutch concerning departures for Luxembourg or Bastogne said, "The 8:45 for Bastogne and the 9:15 for Luxembourg will both terminate at Namur." There was no reason given, and most commuters would have been blissfully oblivious of the savage fury that was being unleashed against four thinly spread US divisions along the whole Ardennes front.

Until that calamitous point everything had gone relatively well for the Allies. Since the breakout from Normandy, Paris had been liberated at the end of August and the Belgian cities of Tournai, Brussels, and Antwerp had been liberated by British troops in early September. US divisions had liberated Mons, Namur, Liège, and the Ardennes during the same month. German units had made a necessary tactical retreat and established their defenses way behind the Siegfried Line.

The First Army of Gen. Courtney Hodges had succeeded in capturing Aachen, while General Patton's Third Army was preparing to invade the Saarland. The general consensus of opinion at Supreme Headquarters Allied Expeditionary Force (SHAEF) headquarters was that the difficult terrain and the onset of winter made it highly unlikely that the Germans would launch an attack on the Ardennes region. The great disparity in opinion that existed between the US and British High Commands at the time only exacerbated their lack of readiness. General Eisenhower was considering the option to invade Germany along the whole length of the front line, while British Field Marshal Montgomery was demanding a lightning breakthrough over more favorable terrain from the Netherlands to Berlin.

Meanwhile, the German army's high command, the Oberkommando der Wehrmacht (OKW), had earmarked Bastogne as a strategic location. The city rests on an elevated plateau in the province of Luxembourg, a few miles from Luxembourg's national border in the south of Belgium and about twenty-two miles west of the German border. Seven roads converged in Bastogne, and according to archival documents it had been a popular market town for many centuries. It was regarded as one of the most important towns in the Ardennes region. Surrounded by gentle rolling hills, prime agricultural land, and a few planted forests that were used mainly for logging, this was the heart of a prosperous farming community.

Bastogne was now relatively quiet save for a few troops from the 28th "Keystone" Division who were still hanging around town and entertaining the locals. A part of Gen. Troy Middleton's US VIII Corps, the 28th Pennsylvania National Guard, were still in the process of replacing casualties incurred during the terrible Battle of Hürtgen Forest, which had reduced the division's number by four-fifths. Due to the massive casualties in the Hürtgen campaign, the Germans had renamed the 28th Division's Keystone arm patch the "Bloody Bucket."

A few miles south of Bastogne in Diekirch, the 28th Division's 109th Regiment was enjoying a USO show that included Marlene Dietrich wowing the troops with her husky Teutonic just-below-the-tone vocals and shapely legs. The "in" joke after the Battle of the Bulge was that the

99th Division strung out on the northern shoulder was expecting Marlene Dietrich but got Schutzstaffel (SS) general Joseph "Sepp" Dietrich and his 6th Panzer Army instead.

In late November and early December Jack Prior found his talents to be in great demand. After a rain-soaked November in Alsace-Lorraine, sickness in the army was rampant. One division had more than three thousand severe cases of trench foot. His other problem was a direct consequence of being within driving distance of Paris. Many GIs opted to spend their furloughs there, and quite a few returned with STDs.

On December 14, 1944, Capt. Jack Prior was assigned as surgeon to the 20th AIB to replace their regular officer, who had been evacuated with pneumonia. That was the official reason. Unofficially the replacement had been made because the officer in question had taken a liking to hard liquor and was failing quite dramatically in his duties.

Jack's appointment gave him command over his colleague, dental surgeon Capt. Irving Lee Naftulin, himself no stranger to intoxicating libations, and about thirty enlisted men who had been trained as litter bearers and first-aid men. The 20th AIB was part of a combat team composed of a tank battalion, an engineer platoon, and a reconnaissance squadron. This team would become known as "Team Desobry" after its infantry commanding officer, the then twenty-six-year-old

Official army photograph of Capt. Irving Lee Naftulin. CREDIT: US ARMY

Maj. William R. Desobry. Desobry was a strong and highly respected combat leader who would ultimately serve thirty-four years, spend time in Vietnam, and retire as a lieutenant general.

Captain Naftulin, known as "Naf" to his friends, was born in Romania in 1907, but his family immigrated to the United States the following year. He had graduated with a dentistry degree from Ohio State University in 1931. He enlisted on December 9, 1941, when he was already thirty-six; had he not volunteered, he never would been drafted, due to his age. He had tried to join an airborne unit and at the time didn't regard being a dentist or being too old as potential deterrents to this ambition. Before he was sent overseas, Naftulin had a reputation for being very keen on physical fitness. He was considered quite militant in his opinions as well as very defensive about anti-Semitism. Joining up was his way of fighting back.

Although Naf and Jack Prior hadn't had much to do with each other up to that point, they acknowledged and respected each other's professions. Jack was given command of the medical unit even though Naftulin had seniority and a higher rank because military regulations stipulated that the post should be held by a doctor or a surgeon, not a dentist.

As Augusta was walking to the bus stop across from the train station in Namur she noticed that large open cattle trucks were being provided to take passengers farther south. There was a large crowd at the bus stop jostling to get on board. It took a long while to load the human cargo onto each truck, and every vehicle that left the station was packed to maximum capacity. The old Bedford truck Augusta boarded rocked and jolted along the cobbled streets as it meandered south in the wake of various US military vehicles.

It eventually terminated at Marché, where Augusta disembarked in search of transport for the last twenty-five miles to Bastogne. She walked a few miles out of the small city, trying to flag down a vehicle going south. A Willys jeep pulled over to the side of the main road and offered her a lift. Augusta gratefully accepted and jumped into the backseat. This took her to Martelange, about thirteen miles south of Bastogne.

In retrospect it would have been better if she'd walked from Marché, as due to a slight communication problem with the soldiers providing the transport, she went farther south than she expected. After waiting a few hours in Martelange she managed to find a bus heading in the direction of Bastogne, but prolific military traffic in and around Bastogne meant the bus stopped about two miles short of its destination.

At that point Augusta noticed an unlocked bicycle apparently abandoned by the side of the road. The reason for its abandonment became obvious when she tried to ride it. The front tire was completely flat, but she decided to ride it anyway. After pedaling strenuously for a couple miles Augusta had no option but to discard the truculent bicycle and walk the rest of the way. She was hungry, cold, and totally exhausted, but with great effort she trudged laboriously toward Bastogne, arriving at her father's home on the rue des Écoles around 11:00 p.m. Her long, arduous journey home to Bastogne had involved tram, train, truck, jeep, bus, bicycle, and shoe leather.

At precisely 5:30 that morning in 1944, the Battle of the Bulge had begun as German armies launched simultaneous attacks along an eighty-seven-mile front. There were only four US divisions in the line at the time, and two of these—the 99th and the 106th infantry divisions—had never fired a shot in anger; they were completely green. The other two divisions, the 28th and the 4th infantry divisions, were refitting after fighting in the punitive, bloody Hürtgen Forest campaign. German intel and recon was good; they knew that these divisions were overextended, and where the gaps were. Ten days before the offensive, the OKW had imposed radio silence to hide the massing of German troops and armor in the west. Although Bletchley Park had intercepted messages prior to the radio silence indicating that German units were being moved from the Eastern Front to the west, this information was dismissed by SHAEF. The general assumption was that the Ardennes was the quiet area, and an attack there was considered unlikely.

On the way to her father's house Augusta would have passed stationary military vehicles parked ad hoc beside the road along with columns on the move. The Americans had been in Bastogne since September and had made their presence known among the locals, particularly the girls.

Germans advancing through the woods near Bastogne, December 1944.
CREDIT: US ARMY SIGNAL CORPS

Many good friendships had been sealed both vertically and horizontally. As far as most residents were concerned, after four rigid years of Nazi occupation these handsome young soldiers were a breath of fresh air.

Winter in the Ardennes always transformed Bastogne from a nondescript market town to a pre-Christmas wonderland. It would never have looked prettier than it did at that moment in 1944. Holiday decorations would have been displayed in shop windows and along the streets, where the old sodium streetlights would have given faces a greenish hue.

Henri Chiwy stood beside his sister-in-law at the door where they'd watched and waited expectantly for Augusta for hours. When she finally arrived, the first thing she noticed was the temporary, self-applied plaster cast on his left arm. He'd wanted those potatoes for a "welcome home" dinner of Flemish stew and fries for Augusta.

Later, after an excellent dinner with the family, Augusta went up to bed. On the wall of her bedroom was a National Geographic Society map of the world, dotted with little red marker flags showing the route to Belgium from the Congo. A blue flag was stuck in the place where she was born. She put her purse and ID card on her bedside table next to an autographed picture of her favorite music artist, Charles Trenet. Briefly revived at being back in her room, she walked over to the shelf that held her record player. Above it was her small collection of vinyl discs. She reached for one and carefully removed a Charles Trenet recording from its sleeve while opening the lid of the player. Within a few seconds, the song "Boum!" drifted from the old machine, filling the room.

She went to bed that night not knowing this would be her last good night's sleep for a long while.

Chapter Three

All Quiet in Bastogne

December 17, 1944

For the second time in less than twenty-five years Bastogne was preparing to deal with all-out war. Augusta's services would soon be called on, but we know she wasn't the only nurse in Bastogne at that time. Nurse Renée Bernadette Emilie Lemaire was also there, visiting her family. Renée was a doe-eyed, shapely brunette who was well aware of her physical attributes and not above using them to her advantage. While she was in Bastogne she stayed with her family above their haberdashery shop in the center of town on the Place du Carré, or Carrefour (today known as McAuliffe Square). The family was well known and liked. Like Augusta Chiwy, Renée was a qualified nurse who lived away from home.

There is no evidence that the two knew each other before their first meeting in Bastogne. It's doubtful that a comfortable, middle-class Belgian family would have had social contact with someone of biracial origins, since the separation of mixed-race and black people had been endemic and institutionalized in Belgium for many years. This wasn't regarded as racism at the time. Nevertheless, Bastogne was a tight-knit, centuries-old community, so it's possible that Renée and Augusta knew of each other's existence purely on the basis that they shared the same profession.

~~~

December 17 was particularly quiet for a Sunday morning. Augusta wouldn't have heard the church bells of St. Peter's announcing mass, but she would have clearly heard the distant dull thud of artillery fire. Around midday Henri Chiwy arrived home after another foraging mission and handed a small brown paper parcel to Augusta. She gratefully accepted. It contained butter, jelly, sugar, coffee, and a few candy bars. These were valuable and much-sought-after provisions, probably traded from US Army supplies. Later that day Augusta decided to visit her brother, Charles, who was staying with friends in the tiny village of Rachamps a few miles north of Bastogne.

When they were children in Bastogne, Augusta was the spirited one but Charles had always exhibited a rebellious streak. He stuck up for what was right, sometimes to his detriment. Henri's occasional intervention had been needed to prevent his son's expulsion from school.

At the age of fourteen Charles had left school under a cloud after breaking the jaw of a renowned local bully. Unfortunately the bully was related to the mayor of Bastogne. Throughout his teens Charles failed to hold down a job for more than a few months at a time, and Henri often berated him for his reluctance to seriously commit to anything. He was a classic "jack-of-all-trades and master of none." By this stage in the war, though, he had committed to the Resistance and was proving himself to be a stealthy, astute, and dangerous adversary for the Germans. One of these organizations, known as "The White Rose," had clandestine cells all over the south of Belgium.

Henri gave Augusta permission to use his bicycle for the short trip from Bastogne to Rachamps. She left Bastogne easily but felt uncomfortable pedaling her father's cumbersome bike. It was difficult to use, and despite the arctic cold she'd already started to work up a sweat under her multilayered clothing. A few miles north of Bastogne, at the small village of Noville, dense fog and snow forced Augusta to take shelter on the porch of the stone church. Clouds turned the sky darker as she sat on the bicycle looking out, waiting for the weather to abate. She removed her mittens and massaged her fingers to get the blood circulating again. Realizing the bike was becoming more of an encumbrance than she'd expected, she decided it would probably be faster to walk, so she left it behind, making it the second bike she'd abandoned in as many days. In the background the sound of artillery fire seemed to be getting nearer and thick fog continued to descend all around her, making it difficult to know if she was heading in the right direction. She quickened her pace and carried on anyway.

Tiny Rachamps is about half a mile to the west of the main Bastogne-to-Houffalize road, just north of Noville. A few small roads and farm tracks head east from there. Considering the weather conditions it was easy to pick the wrong one, and she did.

———

At precisely 3:30 a.m. on December 17, movement orders came over the war-room ticker for the 10th AID. Less than three hours later Jack's unit was clattering down the road, heading north toward Luxembourg. Combat Command A marched seventy-five miles in eighteen hours through the most grueling winter weather to reach their destination. The 20th Armored Infantry was part of Team Desobry.

Around this time Jack got a "Dear John" letter from Marion Golden. She had already alluded to the fact that his absence was definitely not making her heart grow fonder. They hadn't been engaged for very long, but it was obvious from this last letter that her eyes were wandering. If Jack's letters home didn't show him deeply perturbed by the news, it was probably because he had more pressing matters to attend to. If he was upset he kept it to himself, something that seems to have been characteristic of him.

Few things evoke more grumbling than a division about to get on the move. Military engines shuddered and coughed lethargically to life in the subfreezing temperatures. Carving deep furrows in the virgin snow, they moved into position. By early afternoon, Colonel Roberts—a humorless and gutsy individual who preferred deeds to words—and his Combat Command B (CCB) were making their first tentative steps in the direction of Bastogne. They would cross into Luxembourg near the village of Merl. Roberts's command mobilized fairly quickly, but he was still beaten to the punch by his counterparts in Combat Command A, whose superhuman effort got them to Echternach to provide armored support for the 4th Division there.

Jack would have seen the snow-bedecked Luxembourg countryside, because at the time the skies were still relatively clear. Beneath

Maj. William Robertson Desobry (Team Desobry). COURTESY OF MIKE COLLINS

the dim moonlight the vista would have had an almost supernatural quality. Things wouldn't stay pretty for long.

By December 17, 1944, Allied intelligence had a marginally better idea of the strength and objectives of the attacking German forces. As forward elements of the 10th Armored Division drove, skidded, and trudged through blizzard conditions along muddy, snow-clogged roads toward Bastogne, the 101st had been dispatched at speed to accompany them. The 10th Armored's CCB was already divided into three teams, each team named after its respective commander: Team Cherry, Team O'Hara, and Team Desobry. The winter wonderland of Luxembourg with its steep hills and natural forests would have looked great on a postcard, but to the GIs who had to traverse its narrow winding roads between the high pine trees, it just hindered their progress.

The bold German plan was to strike through the Ardennes and cross the Meuse River that stretches from France through Belgium and the Netherlands right up to the North Sea. Then they would retake the city of Antwerp and its port infrastructure to prevent supplies and reinforcements from reaching the Allied armies. Their intention was based on the oldest tactic in military history: divide and conquer. Isolate the Allied armies in the north from those in the south, then force one of them to capitulate in the hope of obtaining the signature of a separate peace on the Western Front. The German army could then be transferred to the Eastern Front to halt the Russian army advance.

Many German generals had secretly voiced reserva-tions about the plan, proba-bly because the eventual suc-

Lt. Col. Henri T. Cherry (Team Cherry).
COURTESY OF MIKE COLLINS

cess of the offensive would depend on several moderately unpredictable factors, like low and long-lasting cloud cover to prevent the intervention of Allied aircraft, a rapid initial breakthrough with the seizure of Allied fuel dumps, and capture of important crossroads. At OKW the generals had also discussed the capture of the key towns of Bastogne and St. Vith as imperative for the German army, but there were major differences between the two places.

Bastogne was French-speaking, while St. Vith was firmly in the German-speaking territory of Belgium, and had only been a part of that country since the Treaty of Versailles in 1919. Since the German inva-sion in May 1940 it had become part of Germany again. Moreover, its rail links to Germany just a few miles to the east hadn't been touched by Allied bombs. Bastogne had only one direct rail link, which went north and south, not east to Germany. Bastogne was no stranger to conflict, though; it had been bombed in World War I and again at the beginning of World War II, but no previous strife was comparable to the ravages it was about to endure.

———

Not far past Noville, Augusta stopped to take a breather and try to get her bearings. In the distance she could still hear artillery, but now she heard another more ominous sound—the menacing, throaty grumble of heavy tanks in close proximity, probably reducing cobbled roads to gravel as they rolled forward. It was enough to give her tired body new impetus to keep moving. She realized at that point that she had made a mistake going out there to visit Charles.

She thought she heard voices through the fog and stopped in her tracks. She looked back, her attention momentarily drawn to the sound of an approaching heavy engine. Whatever it was, however, it was shrouded by the mist. Disoriented and tired, she stubbornly continued in the direction that she assumed was north. Then she froze. Now she could really hear voices, she was sure of it, and they were speaking German. She went over to the side of the road, and found a road sign. Brushing the snow from it, she squinted and could see that it read "Gouvy 3 km."

The vehicle she had heard was now so close she could feel the ground begin to shake. Her eyes widened as a monstrous Panther tank suddenly loomed out of the mist. Augusta dove into the ditch beside the road and, in an attempt to provide camouflage, grabbed some dead twigs and leaves to cover herself. As it passed she could see the black German cross outlined in white on the side of the tank.

Surrounded by the sound of German voices, shivering with fear and cold, she crouched as low as she could get in the narrow ditch. Why was she hiding from the Nazis? She hadn't hidden from them during the occupation, and they hadn't really given her any cause for alarm before. This time she sensed there was something different. These Nazi soldiers were on the move, and she had heard that soldiers on the move were capable of anything.

Augusta felt like she'd huddled there for hours when in fact it had only been a few minutes before she peered carefully from her foliage-covered coat. As soon as the noise abated, when she was sure there was no sign of movement, she got to her feet and began dusting off the twigs and leaves. Suddenly a forceful blow between her shoulder blades sent her flying back into the ditch. She hardly dared to look up to see who had delivered it. A young German soldier gestured to Augusta to get to her feet and she immediately obeyed. Then she tilted slightly to one side and looked her attacker square in the face. He looked very young, and the snow-white camouflage smock he was wearing was obviously four sizes too big for his small frame. His smooth face, which had probably never even felt a razor blade, was pimply and reddened by the cold. He aimed his Mauser rifle straight at Augusta and asked her in broken French what she was doing there. Augusta used gestures to explain that she had gotten lost in the fog. The young soldier appeared to understand. She indicated to him that she was looking for the road to Bastogne.

The young soldier rummaged around in his smock, took out his compass, studied it for a moment, and then pointed. A few seconds later he was hurrying away but before his silhouette was entirely obscured by the mist, a shot rang out that slung him backwards, flipping him facedown on the road with a sickening thud. She ran over to where he lay and rolled him over onto his back. Blood spread from the young man's heaving chest as his labored breathing pervaded the air. His helmet had gone backward on his head slightly, revealing white-blond hair underneath. Augusta brushed it from his forehead and looked into his panicked, teary eyes. He moaned in pain.

Putting a hand to his cheek she felt his fresh face. It was as cold as a glacier. Blood began to trickle in a dark stream from the corner of his full lips but he was still breathing. Augusta reverted to her nursing instinct immediately and opened the front of his smock to find a gaping wound just below his solar plexus. His chest heaved some more, then suddenly a deafening shot rang out. Augusta jerked back as a dime-size piece of the boy's skull flew into the air. Gray brain tissue and blood splattered the side of her face, and the soldier's head jolted back like an electrical charge had just been applied. Augusta looked in the direction of the voices that sounded like they could have been English or American, but she couldn't see anyone. She quickly left the scene, barely believing what she'd just experienced. Throughout the past four years the war had never been this close.

She went up a small embankment on the side of the road, through some snow, and on to a farmer's field that was slightly higher than the road. The snow had been packed hard by livestock, and some sort of wagon had been through recently. Wanting to be seen by neither Americans nor Nazis, she stopped beside a fence post, whereupon she felt a strong impulse to run but her knees were too weak. Catching her breath, she got low to the ground and attempted to suppress the urge to vomit, but then emptied the contents of her breakfast onto the frozen ground.

As a nurse, Augusta had seen blood before—it came with the territory—but usually it was from people who she already knew were sick or needed nursing. This was something different. As she contemplated her next move, she frantically wiped the blood and brain matter from her face with her mitten.

Once again she could feel the ground shaking with the reverberation of more heavy tanks. She waited for what seemed like ages. When things had quietened down somewhat, she decided the visit to see Charles might have to wait. It was getting late in the day; if she could get out of her current predicament, it was probably wisest to head back toward her father's house in Bastogne. She slowly got up and made her way back to the road.

Despite the almost immobilizing cold she could feel beads of sweat rolling down her back under her clothing. Visibility was poor and there were no recognizable features in this landscape. She clenched her teeth and moved forward, every labored step sapping what little reserves she still had left. By now the light was fading, and Augusta guessed it was late afternoon.

Up ahead she thought she could just about make out the silhouette of a building, but the mist was so thick it was difficult to tell. This forced a mild acceleration in her step, but after a few minutes the silhouette was gone.

Augusta knew from years in the Ardennes that the mist could play tricks on a person's eyes, especially when darkness was approaching. It was hard to tell where she was now, and her mind was still distracted by the shocking violence she'd witnessed. She was struggling to suppress the rising panic when suddenly the ground beneath her feet completely gave way, and she slipped down the side of a small hill. The numbing cold had eradicated all sense of time and place as she tumbled downward, her hands outstretched, frantically clawing at thin air in an attempt to stop her rapid descent. There was nothing to hold on to, not a branch, rock, or tree to slow the fall.

She came to a halt as suddenly as she had fallen. After a few moments she composed herself and rose to her feet, checking her limbs. She spit out blood caused by biting the inside of her cheek during the tumble. Clambering back up the hill on all fours, she eventually reached the top and made it back to the road.

She thought she could see the silhouette again. There, right in front of her, was the small church with her father's bicycle still parked on the porch. She was back in Noville. At least the young Nazi soldier had been right in telling her which direction was south. She sighed with relief as she made her way to the stone steps, thumping on the rough-hewn wooden door with every ounce of strength she could muster. It was there while sheltering from the cold that she met Father Louis Delvaux, the village priest. He had a reputation for being a stubborn but compassionate man who was very popular with the community.

From existing photographs and other witnesses who knew Father Delvaux it's possible to ascertain how

Father Louis Delvaux, the priest of Noville.
CREDIT: UNKNOWN

he looked and the type of person he was. He had a large forehead accentuated by a mildly receding hairline, thick, round, black-rimmed glasses, and a prominent Adam's apple protruding from a thin neck above his priest's collar. By 1944 Father Delvaux, then in his early fifties, sported a thick head of hair that was a variegated thatch of gray, brown, and white tufts, topping a square-jawed, heavily grained, pale visage. He wore a bushy mustache that rested beneath his convex nose, which, according to some former parishioners, appeared to twitch as he looked around with short sharp movements reminiscent of a raven.

He'd probably decided that there was no one there when he looked down and saw Augusta's diminutive form huddled in the doorway. The priest gently helped her to her feet and led her inside the church to the potbellied stove in the concierge's quarters. Once there he served Augusta a steaming cup of soup and gave her a thick woolen blanket. She soon fell asleep and didn't wake up until the following morning.

While she slept soundly in the concierge's quarters in the Noville church, she would have had no idea that the Nazi tide of destruction was once again sweeping into the Ardennes and that the race to capture Bastogne was now gathering momentum.

CHAPTER FOUR

The Fog Was So Thick

DECEMBER 18, 1944

THAT MONDAY MORNING IN THE SLEEPY VILLAGE OF NOVILLE, WITH the sound of battle resonating in the distance, good-hearted Father Delvaux gave Augusta what meager rations he could spare and bade her safe journey back to Bastogne. She said good-bye, thanked him for the food and shelter, and then disappeared into the fog. There's only one main road passing through Noville to Bastogne, so at least she wasn't far from home.

It was the same day that Jack Prior and the rest of Team Desobry of the 20th AIB were planning to head in the other direction, passing through Bastogne on their way to their stand at Noville. Augusta didn't meet them on the road but she would have seen some of the column arriving in Bastogne. She would soon get to know these Americans, including Capt. Jack Prior, better than she could have possibly imagined at the time.

When Augusta returned to Bastogne, she was alarmed to see people fleeing the city with whatever belongings they could load onto carts, cars, trucks, tractors, or anything else that had wheels. Those who had decided to remain were taking shelter in the cellars of their homes or in one of the several large communal cellars located throughout the city. Upon reaching her father's house, Augusta found a note. Her father and aunt had already gone to volunteer in one of the public cellars. They left Augusta a Red Cross armband to be worn by medical personnel. It would, in principle, allow her to move unrestricted around the city.

Other elements of the 10th Armored Division were entering the town and taking up residence where they could. Colonel Roberts established his headquarters in the Hôtel Lebrun on the rue de Marche. Simultaneously, the 10th Armored had become the "Ghost Division," which implied that they were not to wear any division patches on their arms or any insignia that revealed their identity. The Allies wanted to prevent the Germans from discovering that one of Patton's armored units was so far north and had arrived before the rest of the Third Army.

During a meeting at the Heintz Barracks, VIII Corps commander Maj. Gen. Troy Middleton asked Colonel Roberts how many teams he had assembled from his available force. Roberts answered that although he only had 2,700 men at his disposal, he had managed three teams. Middleton, aware that Bastogne was the city where seven roads converged, ordered Roberts to use these teams to block the three most potentially dangerous access roads to the city. Roberts then relayed the information to each of the team commanders, with the instruction to assume their positions.

Team Desobry, led by Maj. William R. Desobry, would head north to Noville, while Team Cherry, commanded by Lt. Col. Henri T. Cherry,

Heintz Army Barracks, Bastogne, 1936. CREDIT: UNKNOWN

wheeled east to Longvilly. Team O'Hara, Lt. Col. James O'Hara's group, shifted southeast to Bras. Roberts established his CP at the Hôtel Lebrun just a few yards from the main square, then known as the Carrefour.

When Jack Prior and his present company arrived at the market square in Bastogne, light snow was falling. A staff sergeant walked officiously up to the small group and instructed them to load up and get out to Noville immediately. They diffidently re-boarded the truck and set off down the high street behind the column heading for Noville. Team Desobry consisted of fifteen medium tanks, five light tanks, a company of infantry transported in M3 half-tracks, and a platoon of five M10 tank destroyers. There were accompanied by a unit of mechanized cavalry in three armored cars and six Willys jeeps. Unbeknownst to Team Desobry at the time, the whole 2nd Panzer Division, commanded by Col. Meinrad von Lauchert, was heading in the direction of Noville.

By now about two-thirds of Bastogne's population of nine thousand had fled the city. Of the three thousand who remained behind, hundreds had taken shelter in the space beneath the venerable Sisters of Notre Dame School. Like the thick winter mist that so often enveloped Bastogne, a sense of impending doom had settled over the city. The civilian population was now forced to head to the communal shelters beneath schools and churches or make their own cellars habitable for the duration of whatever was heading their way. Many GIs found accommodation with local families and shared their cellars during the bombardments.

Henri Chiwy and his sister-in-law had volunteered to work at one of the communal cellars beneath the Sisters of Notre Dame School on the rue du Sablon, not far from St. Peter's church on the main street. This was and still is one of the oldest and most revered schools in Bastogne. After returning from Noville and having a short rest, Augusta spent the remainder of the day looking around town, trying to find out which communal cellar her parents were in, and generally getting a feel for the current situation. Although the city wasn't under direct attack at that point, the growing tension must have been palpable. A large number of military vehicles appeared to be converging on Bastogne.

Augusta went over to one of the largest buildings in Bastogne, the seminary building at the edge of town, to see if her father was there. This was also staffed by nuns, two of whom were guarding the entrance to the cellar like stuffed penguins. One of them looked Augusta up and down and then flatly refused to allow her to enter, sending her away with a halfhearted "Hail Mary."

After being refused admission to that particular shelter, Augusta walked over to the Sisters of Notre Dame on the rue du Sablon. That's where she found her parents. The nuns, most of whom were familiar to Augusta, were very busy transforming the cellars beneath their school building into ad hoc shelters that would hopefully offer some protection to the resident students and local civilians in the event of any bombardment. At approximately 3:00 p.m. the first German bombs fell on the city near the chapel of Saint Therese.

The Sisters of Notre Dame School was relatively well provisioned, all things considered. The school had been damaged previously during the German attacks of 1940 and was no stranger to conflict. In the cellars Bastogne citizens Louis Requin and Justin Gierens had organized

The rue du Sablon, Bastogne, 1945. CREDIT: UNKNOWN

a small bakery to provide bread for the population. Granted, their first efforts left a lot to be desired, but they eventually got the hang of it. Moreover, thanks to the hard work of local farmers and Augusta's father Henri Chiwy, there was going to be enough meat to sustain them for the duration. These coordinated and well-organized operations initially provided sufficient food that the locals readily shared with the US soldiers. It's remarkable to note that despite the impending danger the Belgians ensured that their stomachs were well taken care of. As far as they were concerned, food has always been the overriding consideration regardless of any potential adversity.

Team Desobry arrived in Noville at around 11:00 p.m. Upon arrival they set up a roadblock and placed a slender screen of infantry around the village. The initial intention to establish minefields to the north and northeast was abandoned due to the ominous flow of US soldiers from other units falling back from the east on the approach roads through the village. They had already experienced the onslaught firsthand, and after taking some heavy punishment from the advancing Germans, they were happily getting out of the fray. Nevertheless, one platoon from the 9th Armored Division's CCR showed exceptional fortitude and became integrated into Team Desobry for the duration.

Meanwhile, Colonel Roberts had told Major Desobry to draft any men he could use into his organization. It was going to be a case of all hands on deck; cooks, G3 (operations) men, latrine orderlies, and anyone else who could pick up a Garand or a Thompson were requisitioned. Desobry stoically incorporated infantrymen and engineers into the local defense and used engineers to set up obstacles. He ordered his men to let any armored vehicles pass through the lines and continue on to Bastogne. He figured that additional vehicles would merely congest the streets of Noville and increase his vulnerability to enemy artillery fire. Because the team had arrived in darkness, they couldn't immediately take full advantage of the natural defenses of the area. A platoon of armored infantry from CCR, which fell back into Noville near midnight, gave Major Desobry a vivid picture of the enemy forces moving toward Noville from the east. They were preparing to make an epic stand against overwhelming numbers.

Jack arrived in Noville tired and haggard from the long journey and ordered his thirty-five-man crew to disembark and set up shop in what he assumed was an abandoned cafe nearby. In Ardennes, these traditional, no-frills drinking establishments of the day were called "brown cafes," usually one-room affairs with no lounge area. In this one the bare walls were covered with formerly white woodchip wallpaper now yellowing from the nicotine, and an old reversed dartboard hung redundant in the far corner. According to Jack's diary, the good-sized drinking area in the cafe would serve as a perfect location for litter cases.

The cafe's cellar was dreary and freezing cold, but he figured it was probably the safest respite in the whole building. He recorded that the invasive smell of poor drainage and raw sewage made him feel nauseous. Searching around the dank cellar by candlelight he almost jumped out of his skin when he saw two elderly people seated on upturned beer crates in the corner. They didn't speak to Jack, just began saying a rosary repeatedly. Jack attempted to communicate with them, asking if they were the owners of the establishment. The couple just glared at him and shrugged their shoulders. When he asked the same thing again in schoolbook French, the couple looked at each other and then nodded vigorously. Jack apologized for the fact that he was forced to requisition their establishment for the duration. The couple just continued saying their rosaries and virtually ignored him.

He assembled some of the empty wooden beer crates and turned them upside down to fashion a bed for himself, then laid out his sleeping bag on top. Before he could balance himself precariously on this makeshift bed he was interrupted by the all-too-familiar shout of "Medic, medic!"

Jack rushed upstairs to see what the commotion was about. As he emerged into the cafe he was almost blown off his feet, as suddenly the large front window shattered, sending fragments of glass flying in all directions. He quickly dove under a table to escape being peppered by the airborne shards. Two wounded GIs lay on litters in the middle of the cafe. Jack looked around to see who'd delivered them and then crawled out on all fours, keeping his head low as he inspected the nature of their wounds.

The soldier nearest to him had a sizable shard of glass protruding from his abdomen. He wasn't conscious. Jack moved stealthily toward the next patient. He'd escaped the glass but blood was pumping from his exposed aorta; his lower jaw had been almost completely blown away. A look of total fear registered in the soldier's eyes as Jack inspected the ragged, bloody flesh above his neck. He could clearly see that this was a hopeless case. He decided on the humane option and took three vials of morphine from his tunic, ramming them sequentially into the soldier's thigh. Within seconds the soldier's eyes closed and he stopped breathing.

Now dodging stray bullets that flew in through the open window, Jack went to look for water because the taps in the cafe were frozen solid. He stumbled out of the back of the building and gazed around in amazement at the sight that met his eyes. There in the back was a whole ammunition dump. If it were to take a direct hit, it would blow the cafe to smithereens and eliminate everyone within a fifty-yard radius. Moreover, those long-range German artillery shells were getting dangerously close.

At around midnight on December 18, men from the 101st Airborne Division arrived in Bastogne. They had spent almost fourteen freezing hours in the backs of those trucks after being hurriedly sent north from their base in Camp Mourmelon, in northern France. In the absence of Gen. Maxwell D. Taylor, Gen. Anthony McAuliffe was their acting commander. He quickly established his HQ at the Heintz Barracks that had been the previous location of the VIII Corps HQ under Gen. Troy Middleton.

At the time none of the civilians in Bastogne, including Augusta, had any idea of the magnitude of the German attack now getting under way. But they were to discover soon enough.

CHAPTER FIVE

Cafes and Cellars

DECEMBER 18 AND 19, 1944

IT WAS AROUND THIS TIME THAT FATHER LOUIS DELVAUX ENTERED the cafe and timidly offered his assistance to the medical team there. Jack was busy spreading sulfa powder onto a GI's bleeding stomach wound in an attempt to stem the flow when he briefly looked up and saw the priest. Jack asked him what he wanted. Father Delvaux hesitantly moved closer to Jack's patient and offered to help. Jack told him that the offer of assistance depended on two things: First, how quickly could the priest summon help from the Almighty? And second, did he know how to apply a wound dressing?

The priest said that he'd applied the odd bandage before. Jack didn't look up; he just pointed over to the far corner and asked the priest to administer last rites to a badly wounded GI whose intestines were slowly spreading out from his abdomen onto the dirty cafe floor. Jack was a devoutly religious man, and despite the circumstances he was heartened to see Father Delvaux appear on the scene.

The sound of battle was intensifying outside. The most pervasive problem for Team Desobry at that moment was the dense mist that surrounded this location. The village of Noville lies three miles to the north of Bastogne and about a half-mile behind two high ridges that spread out to the northeast and northwest. Behind the village there are a few logging forests that reach almost to the perimeter of Bastogne. This places the village in a shallow valley that is prone to mist emanating from the trees and the ridges at most times of the year, but particularly in late fall and winter.

Airborne troops from the 506th had arrived in Noville and taken up position in close proximity to the two ridges. They were commanded by Lt. James LaPrade, who, much to the consternation of Major Desobry, assumed command of the Noville outpost. They had a brief but fiery discussion as to who was in charge that ended with neither party being entirely sure. They were not aware at the time that two German divisions were closing in, but it's safe to assume that the torrent of shells and bullets landing in Noville would have rendered a long discussion about seniority and rank superfluous.

Jack recounted in a letter home how an Airborne soldier asked him for assistance. Jack donned his Red Cross–adorned tin hat and followed the soldier outside as the priest sat down to read yet another breviary. A few steps away from the cafe entrance they were reduced to crawling to escape the enfilade of bullets and shells raining down around their position. They had only managed to get a few yards down the main road when they were forced to roll into a ditch for cover. The fog only exacerbated the situation, making it difficult to assess the location and direction of both enemy and friendly combatants.

Jack saw the wounded man and crawled over to him. As he inspected the damage a bullet hit the fence post right behind them. Then another one impacted, and another. The paratrooper provided the reason they were being shot at. "Better keep low, Doc," he shouted, attempting to be heard above the tumult of explosions and bullets whizzing by them. "Some Kraut sniper's zeroed that cross on your helmet." As Jack lifted his helmet a bullet went straight through it and churned up the turf a couple of yards away.

Jack turned to the paratrooper and shouted for him to tell his boss that the situation here was becoming untenable, and that the wounded needed to be evacuated as soon as possible. He drove home his request by punching the frozen ground with his bare fist.

The paratrooper acknowledged, and hurriedly left the scene, returning moments later with the information that they were going to bring up four M3 half-tracks and attempt to move some of the wounded as soon as they could. As the paratrooper stood up to leave, a piece of German mobile artillery known as a *Jagdpanther* loomed out of the swirling fog about twenty yards away and fired at almost point-blank range in his direction. The paratrooper's head jettisoned from his shoulders and his lifeless body slumped to the snow like fresh meat on a butcher's block. Two Shermans and an M18 tank destroyer opposite the church returned fire, forcing the German vehicle to reverse into the mist.

The German attack now intensified, and Desobry made an urgent request to Colonel Roberts to withdraw from the situation. Roberts refused to acquiesce, and attempted to reassure Desobry that more reinforcements were on the way. It wasn't until Roberts went over to the 101st Airborne HQ at the Heintz Barracks and spoke to 101st assistant division commander Brigadier General Higgins that Roberts began to realize the gravity of the situation.

Supported by a battalion of paratroopers from the 506th, Team Desobry had been ordered to organize a counterattack. This was initiated but quickly dissolved. Once they realized they were outgunned and outnumbered by the attacking Germans, they fell back in disarray. The main problem the combatants faced was lack of visibility, which made it virtually impossible to gauge the size and strength of their opponents. Although the Germans may have sensed they had a numerical advantage, they nonetheless remained cautious.

A little while later LaPrade and Desobry were examining some topographic maps of the area when suddenly an 88 shell blew out the whole wall where they stood. The explosion killed LaPrade outright, and Desobry was so badly wounded that he required immediate evacuation. He had splinters of shrapnel in his legs and torso; making matters worse, his left eye had popped out of its socket and was resting on his bloodied cheek. Jack ordered an immediate evacuation to the 326th Medical Company, which was operating a division clearing station somewhere in the vicinity of Barrière Hinck, to the west of their current position in Noville. Despite the severity of his injuries, Desobry insisted on first being taken to Colonel Roberts's CP in Bastogne to make his report.

At 4:30 p.m. the following day, December 19, 1944, the 326th's commanding officer had organized a convoy of five ambulances full of wounded, essentially the first evacuation from the division clearing station, and led the way to the 107th Evacuation Hospital at Libin. The evacuation of casualties from the regiments to the division clearing station continued until 9:30 p.m., December 19, 1944. At this time, two vehicles loaded with casualties to be evacuated were sent from the regimental aid station, 501st Parachute Infantry, in Bastogne. When these vehicles didn't return, it was correctly assumed by the command that all was not well. When the evacuation officer of the 327th Glider Infantry Regiment attempted to take more casualties to the division clearing station, he was stopped by the 327th Glider outpost guards and informed that the Germans had apparently captured or overrun the whole area.

At approximately 10:30 p.m., an enemy force consisting of six armored vehicles, a few half-tracks, and a couple of tanks, supported by one hundred infantry soldiers, were proceeding southwest from Houffalize, a town north of Noville, when they attacked the division clearing station of the 326th Airborne Medical Company. The station itself was peppered with machine-gun fire from the half-tracks, and the tents in which medical treatment was being administered were also hit by the machine-gun fire. Six division trucks were set ablaze, lighting up the whole immediate area so that the red crosses on the clearing station tents were clearly visible to the enemy.

During a small cessation a German officer approached the station and questioned the senior US officer, surgeon Lt. Col. David Gold. After a brief discussion with the German officer, the colonel surrendered the 326th Airborne Medical Company. The Germans permitted them thirty minutes to load equipment and personnel onto the remaining vehicles and then escorted them back to their lines. Maj. William R. Desobry would continue his career in the army, but at that moment was among those taken as POWs at Barrière Hinck.

Back in Noville the promised evacuation vehicles hadn't arrived. The floor of the cafe was now so steeped in blood that it stuck to the soles of Jack's boots and made the sound of flypaper separating every time he attempted to move around the place. The thick dust combined with the smell of dead and dying men had transformed a once-amenable drinking establishment into an ice-cold pit of death and misery.

Jack had been on his feet for twenty-four hours straight and hadn't had any decent sleep for more than three days. Despite the fact he was gradually succumbing to the fatigue that threatened to consume his whole being, he kept going. His olive-green tunic now resembled a butcher's bloody apron, but still more wounded arrived. They were placed on and beneath tables, lying shoulder to shoulder on the floor, and piling up in a macabre steaming mound beside the cafe entrance. Rumors had begun to circulate among the ranks that a retreat was imminent, but no direct orders to that effect had yet been issued.

Father Delvaux continued to administer religious rites in the cafe while Jack and his men struggled on unabated. The priest walked across to a freshly arrived young man who was lying prostrate on the floor, shaking but fully conscious, and began reciting the viaticum (Holy Communion for those near death) for the umpteenth time. The young GI recognized the sacrament and joined in, and then asked Father Delvaux if he knew how long it would take for him to die. Jack momentarily caught the priest's attention and shook his head. Father Delvaux turned to the young man and knelt down beside him. He made the sign of the cross and held his hand until the young man released his grip.

A good few hours had now passed since the paratrooper had promised to provide half-tracks to help with the evacuation of the wounded and dying. With the exception of Major Desobry, up until that point evacuation of the many injured had been virtually impossible. Although they did manage to load four patients onto a half-track, just as it lumbered off it had received a direct hit from a German tank and burst into flames. GIs fought through the blaze as the four patients were unloaded and returned to the cafe, which had been transformed into a temporary aid station under the gaze of the German tank commander.

Throughout the morning of December 19 Augusta sat alone in a corner of a small cellar below her father's house in Bastogne. She could hear the German bombs raining down on the city and the US artillery responses as the very foundations of every building shook with each explosion. There was no heating down there in Henri Chiwy's cellar, and light was

A house in Bastogne during the bombing. CREDIT: UNKNOWN

provided by the dancing flame of a solitary candle. Although she did venture up to the kitchen occasionally it was generally accepted that the cellar was the safest place to sit out the bombardments.

The electricity and water had now been cut off, which would remain the case for the next four months. During a lull in the bombing around midday Augusta walked over to the Sisters of Notre Dame to see if she could be of assistance. One of the nuns, Sister Ursula, who remembered teaching Augusta, gratefully accepted her offer and told her that the biggest problem they had to deal with was hypothermia, but there were also serious health concerns related to unsanitary conditions in the cellars. One of the cellars beneath the school was being used to treat wounded GIs who lay on the stone floors among the wounded and ill civilians. This would have been Augusta's first encounter with battlefield trauma, but there is no record of her having assisted with these wounded men at this point. Instead, she spent her time helping the nuns tend the sick, and occasionally she assisted two local doctors, Dr. Heintz and Dr. Govaerts, who had both volunteered their services for the duration.

As the bombardment temporarily subsided, Henri and Charles Chiwy joined other volunteers in an attempt to retrieve dead and wounded livestock from surrounding farms and fields in close proximity to the city. This was a particularly precarious mission to undertake. Nevertheless, they were quite successful in their endeavors, and for the duration of the battle there was ample meat available for the inhabitants of Bastogne. Although meat may have been in abundance, medical supplies weren't; there continued to be a critical shortage of bedding, litters, penicillin, surgical instruments, and surgeons for civilians and soldiers alike.

While Henri was preoccupied with checking and carving up the retrieved carcasses, Charles told him that he wanted to go out foraging on his own. Henri immediately advised against this and asked Charles to return home, or remain in the safety of the cellar. Much to Henri's displeasure Charles left in a huff. His real intention was to go out and rejoin his resistance group, active in the vicinity.

The situation appeared to be deteriorating by the hour as the perimeter defenses gradually shrank under the weight of the German onslaught. In a desperate attempt to escape the fighting, refugees from surrounding villages began to head toward Bastogne. This meant that the communal cellars quickly filled to capacity as people sought shelter wherever they could find it. Augusta could only look on in despair as these additional refugees steadily descended into the cellars beneath the Sisters of Notre Dame, bringing with them stories of terrible devastation and destruction from the surrounding areas.

The people of Bastogne are known as *Les Bastognards*, and they are a special breed. Father Vanderweyden, a priest from the village of Marvie, had urged his parishioners to abandon their homes and seek refuge away from the fighting. Many of these people would never see their homes again. The priest ensured that he was the last person to leave the village before he set out across the fields toward Bastogne. He zigzagged his way to the perimeter of Bastogne, finally arriving at the chapel of Notre-Dame-de-Bonne-Conduite, not far from the cellar where Augusta was working. His progress was abruptly halted when a crew member of a

Sherman tank aimed his grease gun and asked the priest where he was going. The priest replied in perfect English that his village was under attack and he was seeking shelter in Bastogne. The soldier thought it was dubious that this person had come into town from the east, where some of the heaviest fighting was taking place. He suspected that Father Vanderweyden was a Nazi infiltrator, and decided to escort him to the cellar beneath the 20th AIB CP at the Hôtel Lebrun, where he was held captive until the following afternoon.

After he'd proven his identity, Father Vanderweyden was seen going from cellar to cellar offering absolution and attempting to bring some comfort to the desperate civilians there. He eventually worked as a military chaplain and held an open-air Mass over to the east of Bastogne, at the Mardasson Hill. Throughout the Mass he was in full view of the enemy, who fired artillery shells that exploded near his temporary altar, but didn't deter him from completing his service.

Augusta managed to return to her father's house and get a few hours' rest in the cellar that evening, but under the circumstances it must have been very difficult. The bombs were now raining down so close to the Notre Dame School that every nerve-shattering explosion caused clouds of asphyxiating dust to shake loose from the ancient rafters, now illuminated only by sparse candles and narrow shafts of light that occasionally pervaded the murkiness below.

The perpetual resonant screams of panicking children mixing with the agonized wails and moans of the wounded and dying would have tested the resilience of even the sturdiest observers. It was becoming increasingly obvious that no one was safe anymore, yet by the end of the battle for Bastogne, the Notre Dame School would provide refuge for and save the lives of a hundred students, six hundred to seven hundred civilians, and more than fifty nuns.

Chapter Six

No Way Out

December 20, 1944

German artillery shells were now falling on the town of Bastogne with increasing regularity. Almost all the civilians of Bastogne had taken to their cellars to begin a semi-subterranean existence, and they were quite content to share these small spaces with GIs when the need arose, as it frequently did.

Up in Noville, as morning dawned, they were running short of armor-piercing shells. Maj. Charles L. Hustead had been designated to take over command of the armor after Major Desobry had been wounded and taken prisoner. At his HQ in the Heintz Barracks, the former Belgian army barracks in Bastogne, General McAuliffe was wondering whether Noville was worth holding onto.

After hours of unabated combat the time had finally arrived for US forces to pull out of Noville and struggle back to Bastogne. A selection of vehicles was chosen and allocated to provide transport for the wounded. After they were loaded and full to the brim, Jack noticed that there were still many wounded men left in the aid station. Jack told Father Delvaux that he was welcome to join the departing vehicles if he wished, but the priest declined the invitation, preferring to remain with his flock in the now-devastated village of Noville. This courageous decision by the priest was to have severe consequences. Jack also reminded the priest of the couple who were still saying rosaries in the cellar. Then he inspected the remaining wounded and asked for volunteers to stay behind with him until they were all evacuated.

In a last desperate attempt to secure extra transport Jack ran out into the road and flagged down some Sherman tanks. The tank crews were more than ready to offer assistance, diverting their vehicles and driving up to the cafe entrance. Doors were ripped out and secured to the tanks to be used as ad hoc litters as the volunteers quickly loaded up the last of the wounded and moved out. The situation at the temporary aid station in Noville was becoming increasingly precarious as various vehicles pulled away, bearing wounded GIs strapped to virtually any movable flat surface available.

The Germans had now breached the perimeter of the village with two panzers and some infantry, and were only a few hundred yards away from the aid station. Despite this Jack still had a few wounded litter cases that hadn't yet been evacuated. It was at this juncture that he made an incredibly audacious decision, one which he imparted to Naftulin in clear language. Amid the deafening roar of sporadic machine-gun fire and exploding shells, Jack told Naf that he had decided to stay back with the few wounded litter cases that were still in the aid station, allowing himself to be taken as a POW by the rapidly advancing German forces.

Naftulin doubted the wisdom of this decision, and attempted to persuade Jack to leave. His appeals were to no avail; Jack was resolute when he told him, "I'm not leaving my men." Naftulin explained that he would also like to stay behind, but being Jewish, if he were captured he might not suffer the same fate. Jack wasted no time in pulling rank and ordering him to leave immediately. Glancing tenuously out of the doorway of the aid station through the fog Jack could actually see vague silhouettes of German armor maneuvering in his direction. Meanwhile, Naftulin threw himself into a passing Willys jeep with such force that he almost unseated the occupants.

Anxious moments passed as Jack resigned himself to capture. He set about making his patients as comfortable as possible before the Germans arrived on his doorstep. It was just then that a GI appeared in the doorway and shouted at Jack that it was high time to get the hell out while he still had a chance. Jack looked up and shook his head, but suddenly saw an M3 half-track that had stopped directly opposite the aid station. He commanded the GI to assist him in loading up the last of the litter cases. The GI agreed, but only under duress from Jack.

Ducking shrapnel they hurriedly hauled out the wounded men one by one and loaded them onto the back of the M3. Then with machine-gun bullets ricocheting off the rear doors, Jack squeezed into the passenger seat at the front as the M3 arduously spluttered and belched to life. While it was pulling away all of the occupants heaved a mighty sigh of relief. Seconds later as they drove away toward Bastogne, an enormous explosion resonated from behind the aid station cafe. The ammo dump located there had just taken a direct hit.

The M3 caught up with other vehicles heading south but were harried throughout the entire short journey by German mortar shells landing in close proximity. On the way back to Bastogne the convoy ran into even more problems. Team Desobry had retreated from Noville only to discover that Germans had occupied Foy, a village a couple of miles north of Bastogne that was on their direct route. A nervous situation ensued when the remnants of Team Desobry, arriving in Foy, were nearly caught between the 77th German regiment and the 26th Volksgrenadier regiment. This subjected the fragile convoy to yet another running battle as they attempted to reach the relative safety of Bastogne.

The other teams that had been charged with the task of stopping the German advance were also experiencing serious problems. Team O'Hara had so far failed to stop the flow of German troops and vehicles heading toward Bastogne, and out in Longvilly, Team Cherry was faltering. Due to various misadventures, Team Cherry could no longer tackle the approaching enemy and now had to refocus their energies on saving its remaining elements and covering its flanks and rear. Whether the German advance into Bastogne from the east could be checked now remained to be seen, but as each hour passed it became increasingly unlikely.

Throughout the whole day the Germans mounted continuous attacks in an attempt to penetrate the US Army defenses to the east of the city. However, eleven strategically placed artillery units and machine gunners on the approach roads to Bastogne maintained a constant barrage that effectively deterred the attacking forces. In addition to this, and despite being forced to retreat from Noville, Team Desobry/Hustead had stopped the whole 2nd German Panzer Division in its tracks, which had assumed it was opposing a much stronger force. Outnumbered ten to one, the Noville defenders knocked out thirty-one enemy tanks in two days.

Bastogne at this time was intact, but due to the underground existence of its inhabitants, it appeared to be a somewhat deserted city. The sight of abandoned streets still festooned with Christmas decorations must have been generally regarded as an unpromising sign for the survivors of Team Desobry as they gradually rumbled into the war-torn city.

The temperature had dropped quite a few degrees since the withdrawal from Noville; the weather was bitterly cold, and there was a good layer of snow on the ground when they arrived. Jack's new temporary aid station was initially established in an abandoned garage on the rue du Vivier, just off one of the main streets in Bastogne. He didn't plan on staying there long, however.

While Jack Prior was tending his wounded men in the temporary aid station, he realized that the only prospect for patients who had head, chest, and abdominal wounds was a slow, painful death; this was because although operations were carried out, under the present arrangement there was little chance of conducting complex surgical procedures. The extremity wounds were irrigated with a dwindling supply of precious hydrogen peroxide in an attempt to prevent Group A streptococcal disease (GAS) infections, better known as gangrene. Many other weather-related conditions such as frostbite, trench foot, and hypothermia were treated as best he could. It wasn't unusual for Jack to help a GI remove his boots only to discover that one or more of the soldier's toes had frozen off. He desperately needed assistance, but at that point in time he had no idea when or indeed if it would arrive. What Jack really needed was some serious help, but so far it looked like he was on his own. Exacerbating his situation was the recent drop in temperature to below-freezing conditions, augmented by the first snowfalls.

German soldiers had winter smocks and other appropriate clothing to deal with the weather. US troops in and around Bastogne didn't have this luxury, so they did what every good American soldier did frequently in World War II: They improvised. Many of them began to resemble people who'd just run through a clothing store during a hurricane. Blankets became erstwhile ponchos, while cotton pillowcases covered their helmets perfectly.

While Jack was struggling to meet the growing demands of the wounded, Augusta wasn't faring much better. Despite ample rations being available, she hadn't eaten properly for a few days, and the almost constant racket of artillery exchanges had deprived her and all the other Bastogne inhabitants of much-needed sleep. Still, she returned to the Notre Dame School and continued to tend to the civilians in the cellars there. Wearing two thick overcoats above her own nurse's gabardine, she darted from one patient to the next, checking temperatures and administering what medication she could procure.

One of the nuns, Sister Emmanuel, the Mother Superior, went to pray in a temporary oratory in the coal cellar when a shell fell on the sidewalk outside. A piece of shrapnel crossed the cellar, went through the wall behind the tabernacle, then through the ciborium (a container used to hold the hosts for the Eucharist) and the tabernacle door, striking Sister Emmanuel in the heart. She died instantly. Today, the current teaching staff at the school has a glass cabinet on display with the damaged ciborium beside a photograph of Sister Emmanuel.

Outside the fog still hadn't cleared and the city of Bastogne was beginning to resemble a forsaken gothic ruin. It was the children and the elderly that worried Augusta the most. They didn't have the resilience or stamina to stave off the bitter cold and weather-related conditions, such as hypothermia, frostbite, and pneumonia. Dr. Heintz had given Augusta a vitamin supplement to keep her active, but the strain was already beginning to show. Although she was used to pulling long shifts at St. Elizabeth Hospital, the present conditions were enough to test anyone's endurance. Adding to Augusta's woes was the news that her brother Charles hadn't returned from the foraging mission he'd said that he was going on. The possibility of being captured or killed by the advancing Germans was a real one, especially since he was a known member of the Resistance, having happily brandished his Lee-Enfield rifle and celebrated when the Americans had liberated Bastogne in September.

The armed Belgian resistance movement, "La Rose Blanche," had established itself in the Ardennes region of the country. Although there's no direct evidence linking Charles Chiwy to the group, it's more than likely he was active there. British records from 1942 show there were more clandestine transmitters in Belgium than in any other occupied country, and 80 percent of all the intelligence gathered by all resistance movements in all occupied countries that year came from there. In particular, the reports sent through regarding the placement of German radar were vital to the Allies' bombing campaign.

The scene below the Sisters of Notre Dame School now presented a hellish, grim tableau. The sound of children crying incessantly as mothers and fathers attempted to pacify them was interspersed by the wretched groans of the sick and dying. This continuous drone was punctuated only by the resounding boom of nearby explosions. Each petrifying blast shook the very foundations, adding to the terror and exacerbating an already-bad situation. People were huddled together in small groups speaking in hushed tones, flinching and cowering every time a bomb fell in the vicinity. So far they had all endured the siege with resigned dignity and courage, but the latter was dwindling among soldiers and civilians alike. Kneeling beside a sodden mattress on the freezing stone floor, Augusta continued to check temperatures and administer scarce medications.

───◆───

Just a few streets away from Augusta, Dr. Jack Prior had already relocated and was tending his wounded men in the new aid station on the rue de Neufchâteau. It was Naftulin who had discovered the new location, but now he was away on another mission. Naf had complained vociferously about the menial work that he was forced to do, probably because there wasn't much call for dental treatments at that time. So instead he used what medical training he had to perform jobs such as suturing and applying wound dressings, which proved to be of invaluable assistance to Jack. Jack was operating the 20th AIB's only such facility, and found himself in charge of over a hundred patients. About thirty of these men were very seriously injured litter cases that needed to be evacuated to a better facility. With Bastogne becoming surrounded, however, that option was no longer viable.

Meanwhile, haggard and exhausted, Augusta struggled back to her father's house and took refuge in the cellar there. All she needed was a few hours' respite from the incessant, calamitous drone of the crowded Notre Dame School cellars. There was still no news from Charles, but Augusta assumed that he would be all right. Henri Chiwy and his sister-in-law had also made it back to their home cellar. They placed mattresses and blankets around the floor and attempted to make it as comfortable as possible. They hadn't been down there long when a neighbor returned home to discover that his house had taken a direct hit and that his wife and three-month-old baby were trapped beneath the rubble.

Augusta went with her father to inspect the damage, but there was little they could do. The place was gushing flames and completely destroyed. As Henri Chiwy restrained his neighbor Augusta shouted around for assistance, yet there was none to be had. Suddenly the neighbor broke free and dove headfirst into the burning embers never to be seen again. To Augusta it felt like everyone was slowly but surely going insane, and just when she felt that the situation couldn't get any worse, it did.

CHAPTER SEVEN

Welcome to Hell

DECEMBER 21, 1944

AUGUSTA HAD BEEN LENDING A HAND, TENDING THE SICK AND DOING what she could for the people beneath the Notre Dame School, but as German artillery bombardments intensified it was becoming far too dangerous to keep venturing to and from the cellar of her father's house. So far the people who had remained in Bastogne had displayed great courage and fortitude, but the deteriorating situation was enough to break anyone's resolve. Feeling utterly exhausted through lack of sleep, Augusta managed to take a few books down to the cellar. Every so often she would peer through the pages by candlelight as she resigned herself to the possibility of staying down there for the duration, however long that would be. She had no idea; nobody did.

Now and again Augusta would hear thunderous bangs and feel the percussion waves from nearby blasts shaking the whole house to its very foundations and churning the contents of her stomach. Most of the windows had been blown out, along with bits of window frames and masonry that littered the rooms above the cellar, but there was neither the opportunity nor the inclination to clean up. Everyone lived in constant dread and trepidation of the next barrage, never knowing if it would be their last. Many were pushed over the edge.

Down in the cellars of the Notre Dame School Sister Ursula had managed to get a message to Henri Chiwy that Augusta's services were urgently required. Reluctantly Augusta donned her gabardine and waited for the bombing to abate before venturing out into the rubble-strewn

59

streets. She stepped awkwardly over tangled wires that had supported Christmas lighting and took care not to trip or twist her ankle on the dislodged cobblestones that surrounded the impact craters on the main street.

When she arrived at the school, she quickly made her way to the cellar where Sister Ursula was kneeling and inspecting the condition of two seriously ill young sisters. Augusta walked over and tapped her gently on the shoulder. The nun looked up, pressed her ill-fitting bifocals back from the bridge of her nose, and turned her head slowly toward Augusta while explaining that one of the doctors, Dr. Heintz, suspected tuberculosis. Augusta took out a thermometer, checked the temperature of one of the girls, and listened to her heaving chest. After a few moments she moved to the other girl, whereupon she confirmed that, on the basis of her knowledge, their symptoms appeared consistent with the early stages of tuberculosis. However, she reminded Sister Ursula that she was only a nurse and wasn't totally sure.

Sister Ursula listened attentively to Augusta's diagnosis and then, again pressing back her bifocals, beckoned Dr. Heintz over. She insisted that Mrs. Petit's young daughters be moved immediately to another location to avoid any contamination. Dr. Heintz nodded and reluctantly agreed to her request. Every time a bomb fell in the vicinity, more dust was being released into the dank cellar, which was beginning to adversely affect those with respiratory problems. This was further exacerbated by the ever-present cigarette smoke and other nauseating fumes permeating every corner of the crowded cellar.

The doctor inquired as to where the nun was planning to move the children, and Sister Ursula replied that she intended to take the children over to the cellar beneath the chapel. This cellar was actually a crypt, but it was empty, and the conditions there were a little more sanitary. The doctor warned Sister Ursula that he couldn't spare any medication or bedding. She paid little attention to him. She was already bundling up one of the youngsters in her arms while Mrs. Petit picked up her other daughter. Augusta offered to accompany them.

She walked closely behind the two women as they carefully ascended the steep stone steps that led from the cellar out into the adjacent court-

The inner courtyard of the Notre Dame School prior to the siege. CREDIT: UNKNOWN

yard. Although covering any distance in the open was precarious at that time, it was only about a hundred yards to the chapel. Augusta peered nervously out from behind a heavy oak door as the two women prepared to scurry across the cobblestone courtyard. She planned to wait until they'd reached the chapel before running over to join them.

In an attempt to break the resolve of its population and its defenders, the Germans now commenced twenty-four-hour shelling of the city. The bombing didn't always have the same intensity and could be quite sporadic at times, since the Germans were also experiencing supply problems. Out on the streets of Bastogne wreckage from the shelling was everywhere and bodies lay where they had fallen, frozen into incongruous shapes in the snow, more reminiscent of the Russian front than the Western one.

Augusta stared incredulously as Sister Ursula and Mrs. Petit, carrying their tightly wrapped human bundles, timidly emerged from the safety of the cellar and set off in the direction of the chapel, dodging the bomb craters along the way. Only a few yards from the cellar door they were forced to stop and crouch down to avoid shrapnel. Now outside in the open they were vulnerable and exposed to flying debris and flame as yet more shells began to descend on the city.

Suddenly there was an explosion in the courtyard and Sister Ursula appeared to stumble. Extending a hand to prevent herself from falling on her face, she held the child firmly but somewhat awkwardly under her arm and then managed to struggle to her feet. Her bifocals fell off completely as she recovered her balance. While Augusta shouted encouragement from the doorway, Sister Ursula wiped the dust from her eyes on the back of her sleeve and squinted toward her destination. It wasn't far anymore, but a second explosion caused Augusta to recoil behind the door. Seconds later she peeped out and scanned the courtyard, only to discover that where Sister Ursula had been holding the child there were only flaccid shards of flesh and torn clothing. She couldn't see Mrs. Petit.

The percussion from the blast had caused Mrs. Petit and her other daughter to slam against the high wall of the courtyard. She was still standing up straight but had dropped her daughter onto the cobblestones. In one move she quickly bent down low, gathered the small, inert frame up in her arms, and clasped the girl tightly against her bosom before setting out again. Augusta could clearly see that the child wasn't moving and a dark stain had begun to appear on her back. Still peering out from behind the door she screamed for Mrs. Petit to hurry. Just a few feet from the entrance to the chapel she fell to her knees and began to shuffle laboriously toward the door. Within moments Mrs. Petit had reached the chapel entrance and, using the door handle for leverage, she dragged herself upright. Then she forcefully kicked open the door and was just preparing to enter when the small building took a direct hit. Neither body was ever recovered.

Dr. Heintz heard a coarse, feral sound emanating from somewhere else so he ascended the stone steps to see what had occurred. He saw Augusta slumped onto her haunches, pressing her forehead against the back of the door and sobbing. Her tears coursed freely down her cheeks, making a path through the dust and grime on her face as she crouched there, wailing like a banshee. The doctor helped her to her feet and got someone to take her back to her father's house. After that Augusta never returned to the Sisters of Notre Dame School.

—◦—

Back in Noville, acrid black smoke still belched from the ruined buildings as the Gestapo arrived to interrogate the remaining villagers. They immediately arrested twenty-three men who had just left the relative safety of their cellars or returned from the surrounding woods to discover their homes in ruins. The suspects were taken to the municipal building for questioning. Some French-speaking Gestapo agents maintained there was a transmitter in the church tower, while others fiercely berated them for having celebrated the arrival of the Americans in September.

Although it was clear that they were mainly after members of the Resistance, none of the specific accusations made any sense to the accused. When they had finished interrogating the suspects, the Gestapo marched the men to the main road in groups of three. There they made them scoop mud and debris with their hands. The suspects were in fact being forced to dig their own graves. After enduring about fifteen minutes of this humiliation, the Gestapo took the men back to the municipal building.

Then they told six of the younger men to stand apart from the others and motioned for the village priest and the schoolteacher to join them. The eight men were marched off with their hands behind their heads. The Gestapo, in playing judge, jury, and executioner, decided that the penalty for collaboration with the *Amis* (Americans) was to be instant death. They took the men to a small clearing just off the main Bastogne road and told them to kneel down. A Gestapo officer placed his Luger in the mouth of one of his victims and pulled the trigger. The victim dropped like a stone as a jet of blood and brain tissue flared out from behind his head. The officer then turned to Father Delvaux and motioned for him to leave the group.

The priest began protesting. "What in the name of God are you doing?" he yelled. "Stop this madness immediately. You are not acting like men."

The Gestapo officer motioned again for the priest to leave the group but Father Delvaux remained where he was and looked to the other men. According to a local witness, the priest said, "Don't show these cowards any fear, my children. We are all going to meet our maker now. Go to him with a clear heart and the blessing of his humble servant here on earth." Then Father Delvaux walked up to the Gestapo officer and nodded his acquiescence. "Kill me then, if you must. I'm not afraid of you."

"I don't care," said the Gestapo officer belligerently. "You're all the same traitorous scum to me. You have all actively collaborated with the US Army and will therefore pay the price."

Just then a villager stepped forward and offered to take the place of the priest. Father Delvaux shook his head and a wry smile cracked his wrinkled visage as he told the man to go home to his family. He immediately added in a whisper that the man should get away from the area as soon as possible.

Artist's depiction of the execution of Father Delvaux and other citizens of Noville.
CREDIT: DARRIN HOOVER, PHIL GEGNER, AND SHAWN TETGEMEIER. COURTESY OF JASMINE AVENUE HOLDINGS

Delvaux looked around at his fellow victims and the German guards and said to them, "Courage, my sons. God is waiting to receive your souls." Then he closed his eyes and felt the barrel of the Luger press against the back of his head. That was the last thing he felt.

The victims were Father Louis Delvaux (age fifty); Auguste Lutgen (forty-five); brothers François and Felix Deprez (thirty and thirty-five); Joseph Rosière (thirty-five); Romain Henkinet (forty-two); Roger Beaujean (twenty-one); and Michel Stranen (thirty-nine).

The father of the two brothers was a witness to their execution.

During a small intermission between bombardments, Henri Chiwy pottered around the first floor of the house, picking up fragments of glass from a shattered window, while in the basement Augusta sat quietly on her mattress reading a book by candlelight. Her brother, Charles, had only gotten as far as Sainte-Ode before realizing that all the roads were blocked by the Germans and that he was going to have to return to Bastogne.

At the same time, Lee Naftulin had made his way to a communal cellar and asked some of the locals if they knew of any medical personnel in Bastogne. One man rose to his feet and stepped forward to provide information. A little while later Naf was knocking at the door of Gustave Lemaire's haberdashery store on the main square, then known as the Place du Carré (today it's McAuliffe Square). Gustave's daughter, Renée, answered the door and then called to her father. Naftulin slowly explained his current predicament to Gustave as Renée took her coat and bag and prepared to follow him to the new aid station around the corner on the rue de Neufchâteau. (Renée Lemaire and Lee Naftulin would later be seen walking often together through the streets of Bastogne by 10th Armored veteran William Kirby.)

On the way there Renée told him about another nurse who also lived in Bastogne. "I should point out, Doctor," she said, "that she isn't white." This was the first and only real indication that Renée was conscious of Augusta's ethnic identity.

Naftulin introduced Jack to Renée and then showed her around the aid station while Jack went over to where Augusta lived and knocked on the door. He thought that the building had been abandoned because no one answered. What he didn't know was that Henri Chiwy had left to see if he could find out any information about Charles while Augusta remained in the cellar with Mama Caroline. Augusta heard the knocking and timorously ventured upstairs to see who it was. Jack tried the door handle, but although it appeared to have been kicked open it was still blocked from the inside as if something heavy had been placed against it. After a while he walked around the back of the house and peered through a cracked window.

Within a few moments Augusta walked to the window where she saw Jack for the first time. He looked disheveled and unshaven, and Augusta was at first hesitant about talking to this unkempt-looking individual. She didn't speak particularly good English at the time but apparently understood a lot more than she could speak. She opened the window and stared past Jack. The first thing that he uttered was *"Parlez-vous anglais?"*

Augusta replied that she didn't speak it very well, and Jack said he had the same problem with French, although in fact he had quite a command of the language. At the time Augusta's knowledge of English was apparently sufficient for them to communicate, and Jack told her that there were a lot of young American men wounded and dying just a few hundred yards away. He added that even though he didn't have many medical supplies, he was sure that Augusta could help to ease their suffering.

Eventually Augusta went around to the front door and let Jack inside. There was nothing to offer him except her time. They went down to the safety of the cellar and sat silently facing each other for what seemed like an age. Then Augusta rubbed her bloodshot eyes and looked shyly at the doctor. She agreed that if her father gave her permission she would be glad to help out. She asked Jack why the Americans and Germans were fighting in Belgium, adding that Belgium was only a little country that had nothing to do with the war. She said, "Why can't you go and have your damned war somewhere else?"

Jack concurred with this sentiment and assured her that it was actually a "world war," and that the Allies were fighting just about everywhere else too. Then he went on to explain that nurse Renée Lemaire had already joined him over at the aid station, but another pair of soothing hands would really help. Augusta told him that she knew Renée a little. While they were talking, Henri returned with Charles. Augusta heard her brother's voice and excitedly ran up the cellar steps with her aunt. They both hugged Charles and then Augusta began rebuking him. Charles told her that after returning to Bastogne he had hidden in a cellar on the rue du Sablon. Henri Chiwy looked wide-eyed at Jack as Augusta explained the current situation at the aid station. Henri Chiwy told Augusta that it had to be her decision.

She decided to go and assist even though Henri had reservations. Unfortunately he wasn't able to articulate these to Jack at the time. He was worried about Augusta and wanted Jack to give him some guarantee about her safety, but he couldn't make himself understood. Moments later Augusta stood up and took her blue gabardine from the hallway. Jack took this as his cue to lead the way. They hurried together to the aid station, and when they arrived Augusta claimed that she could actually smell the place before she got to the entrance. Jack stepped over the threshold and Augusta followed him inside.

Though it had only been operational for one day, the constant arrivals of wounded GIs had reduced the US Army aid station, located at the former Sarma supermarket on the rue de Neufchâteau, to an unsanitary hovel. Here, the able-bodied waded ankle-deep in dirty bandages and human viscera while shreds of discarded clothing were thrown around in heaps that littered the grimy flagstone floor. In some places, blood had collected in shallow pools, slightly diluted by melted snow brought in on the boots of the wounded and their litter bearers. Like all the other places in Bastogne at that time, there was no electricity and no running water. The bedridden still wore remnants of uniforms that were stiff with dried blood and gore. Strategically placed candles cast a dim yellow glow that barely illuminated the haze caused by the condensation from open wounds and desperate breathing. Augusta described it as "the devil's breath," and Jack concurred when he turned to Augusta and said, "Welcome to Hell."

Within minutes of entering the building Augusta had rolled up her sleeves and gotten right to work, tending the many wounded. As she looked around the place she attempted to assess the condition of some of them. She noticed that some of the soldiers were sitting up, shaking uncontrollably, while others either lay writhing in pain or remained ominously dormant.

After only a few hours both Renée and Augusta were proving themselves to be attentive, professional, and dedicated nurses. Surviving in a city without electricity, water, food, and medical supplies was a daunting challenge, but the team carried on and did their absolute best despite all the adversity. While Renée preferred to circulate among the litter patients, sponging, feeding, wiping fevered brows, and distributing the few medications that were available, such as sulfa pills and plasma, Augusta proved herself to be extremely adept at dealing with the blood and gore caused by bullet, shrapnel, and shell wounds.

Sulfa—or rather, sulfanilamide—greatly affected the mortality rate during World War II. American soldiers were taught to immediately sprinkle sulfa powder on any open wound to prevent infection. Every soldier was issued a first-aid pouch that was to be attached to the soldier's waist belt. This pouch contained a package of sulfa powder and a bandage to dress the wound. Some of the main components carried by combat medics during World War II were sulfa powder and sulfa tablets.

Having used up nearly all the morphine, Renée was spoon-feeding four-star Cognac to some of the patients. Two previous recipients had even started singing on the strength of it. A third had reportedly gone AWOL. Both Renée and Augusta even used the Cognac to disinfect their hands. On one occasion as Renée peeled away a soiled wound dressing, the soldier turned his head and suddenly, like a geyser erupting, a spout of blood gushed from a hole in the right side of his neck. The young soldier screamed as his hands clawed desperately at the air. Jack rushed over and stuck a pair of forceps along with his index finger into the wound, blocking off the severed artery. Renée recoiled, holding her hand over her mouth as Augusta rapidly intervened and immediately began threading a suture needle. First Jack stemmed the bleeding and sealed the artery; then Augusta repeatedly forced the needle into the wound of the semiconscious soldier until it was well and truly closed up. Around one-tenth of all deaths in World War II were caused by hemorrhage from extremity wounds.

Jack noted in many letters that although her presence alone was greatly welcomed by the wounded men, Renée always felt awkward and uncomfortable at the sight of so much blood. Nevertheless, he wrote that the presence of Renée and Augusta was a morale factor of the highest order, even if the deteriorating medical situation was ever worsening, with little hope for the surgical candidates, and any superficial wounds beginning to develop GAS infections.

—◦—

Naftulin was becoming increasingly fond of Renée to the point of obsession, and he made his affections known in many ways. Being an expert procurer of whatever was required, he made sure that Renée received ample supplies of chocolate and cigarettes for the duration. He even managed to get her some nylon stockings. They were seen in very close proximity on more than one occasion, and Renée for her part was very aware of the power of her feminine wiles. She wasn't above a bit of flirting when the situation required it. To a young dentist far from home, this was encouragement enough as far as he was concerned. Naf appears to have displayed double standards, though, because he mentioned to Jack that he wasn't comfortable with him being so friendly to Augusta. He didn't go so far as to confront Jack on the subject, but he did make his opinions known.

Meanwhile rumors were circulating around the GIs out on the perimeter that the Germans were actually using children to infiltrate the US line. This must have induced some marked paranoia among the ranks, because later that day Jack witnessed a cold-blooded murder right before his eyes. One of the most highly decorated soldiers in the 20th Infantry Battalion shot a civilian boy in the back, right in in front of Jack's aid station. Jack promised that when it was all over he would personally see to it that the GI received a dishonorable discharge for shooting a non-combatant.

At the aid station all the serious cases had been assembled on the first floor, while the rest were dispersed around the cellar directly below. There were well over a hundred patients by this time. While doing his rounds Jack leaned over one of his patients and sniffed the dressing on his leg.

The smell that permeated Jack's nostrils caused him to throw back his head in disgust. He shouted for Renée, who was tending a patient at the other side of the room, and asked her to smell the dressing. She nodded her head vigorously and concurred that the abhorrent odor was probably caused by a GAS infection. The same smell appeared to be coming from the wounded man's bandaged hand, as well.

There was still no morphine or any kind of pain relief in the aid station. As previously mentioned, hygiene and even anesthetic had been reduced to administering large doses of four-star Cognac, which had been procured by Lee Naftulin and was now available in abundance. Jack rummaged through his medical bag until he found what he required: an army knife with a serrated edge. Much to his own dismay he realized that he was going to have to utilize this rudimentary means to amputate the infected limbs, "Civil War" style. Renée stroked the wounded man's forehead while Jack told her what he required.

She recoiled at this and suggested that he ask Augusta instead. Augusta was fast asleep on a woolen blanket on the bathroom floor, covered only by her trusty old blue nurse's gabardine. Jack patted her shoulder gently and she awoke with a start. Jack quietly asked her to assist with a vitally important surgical procedure. Augusta rubbed her eyes and groggily eased herself to an upright position. It was around 4:00 a.m. when Jack explained the problem to her. Jack's face looked like all the blood had drained from it; he desperately needed to get some rest, but that simply wasn't possible under the circumstances.

Jack and Augusta walked over to the wounded man and began to prepare him for surgery. First Jack sterilized his only implement, his army-issue dagger, and then he and Augusta gathered the suturing materials and bandages that would be required after the limbs had been removed. Although the wounded man was barely conscious, he was still aware of what was going on around him. He protested weakly and tried to call for help. Jack held the bottle of Cognac to the patient's mouth and poured it in like he was funneling gas into a tank. The viscous liquid dribbled out of the sides of the man's mouth and collected in a small pool at the base of his neck. He asked Augusta for a fresh bottle and held out the empty one for a replacement. She soon returned with a full bottle.

Jack explained that this was going to be a double amputation. The wounded soldier's hand and foot had to be amputated in the shortest possible time to avoid the patient going into shock.

The wounded man muttered insensibly as the alcohol kicked in. As Jack carefully removed the field dressing from his foot, two rancid, gangrenous toes actually came off with it. The foot was black and festering badly. Augusta had never seen live maggots eating putrefied flesh before, but she firmly fixed her hands around the man's ankle and Jack set to work immediately. The wounded man jolted and blood spurted out in a dark stream as the knife made a deep incision just above the infected flesh. Speed was of the essence; as Jack sawed away frantically, the wounded man screamed and writhed in agony. Jack said that this was a good sign. Augusta held on tight. The wounded man squirmed and struggled but within a few seconds the first limb had been successfully removed and he'd lost consciousness. Then Jack set to work on the hand, cutting with the same speed and precision he'd employed with the first amputation.

Within a few minutes it was all over. Augusta irrigated the wounds with the last of the hydrogen peroxide, then sutured the extraneous jagged flesh on both limbs and expertly bandaged them up. After this she took some towels to mop up the pools of blood that had collected on the tiled floor around the litter. Jack arched his back and wiped a bloody hand on his tunic as he turned to Augusta, who was working away to clear the stain.

"Nice work, Augusta. What really bothers me is that if we don't get some antibiotics soon, he will die anyway."

Augusta was touched by the depth and sincerity of Jack's compassion for his patients. He wasn't just going through the motions, doling out whatever he could; he genuinely cared for these young men who were far from home, fighting for survival in a land that wasn't theirs. It was incomprehensible to Augusta at the time that these strangers would risk life and limb to liberate people they didn't even know.

The bombing intensified and some shells were falling dangerously close to the aid station. Precisely how close would soon become apparent to everyone confined within the walls of that abandoned grocery store. Outside the fog still hadn't cleared, but rumors that the weather would improve were circulating at the time. Augusta's clothes were now dried stiff with congealed blood and grime; she had no alternative but to work, sleep, and eat in them. Her hair was so dirty that it felt as if it were stuck to her head like a scouring pad. Renée Lemaire's attire wasn't faring much better, but she still looked good despite everything.

Renée was obviously more popular with the patients than Augusta. There were even a few patients who refused to be treated by Augusta because of the color of her skin. Due to racial segregation laws at the time in some of the Southern US states, there were always going to be some dissenters among the wounded who were very reluctant to be touched by Augusta. However, that didn't appear to distract her in the slightest. Belgium had treated her as a second-class citizen for as long as she could remember, so a few racist remarks from culturally vacuous soldiers didn't break her stride.

Jack made a concerted effort to continually remind the soldiers that Augusta was a volunteer and she didn't have to tend them if she didn't want to. She was there by choice. She hadn't been drafted or inducted into the ranks; in retrospect, that would have been an altogether different situation. Due to strict segregation policies in the US Army, while whites could go to black hospitals for treatment, the reverse was not true. Even the donated blood was kept segregated.

On one occasion Jack berated one of these men quite severely, telling him that if Augusta wasn't good enough to treat him, then he was welcome to join the pile of frozen stiff corpses outside. The wounded man's racially motivated reluctance soon dissolved.

CHAPTER EIGHT

Whose Nuts?

DECEMBER 22, 1944

ON THE MORNING OF DECEMBER 22 JACK OFFERED AUGUSTA A CUT-down army uniform to replace her own clothes. Augusta wasn't too happy about putting it on at first, because even with the ad hoc alterations it was still four sizes too big for her diminutive frame. Her own clothes, however, were so bloodstained and grimy they were no longer wearable. Sleep deprivation and fatigue were now taking a heavy toll on her, but she was determined to carry on regardless. Jack had already expressed his profound admiration for August's talents, and he was even more amazed by her continuing fortitude and tenacity. It was as if she was impervious to her surroundings and situation. She just labored on unabated.

On the perimeter, in the foxholes and slit trenches, GIs shivered and huddled together in a vain attempt to stave off the encumbering cold. The scarcities that they shared and endured back then formed a bond of friendship among the survivors that appear in some ways to supersede the experiences of other veterans who fought in other theaters. In our ignorance we cannot begin to imagine how much these people suffered during this battle. The place was still shrouded in dense fog, and over a foot of snow had accumulated over the past few days, exacerbating an already bad situation. Some artillery units were down to their last shell, and all stocks of ammunition were becoming seriously depleted. Resupply was now a matter of great urgency to all concerned.

A Nazi surrender party, consisting of two officers and two senior enlisted men, approached the lines of the 327th Glider Infantry Regiment to the south of the city, between Marvie and Assenois. The noncommissioned officers each carried a white flag, while one of the two officers carried a briefcase under his arm. In their long overcoats and shiny black boots, the enemy soldiers confidently walked past a bazooka team, then stopped in front of the foxhole of Priv. Leo Palma, a Browning automatic rifle (BAR) gunner. Palma was so stunned that he didn't even raise his rifle. The Nazi lieutenant spoke to him in English.

"I want to see the commanding officer of this section."

A staff sergeant who had been manning a position nearby walked out to the road and called the group over to him.

"So you Heinies finally decided to surrender, is that it?" he said sarcastically.

"Take me to your commander" was the curt response.

The enemy party was taken to a nearby platoon command post, and while the enlisted men were detained, the officers were blindfolded and taken to the unit's commander. Here, they formally presented their commander's surrender ultimatum to American forces. The demand quickly made it to General McAuliffe's division headquarters across town at Heintz Barracks.

"They want to surrender to us?" he asked his chief of staff, Lt. Col. Ned Moore.

"No, sir," Moore responded. "The Nazis are demanding *we* surrender to *them*."

McAuliffe laughed out loud. Not known as a profane man, he said: "Us? Surrender? Aww, nuts!"

McAuliffe's staff just stared at him, not sure what to say. McAuliffe got the distinct impression they were sure he'd surrender. "We're not surrendering, gentlemen," he said. "Now, the question is, how do we articulate that to the German commander?"

The room went quiet again.

"Well, sir," Lt. Col. Moore finally responded after a pregnant pause, "I think your first response is quite appropriate."

"What?" McAuliffe asked, unsure of Moore's meaning.

"Nuts, sir."

"Nuts?" McAuliffe asked.

"Well, yes," Moore said. "It's what you always say in these situations. We ought not to waste time drafting an eloquent response. Why not tell the Krauts what you really think of their request, General?"

McAuliffe stared off and thought for a moment, chuckling under his breath.

"Nuts . . . ," he muttered to himself. "Okay, Ned. Type it up."

A few minutes later, the commander of the 327th Glider Infantry Regiment, Col. Bud Harper, who had received the original surrender demand from the Nazis, carried McAuliffe's typed message back to the company command post where his men had detained the two German officers.

"Gentlemen," he said to them. "I have my commanding officer's reply."

In thickly accented English, the German lieutenant asked, "Is it written or verbal?"

"It is written, Lieutenant," Harper said, adding, "I will place it in your hand."

"Is the reply negative or affirmative, Colonel?" the Nazi officer asked. "If it is the latter, I am authorized to negotiate further."

Colonel Harper, clearly annoyed, responded, "The reply is decidedly not affirmative, Lieutenant."

The enemy officer unfolded the paper, read the single-word response from McAuliffe, and then looked back at Harper, appearing quite confused.

"What is, 'nuts'?"

"Gentlemen," Harper said, "your commander would be wise to stop this foolish attack before your army is soundly defeated."

The colonel spun around to one of his staff officers.

"Captain," he said. "See to it that these fine men are escorted back to their lines."

"Yes, sir."

"And if you don't know what 'nuts' means," Harper said, turning back to his adversaries as they prepared to walk out, "in plain English, it is the same as 'Go to hell.' Please make sure your commander understands that."

The German officers saluted stiffly.

"We will kill many Americans," the lieutenant said, now appearing quite nervous. "This is war."

"Well, good luck to you," retorted Harper, grimacing.

He always regretted saying that.

———

This simple response from 101st Airborne general Anthony McAuliffe was an idiom, so it's no wonder the Germans at Bastogne were confused by General McAuliffe's one-word answer to their ultimatum for surrender. McAuliffe was not given to profanity; still, whatever "Nuts" may have meant to the Germans, it was clear the Americans weren't about to surrender. The message may have been initially misunderstood by the recipients, but one German officer who had a comprehensive understanding of the English language reliably informed his superiors that the American general was in fact making a blatant riposte to the German ultimatum.

The news that McAuliffe had said "Nuts" to the Germans spread like wildfire around the ranks, and was a great boost to the defenders' morale. It became a rallying cry to those US troops attempting to break through to Bastogne.

Later that morning a paratrooper from the 101st Airborne entered the aid station and approached Jack Prior as he attempted to get frozen plasma running in a drip. The corporal asked if Jack was the man in charge. Jack looked up and surveyed the paratrooper. He looked young, probably not a day over twenty, if that. His face was a veritable collage of dirt, three-day-old whiskers, and dried blood. He held his M1 carbine loosely at his side and was darting glances around the place as if on guard. Since the action at Noville Jack had grown to respect these baggy-trousered troops and the job they did. The corporal told Jack that there were around six men down just east of the Mardasson Hill, and that they were in need of urgent medical attention. Jack asked him if he had transport and the corporal told him that he would requisition a truck for the duration.

Jack asked Lee Naftulin to hold the fort and then turned to the two nurses to tell them that he needed one of them to assist. Renée was in close-enough proximity to hear the request but didn't particularly care to participate, so she looked away and continued sponging down a patient. Augusta turned to Jack and told him that she would volunteer. The paratrooper returned with a requisitioned deuce-and-a-half truck and within minutes they were all loading up. Jack took the wheel, and Augusta sat wedged between him and the paratrooper as they drove east on the rue de Clervaux. As they approached the Mardasson Hill they could clearly hear the sound of battle drawing ominously nearer. Jack put a reassuring hand on Augusta's shoulder and instructed her to keep her head low because there could be firing involved.

The truck pulled up beside a small copse of Scots pines and everyone disembarked. As they did German bullets whistled past the canopy of the truck, some even tearing holes in the canvas. The paratrooper responded with a few rounds from his M1 carbine. Then the paratrooper signaled to other men from his company that he'd returned with a medic and a nurse. Jack and Augusta crawled apprehensively behind the paratrooper to an open area where some of the wounded men were lying in the snow. Due to drifting, the snow was now waist-deep in some parts, and there was still a thick mist providing good cover as they cautiously progressed to the wounded. Jack began to make his assessments of their respective conditions.

The first case Augusta approached was a paratrooper with a serious head wound that she considered beyond help. She carefully put the dead soldier's brains back into his skull cavity and wrapped a bandage around it to keep them in. The next man was lying in a pool of blood that was still gushing from his neck and chest. Jack quickly examined him with Augusta, but the patient's eyes were enough to communicate that any attempt at a repair job was superfluous. Jack checked his heartbeat and Augusta closed the man's eyes. Distant flashes of artillery and machine-gun fire reminded them that this was an active battlefield. Jack rolled over in the snow to the next wounded man. He took out his torch, and as he checked the man's eyes he noticed that the pupil of his right eye was dilated. Jack could feel swelling around the back of the man's head. He called back to the paratrooper to ask if he had a corkscrew on him.

The paratrooper crawled quickly over to Jack and, lying on his back in the snow, rummaged around his capacious pockets and produced the requested item with a flourish. Jack snatched it out of his hand and began screwing it into the wounded man's skull. Seconds later a torrent of blood gushed about two feet into the air, only just missing Jack. It quickly diminished to a dribble as Augusta took over and closed the small wound with silk sutures. Jack marveled as she performed this task unflinchingly.

Jack shouted to the paratrooper to get the soldier over to the truck. Bullets now whizzed past them with increasing frequency. The Germans had zeroed on their position and any minute now mortars and 88s would be tracing a deadly path to their location. Two other wounded men had managed to get to the truck when suddenly a mortar shell landed among the trees and the paratrooper poleaxed backward onto the snow. Jack, who was assisting a walking wounded, looked around, startled. He dashed over to the paratrooper who was lying prostrate beside the stump of a fir tree and shook his shoulder. The paratrooper blinked open his eyes, looked around, still a little stunned by the explosion, and told Jack that he was just winded.

The paratrooper got to his feet and sashayed behind a tree to catch his breath. Augusta noticed that the ground around her appeared to be getting torn up but she didn't assume that this was caused by machine-gun bursts until she surveyed the two fresh bullet holes in the hem of her blue gabardine. She just exhaled sharply and continued working undeterred, carefully dusting sulfa powder on the thigh of a wounded soldier who'd caught some shrapnel from a tree burst. Augusta then expertly applied a bandage before asking him if he could walk. The soldier replied that he could crawl if she helped him, so together they moved laboriously, inch by inch, through the snow toward the apparent safety of the truck. As they approached Jack noticed the holes in Augusta's gabardine and said, "Nice work, Augusta. Looks like they almost got you. It's a good job that you're small; that's probably why they missed."

She dismissively replied, "And a black face in all this snow isn't an easy target? Those Germans are just bad shots."

Bullets and shrapnel continued to impede their work but they carried on, undaunted, until all the wounded in the immediate vicinity were cleared. Then the guttural rumble of approaching engines forced them to abandon their tasks and get back to the truck as fast as possible. Jack drove away from the scene with all haste, and around twenty minutes later they were safely back at the aid station. Augusta inspected the bullet holes in her gabardine again and then told Jack that she had never really liked that coat anyway.

— • —

Left to his own devices, Naf's blatant advances toward Renée were becoming more fervent, but Renée was a woman who knew how to handle herself. Although she may have flirted occasionally, she wasn't someone that could've been referred to as promiscuous. Those young, handsome GIs were indeed very popular with the ladies of Bastogne, and there's no doubt that some of the relationships did develop a physical element. Belgium, however, was still a devoutly religious country, and most of the girls there would, like Augusta, have been educated in strict convent schools and subjected to rigorous moral guidance by the nuns. This would have undoubtedly governed the way they led their lives, as the church was still powerful during the war.

When they entered the aid station Jack advised Augusta to get a few hours' sleep while Renée pulled the night shift. Naftulin told Jack about McAuliffe's response to the Germans, which raised a smile on Jack's bloodstained face. Then he looked straight at Augusta, rubbed his chin pensively, and told her that she was a great nurse. Augusta dismissed the compliment, saying she was only doing her job. She wanted to tell him that she was terrified throughout the whole ordeal, but couldn't find the words to adequately articulate how she'd really felt about the situation.

Jack reverted to sign language before he stopped, took a breath, and suddenly turned to Augusta. He reached out his arms and delivered a mighty hug that took Augusta completely by surprise. Her first instinct was to recoil, but feeling his powerful arms around her small frame made her feel safe for the first time in days. Augusta reciprocated by reaching up onto her tiptoes and planting a moist kiss on Jack's stubbly cheek. For a few seconds they held each other close, oblivious to the world around them. In that moment there was no war or death to distract them; their lives were blessed and blighted in the same breath. They were just two vulnerable human beings enjoying a rare moment of tenderness normally denied in such situations. Augusta looked deep into Jack's eyes and noticed something that she hadn't seen before. He looked defenseless, and there was definitely apprehension there too. He parted his lips to say something but no words escaped. From that instant Augusta deduced that, although so far he'd successfully managed to conceal his fear, Jack was just as afraid as the rest of them. Augusta had never had a boyfriend as such, and this was a completely alien experience to her, but she felt closer to him at that moment in time than she'd ever felt to any other living soul. For the first time in her young life she felt loved.

Augusta quickly regained her composure and pulled away hastily. The moment had passed, but it had left an inedible stamp on her heart that she would never forget. Augusta realized that she was beginning to like Jack Prior a lot. That evening, during a brief respite, she stood looking out the window for a moment. Jack tapped her on the shoulder and asked if she could see the stars. Augusta shook her head. Then Jack pointed skyward and said that he thought he'd just seen one, but he wasn't sure. He reminded Augusta to get some sleep, and thanked her again for the day's work.

Augusta's gaze drifted from the heavens until she was staring directly at Jack. She felt sure there was something in his eyes—that he was trying to communicate something to her that he dared not say out loud. She pressed her index fingers against the corners of her eyes to remove the dust, and when she looked again a second later Jack was gone. Were the clouds finally clearing?

Belgians are very tactile people, and those in the French-speaking part of the country, particularly, have a tendency to be overtly emotional. They wear their hearts on their sleeves. Jack didn't. In many ways he was emotionally retentive, preferring to internalize his feelings as opposed to letting them be known. He regarded himself as a leader, and probably in his opinion leaders weren't the kind of men who allowed emotion to cloud their judgment.

While the fighting that occurred during the battle for Bastogne devastated this centuries-old market town, many deep and lasting bonds of friendship evolved between the American soldiers and citizens of Bastogne. Suffering the same deprivations drew them together even though the fighting was far from over, and the worst was still to come.

⸻

On that same day, with the help of Naftulin and Jim Revell, a supply officer, Jack delivered a baby in Bastogne. After it was delivered Jack asked his assistants what they'd done with the afterbirth.

"Gee, what's that, Doc?" was the reply he got from Jim Revell. Jack noted that the woman was probably still walking around somewhere with the placenta still intact.

Something that Jack also acknowledged at that time was Augusta's speech patterns. She began stuttering slightly and flinching at every loud noise, even when the explosion wasn't in close proximity. A new batch of wounded had arrived at the aid station that evening and fresh blood had pooled on the floor, mixing with water from the snowy boots of soldiers constantly transiting in and out. With little hope for the surgical candidates, even the superficial wounds were now at risk of developing gangrene. The overpowering stench inside the aid station was becoming more reminiscent of an abattoir than a medical facility.

Jack thought of this situation, then and later, as a low point in the history of the US Army. He continued to marvel at how Renée and Augusta kept going despite the deteriorating conditions there. All the medical supplies were used up and there was no indication that they were going to be resupplied in the near future. They'd reached the bottom of the pit.

CHAPTER NINE

Blue Skies Smiling at Me

DECEMBER 23, 1944

THE BESIEGED RESIDENTS AND DEFENDERS OF BASTOGNE HAD ALMOST reached their nadir. Life in the city had long since lost any semblance of normality, but the situation was now at its absolute worst. The absence of running water and electricity at the aid station, compounded by a total lack of medical supplies, pushed everyone to the limits of their endurance. Naftulin had procured what he could from the 101st Airborne HQ, but they couldn't spare much either. At least the skies appeared to be clearing.

Augusta stepped outside the aid station briefly for some air and to attempt to get the all-pervasive smell of death out of her nostrils. She looked up and saw the very same skies she'd studied with Jack the night before, but didn't experience any great feeling of elation. All she had to do was turn around and look inside the aid station to see death and dying. It plundered her senses and subdued any feeling other than one of utter despondency. She felt empty and drained. Since working at the Notre Dame School, her emotions had been hovering in suspended animation. She had shed some tears for the people of Bastogne and for those young men whose lives had been prematurely stolen, but the well that held those feelings was almost dry.

Renée had demonstrated much more emotion than Augusta. Renée had become the Angel of Bastogne while Augusta carried on, almost unnoticed except by the soldiers she was treating. Some US soldiers continued to refuse her when she tried to treat their wounds because she was black. She had been hurt by this treatment, based purely on the color of her skin, and this had caused her even more emotional turmoil. Even Jack Prior appeared to be biased toward Renée, the nurse who hated the sight of blood. Augusta didn't mind it; after all, she had spent the last few days up to her elbows in it, along with every other kind of human effluence.

The one condition that she didn't know how to treat was shell shock. When young men were brought to the aid station, shaking or immobilized by severe trauma, Augusta didn't know how to deal with them. There was no respite, and of course, no medication that the staff could administer. They were continuing to ply the wounded and badly traumatized with alcohol.

Lee Naftulin thought that Jack was casting more than a concerned eye in Augusta's direction, and even mentioned it to him. Jack naturally denied anything more than a professional regard for his nurses. He said that one would have to be pretty determined to consider anything more than that under the present circumstances, but Naf didn't believe him. It's possible that Naftulin was attempting to distract from the fact that he'd been spending almost all of his time in close proximity to Renée.

Jack helped wrap up one of the previous night's amputees in a makeshift body bag. There were no real body bags left; they had all been used. Very early that morning before sunup he'd decided to attempt to get out to the 101st aid station located inside the Belgian army barracks on the outskirts of town. Outside on the rue de Neufchâteau, bombs were still falling, but they'd been a little more sporadic during the past few hours. Jack deduced that this could be for one of two reasons: Either the Germans were running out of ammunition, or they were saving it for a new offensive. He suspected the latter.

Jack decided to go over to the 101st HQ at the Heintz Barracks on the other end of town to try to procure some provisions. He arrived there at about 8:00 a.m. and immediately sought out Davidson, the chief surgeon there.

Although they had never met personally before, each was aware of the other's reputation. Dr. Douglas Davidson sat behind his desk in the cellar of one of the barrack buildings. Jack formally introduced himself and was warmly greeted by the doctor, who immediately ordered coffee for the two of them.

"How's it feel to be surrounded, Major?" asked Jack.

"Call me Doug; we can dispense with formality for the time being," he replied. "Well, we survived Normandy and Holland, and according to the rulebook, we're supposed to be surrounded, so situation normal by our standards."

Jack pulled up a wooden chair, clasped his hands, and rested his elbows on Dr. Davidson's desk as he said, "Well, no point in beating about the bush, so I'll cut right to the chase. I've come to bum some supplies off you, Doug."

Dr. Davidson replied that he would love to help out, but warned Jack there wasn't much to spare because their entire medical company had been captured by the Krauts a few days earlier. Then Dr. Davidson slowly rose from behind his desk and asked Jack to accompany him over to the main area being used to accommodate the wounded.

While they were walking across the parade ground Jack noticed the various signs written in gothic script on the walls of the barracks. During the occupation it had been used by the German army as a training depot for new recruits. They approached a large redbrick building, and as Dr. Davidson opened the door and led Jack inside they were confronted with a gruesome tableau. There, in something that resembled an aircraft hangar, were over six hundred litter cases, not counting the walking wounded and the psychiatric cases that hung around the perimeter of the former Belgian army "Riding Hall" of the Heintz Barracks.

Dr. Davidson told Jack that he had heard the previous day there could be a supply drop coming their way at any moment. He added: "I've got my reservations, though. The Krauts are going to do their damnedest to shoot down anything that even attempts to fly over Bastogne."

"Well, it looks like the skies are clearing, so who knows?" Jack said. "This could be our lucky day."

Jack loaded what provisions the 101st could spare into the back of the truck and set off.

When they got to the aid station, two GIs from CCB 10th Armored Division were waiting outside. They asked Jack if he could pick up some wounded a few miles down the road at Marvie. Augusta was nearby and overheard; without being asked, she immediately donned her coat and rushed into the truck. Jack thanked her for gracefully accepting yet another invitation to see the war up close. Jack also asked Naf straight out if he would join them. Naftulin somewhat reluctantly joined the group heading out.

The road east was difficult to traverse due to the drifting snow and numerous abandoned and burnt-out US and German vehicles blocking the way. Moreover, it was difficult to discern the national identities of the bodies lying at intervals, frozen and splayed in grotesque positions on both sides of the road. The countryside to the east of Bastogne is a patchwork of small woods, open, gently rolling hills, and, on a clear day, excellent views. There was still a light mist and about two feet of snow on the ground as they slowly bumped their way toward the tiny village of Marvie.

Sporadic machine-gun fire whizzed by above the truck as it approached the village. The Germans had set up a machine-gun nest and a battery of 88s on a hill overlooking the village, providing them-selves with an excellent 360-degree view of the surrounding area, where they could shoot at anything and everything that moved, including the approaching deuce-and-a-half.

The team quickly disembarked and got to work attending wounded GIs. There were two wounded Germans among them. Jack insisted on respecting the terms of the Geneva Convention and assisted these men, as well, much to the disgust of Lee Naftulin, who yelled, "Leave those goddamn Krauts till last!"

Jack immediately intervened and told Naftulin that, although he wouldn't be required to extract any molars or wisdom teeth, the German wounded were to receive the same care and attention as the US soldiers. As he imparted this information the truck took a direct hit from an 88 and exploded just a few yards away from the group. Naftulin was quick to point this out as an example: Most Germans didn't give a hoot about the Geneva Convention. Jack explained this away by saying that there was no red cross on top of that vehicle, so the Germans wouldn't have known it was being used as an ambulance. Naftulin protested that it wouldn't have made any difference if a Red Cross barrage balloon had been tied to it. In his opinion, the Germans would still have shot it up anyway.

Jack managed to acquire an M3 half-track with a .50 caliber machine gun on a raised, armored pulpit mount for the return journey. As they set about loading up the wounded, Jack continued to insist that despite what Naftulin thought about the Germans, he was going to observe the terms of the Geneva Convention. He also reminded Naftulin who was in charge.

Augusta was busy shaking what little sulfa powder she had left onto a stomach wound when Jack approached and asked her if she'd have a look at the two Germans after she finished up. Augusta explained that she had already attempted to provide some first aid to them, but both Germans had refused to allow her to touch them. This enraged Jack so much that despite the din of artillery shells flying over his head, he stormed over to the wounded Germans and asked if either of them could speak English. One of the Germans nodded. Jack then asked why he hadn't permitted his nurse to do her job. The German retorted indignantly that Augusta was a *Schwartze*, "a black one," who could not possibly take care of soldiers of the Reich. Jack assumed an authoritative stance and considered remonstrating with the Germans, then decided against it.

"Well, fucking die then, you dumb sons of bitches," he snarled within earshot of Naf, who, while looking over the side of a requisitioned M3 half-track, smugly asked, "What was that you said about the Geneva Convention, Jack?" He didn't wait around to hear the colorful reply.

With the assistance of some GIs from the 10th Armored, they managed to load up most of the wounded, including the Germans, and set off. Augusta sat in the front beside Jack while Dr. Naftulin negotiated the debris-strewn road back to Bastogne. They had only traveled a mile or two down the road when mortars began exploding around the vehicle. Naftulin slammed his foot hard on the gas pedal, but as the half-track wasn't built for speed, they remained a viable and vulnerable target. Jack told him to pull over beside some high hedges until the shelling stopped. As they did a Panther Mark IV drove directly into their path, accompanied by around twenty soldiers from the infamous Panzer Lehr.

A German Panther tank preparing for the Battle of the Bulge. CREDIT: UNKNOWN

Naf begged Jack to let him turn around as fast as he could so they could return to the US line, but Jack refused on the premise that they were transporting wounded, reiterating that they were protected by the Geneva Convention. Despite Naftulin's protests he insisted that his colleague stop the vehicle. They watched as a German officer cautiously approached with four soldiers all wearing winter camo smocks. With hardly a trace of an accent the German officer ordered the M3 half-track's occupants to step out of the vehicle immediately.

Jack bravely stepped out of the half-track and with his hands held high, approached the German officer and informed him that they were taking wounded men back to the aid station in Bastogne. He also mentioned that under the terms of the Geneva Convention they were allowed to do this unimpeded. More German soldiers gathered around the half-track as Naftulin and Augusta also disembarked. The German officer said that he could use a doctor, but then he pointed toward Augusta and asked what she was doing with the party. Jack explained that she was one of his nurses.

The German officer laughed raucously and made a snide remark about Jack probably being a "witch doctor." He also insinuated that the US Army must be really desperate for nurses. Other German soldiers who probably hadn't even understood this base attempt at jocularity joined in the laughter as Augusta hung her head and maintained a silent dignity throughout. Jack put his hand on her shoulder and told the Germans that Augusta was the best nurse he had.

The German officer told him that such a remark could cost him his life, and then, reaching for his Luger, he demanded that they hand over all their weapons, adding that they were all now prisoners of war. Jack interceded and told the officer that there were two German wounded among the cargo. This appeared to diffuse the situation somewhat. The German officer stepped up to the half-track and opened the back door to see for himself. Presently a few of his men helped the two German wounded off the vehicle. Using the temporary diversion, Naftulin went around to the other side of the M3 half-track and snuck inside the back where he could creep up to the small turret and man the .50 caliber machine gun. What followed was probably a panic reaction, but Naftulin shouted something to the effect of "Hey, look what I got you for Christmas, you Heinie bastards" as he pointed the machine gun directly at the group of German soldiers, who to a man aimed their weapons right back at him.

In an effort to alleviate the standoff Jack proposed a small truce. He asked the German officer to respect the Geneva Convention and let them pass. The German officer looked him straight in the eye and told Jack that he'd served with Rommel in the desert. He went on to say that Rommel always told his men that they should treat their prisoners the same way that they themselves expect to be treated. Then the officer told Jack to get on his way before he changed his mind. Jack extended his hand to shake the German officer's but thought better of it as he jumped into the half-track beside Augusta, where he took the wheel while Naftulin remained at the .50 caliber gun.

Jack drove and talked to Augusta as the truck jostled and jolted its way back to Bastogne. He said the war would be over soon, and despite the current situation, he insisted that the Germans were going to lose. Then he said that he didn't know if the world would be a better place when they'd been defeated, but he was convinced that it couldn't be any worse. In his opinion the most frightening aspect of any society is the one that regards others, those who are different, as being "less than human."

Augusta nodded and forced a half-smile before turning her attention back to the war-ravaged winter scenery. She wanted to tell him that she appreciated what he'd done for her, but again she simply couldn't find the words, so she just squeezed his hand. In the short time they'd been working together they had developed a very close affinity. There was already a depth and regard to their relationship that transcended the deprivations and dangers they had both been forced to endure. This mutual admiration and respect hadn't manifested in any real physical sense yet, but it was there, and almost palpable whenever they were in close proximity to each other, which under the present arrangement was most of the time.

Jack looked at Augusta, winked reassuringly, and then bellowed out of the window to Naftulin not to pull any more dumb-ass stunts. Naftulin retorted: "You don't need to look for trouble when you're sharing a ride with a black nurse and a Jewish dentist."

Jack didn't have any gloves at the time, and with temperatures beginning to dip below minus-4 degrees Fahrenheit, his fingertips were turning black with frostbite. All he could do to stave off the immobilizing cold was vigorously rub his hands together as often as he could during the journey back to Bastogne.

Frostbite occurs when skin and body tissues are exposed to a cold temperature for a prolonged period of time. Hands, feet, nose, and ears are most likely to be affected. The first symptoms are a "pins and needles" sensation, followed by numbness. Frostbitten skin is hard, pale, cold, and has no feeling. When skin has thawed out, it becomes red and painful (early frostbite). With more severe frostbite, the skin may appear white and numb (tissue has started to freeze). Very severe frostbite may cause blisters, gangrene (blackened, dead tissue), and damage to deep structures such as tendons, muscles, nerves, and bone.

As the small group neared Bastogne all eyes looked heavenward as the skies above began to fill with squadrons of C-47s roaring into view

US Army medics treat frostbitten toes and feet, December 1944. CREDIT: UNKNOWN

and dropping different-colored parachutes. The chutes were color-coded to indicate their contents: medical supplies, ammunition, food, etc. The Bastogne resupply mission—Operation Repulse—used 927 C-47s and 61 gliders, but only incurred total losses of 19 C-47s. During the afternoon of December 23, three 9th Air Force fighter groups provided tactical support. At the start of the mission Pathfinders were dropped from two C-47s to mark the landing zones (LZs) and drop zones (DZs). The first of the carriers dropped its six para packs at 11:50 a.m., and in little more than four hours 241 planes had reached Bastogne. Each plane carried some 1,200 pounds, but not all reached the drop zone, nor did all the para packs fall where the Americans could recover them. Despite this, it would go on to be considered the most accurate supply drop of World War II.

Jack sang the words of a song called "Blue Skies." "Blues skies smiling at me," he bellowed in full voice as the M3 plowed along the old farm track back to Bastogne. Naftulin joined in from the machine-gun pulpit. It must have been surreal, these two young Americans singing in full voice to the accompaniment of exploding shells and dive-bombing P-47s strafing German positions. On more than one occasion they had to dive for cover as the fighters swooped down on their half-track. It didn't stop them singing, though.

When the small group disembarked outside the aid station on the rue de Neufchâteau, they immediately set about helping to get the wounded inside. Jack scanned around the dank interior looking for Renée, but she was nowhere to be seen. He asked one of the conscious wounded men if he'd seen her. The man told Jack that she'd put her coat on and left about ten minutes earlier. Before he had time to send out a search party Renée appeared at the entrance looking windswept and a little crestfallen. Jack asked her where she'd been, and she replied that she had been attempting to retrieve a parachute from the field down the road. Renée looked intently at Jack and asked him if there was going to be another parachute drop tomorrow. Jack replied that he didn't know, noting that she appeared pretty determined to get some of that parachute silk. Renée told him that she wanted the silk to make a wedding dress. Jack asked her politely if she would stay with the wounded in the future, and he would see what he could do to comply with her request.

As December 23 drew to a close, fresh supplies arrived at the aid station, allowing the team there to administer anesthetics and other medications for the first time in days. All units in and around Bastogne received much-needed ammunition to continue their dogged fight against the opposing army. Two C-47s from IX TCC Pathfinder Group had arrived as early as 9:30 a.m. and dropped ten men each in the area where Colonel Harper's 2nd Battalion, 327th Glider Infantry Regiment was deployed. The Pathfinder team dropped inside the perimeter and set up the apparatus to guide the C-47s over a drop zone between Senonchamps and Bastogne. The para packs did a great deal to help alleviate some of the terrible suffering that was being endured by military personnel and civilians alike.

Troops all along the front lines saw the formations coming, and considered it "the most heartening spectacle of the entire siege." Though the initial parachute resupply missions had given the defenders of Bastogne a vital shot of hope, the need for resupply was still considered a dire emergency by all. Supplies of ammunition had been running dangerously low, and the artillerymen were down to a few rounds. The resilient commanders of Bastogne were certain that as long as the artillery ammunition lasted, Bastogne would hold indefinitely. It was an optimistic prognosis, but enough to sustain the fighting spirit of the defenders, who hadn't had much to cheer about in recent days.

CHAPTER TEN

What's Merry About All This?

DECEMBER 24, 1944

AS DAWN BROKE ON THE MORNING OF DECEMBER 24, A PALE SUN
cracked shards of light across the horizon and hesitantly emerged
through a freezing haze to announce another bitterly cold day in Bastogne. Another day to fight and die, another day to struggle and cower in
the dank confines of a freezing cellar, another chance to live and survive.
Within an hour the sun was gone, replaced by low pregnant clouds that
released large swirling snowflakes onto the pummeled buildings below.
The streets were deserted save for the odd wraithlike inhabitant wandering like a lost soul between the ruins of a once-beautiful city. Smoldering
embers permeated the stale, damp air, mixing with the nauseous stench of
decaying corpses; starving stray dogs and cats foraged frenetically among
the piles of rubble that were once homes, shops, and businesses.

Augusta heard Bing Crosby's "White Christmas" crackling mock-
ingly from a requisitioned gramophone. It was difficult to imagine that
less than a week ago the place had been festooned with decorations in
anticipation of the approaching festivities. Now the illuminations were
dead, and bunting was scattered like discarded confetti around the shell
holes and debris that littered the sidewalks and roads.

Bastogne had been under siege for almost four days, and though
reports about Patton's advancing Third Army were encouraging, it
brought little comfort to those having to fight it out inside the perimeter. Their cause, however, began to take on increased significance as
the world's free press hammered home the story with headlines such as

"The Brave Defenders of Bastogne," "Remember the Alamo," and "Siege City Holds Out." This kind of propaganda was galvanizing the Allies as they raced from the north and south to deal with the situation. It hadn't escaped the attention of Hitler, either, who, despite his shortcomings, genuinely understood the meaning of propaganda. Patton was now a man with a mission, and no effort would be spared to save those poor "Battered Bastards of Bastogne." Gen. Anthony McAuliffe's famous "Nuts!" riposte to the German ultimatum was now followed with a poignant and stirring Christmas message to the men involved in the fight:

From the office of the Division Commander, 101st Airborne Division December 24, 1944

What's so merry about all this, you ask? We're fighting, it's cold, we aren't home. All true, but what has the proud Eagle Division accomplished with its worthy comrades of the 10th Armored Division, the 705th Tank Destroyer Battalion, and all the rest? Just this: We have stopped cold everything that has been thrown at us from the North, East, South, and West. We have identifications from four German Panzer Divisions, two German Infantry Divisions, and one German Parachute Division. These units, spearheading the last desperate German lunge, were headed straight west for key points when the Eagle Division was hurriedly ordered to stem the advance. How effectively this was done will be written in history; not alone in our Division's glorious history, but in world history. The Germans actually did surround us, their radios blared our doom. Their commander demanded our surrender with the following impudent arrogance.

To the USA Commander of the encircled town of Bastogne December 22, 1944

The fortune of war is changing. This time the USA forces in and near Bastogne have been encircled by strong German armored units. More German armored units have crossed the river Ourthe near Ourtheville, have taken Marché, and reached St. Hubert by passing through Hombres Sibret–Tillet. Libramont is in German hands.

There is only one possibility to save the encircled USA troops from total annihilation: that is the honorable surrender of the encircled town. In order to think it over, a term of two hours will be granted, beginning with the presentation of this note.

If this proposal should be rejected, one German Artillery Corps and six heavy AA Battalions are ready to annihilate the USA troops in and near Bastogne. The order for firing will be given immediately after this two-hour term.

All the serious civilian losses caused by this artillery fire would not correspond with the well-known American humanity.

The German Commander received the following reply:

To the German Commander
December 22, 1944

NUTS!

The American Commander.

Allied troops are counterattacking in force. We continue to hold Bastogne. By holding Bastogne we assure the success of the Allied armies. We know that our Division Commander, General Taylor, will say: Well done!

We are giving our country and our loved ones at home a worthy Christmas present, and being privileged to take part in this gallant feat of arms are truly making ourselves a Merry Christmas.

A. C. McAuliffe
Commanding

In late fall of 1944, Brugmann Hospital, where she worked, had given Renée Lemaire permission to spend some time in Bastogne with her family. After four long years of repression and occupation, the Lemaires heartily welcomed the American soldiers who had liberated Bastogne that September. One soldier by the name of Jimmy was a frequent visitor to their house. Some historians believe that Renée and Jimmy fell in love, and may have been engaged to be married.

On December 17, 1944, Jimmy's unit had sudden orders to leave, but he promised to be back. Although the surname of this soldier isn't known, it's safe to assume that he was probably from the 28th Division, who were in and around Bastogne at that time.

Renée had no idea of Jimmy's whereabouts, but she clung to the vain hope that they would eventually be reunited. Maybe she wanted to make a wedding dress for eventual nuptials with him? We'll never really know. The one thing we can be certain of is that she never had an affair with *Band of Brothers* character, Doc Roe. Although Tech 4 Eugene Gilbert Roe Sr. was a real person, the meeting that took place between him and Renée in the TV series was pure Hollywood conjecture.

Despite the adversity of working in a filthy, overcrowded aid station, Renée maintained the capacity to wear a cheerful smile and offer some comfort to those wounded young men miles away from their homeland. This was the characteristic that endeared her to everyone in her immediate environment. She was always ready to share a piece of her beloved Belgian chocolate or listen to the concerns of her patients.

Christmas Eve arrived at the aid station without much ceremony. Renée had borrowed a Christmas tree from her father's hardware store and adorned it with a colorful array of items, from K-ration tinfoil wrappings to surgical scissors. It didn't add a great deal of Christmas cheer to the proceedings, but it was a brave effort nonetheless. As news of the latest airdrop circulated, Renée asked Jack if she could go and see if she could find a parachute. Jack agreed to let her go, but only moments after leaving the aid station she returned empty-handed, looking more deflated than the grounded parachutes she so badly wanted. Anticipating this result, Jack had asked Naftulin to procure one, and without a moment's hesitation he'd done precisely that.

Earlier that morning Jack had neatly folded the chute into a small brown paper parcel that he intended to give Renée as a Christmas present the following day. He'd also managed to get hold of a woman's army greatcoat for Augusta, to replace the tattered old one she had been wearing. The day passed uneventfully save for the odd bomb falling in their vicinity, but there were still casualties arriving and wounded to attend to.

Later that day Jack was in a building adjacent to the aid station, preparing to go next door and write a letter for a young lieutenant to his wife. The lieutenant was dying of an infection caused by severe shrapnel wounds to his stomach and chest. These were the jobs that Jack hated. He had a set of sentences in his head that he always used on these occasions, but they never articulated how he really felt. This was the case on Christmas Eve, as well. No words of comfort could ever pacify a broken heart as far as Jack was concerned. Loss was loss, and it was going to change lives forever and cause floods of tears whatever the wording of his official military letter of condolence. No matter how many times he wrote this kind of letter, and how many different ways he attempted to express his condolences, the words still felt empty and superfluous.

The soldiers who had delivered this young man to the aid station were part of CCB 9th Armored, which had been recently dissected and reallocated. They told Jack that the wounded soldier had been a part of Team SNAFU. Jack concluded that the acronym accurately summed up the whole current situation.

⌒⌒

Out to the east a squadron of Luftwaffe bombers was heading for Bastogne. They hadn't come far since launching from Dedelstorf, just over the German border. Despite the more-streamlined fuselage of the Junkers 88 S-3s, their smaller bomb loads, and the stripping down to the bare essentials of equipment, these bombers were already down to a little over half their fuel reserve. They flew low, following the road network while maintaining radio silence. Beneath their wings they carried five-hundred-pound messengers of imminent death.

⁓

Augusta sat nibbling on a piece of K-ration chocolate, taking a short pause while Jack chewed on a pencil and consigned yet another crumpled piece of paper to the growing pile on the floor. He hated writing these letters to mothers and fathers, sisters and brothers, and any other living relatives of the recently deceased. He paused for a moment and looked over at Augusta sitting silently by the window, her mind obviously somewhere else. She looked completely drained. He was planning to go over to her when suddenly a young lieutenant from the 10th Armored appeared at the door of the aid station and asked if Jack would like to join him for a glass of champagne.

Jack thanked him for the invitation and looked around for Renée and Naftulin. When he didn't see them, he graciously asked Augusta if she would accompany him. Augusta nodded, got to her feet, and followed Jack and the lieutenant to the kitchen in the house adjacent to the aid station. The lieutenant ceremoniously opened the champagne with an army-issue dagger and poured himself a full cup. He handed the bottle to Jack, who walked over to Augusta and poured some into the tin cup she was holding. She looked at Jack and then the lieutenant before slowly raising the cup to her dry lips, wincing as she sipped a little of the effervescent liquid before putting it down again.

They all looked up as the sound of aircraft engines began to fill the night sky. Most of them assumed they were C-47s making another drop, but it was difficult to tell.

While Jack and Augusta were next door enjoying a glass of champagne, they were oblivious to the situation developing at the aid station. A few incendiary bombs had already fallen and a small fire had broken out. These were probably intended as target markers for the following wave of bombers. Renée was unsuccessfully attempting to douse the flames with melted snow. She ran out into the street looking for assistance, with Naftulin chasing closely behind. Stopping in the middle of the street, she began screaming for help as the hum of enemy planes started to become more menacingly audible. Naftulin quickly caught up to her and attempted to rush her back inside, but she initially resisted his attempts to get her to safety. Step by step he gradually managed to move her back toward the aid station.

As they reached the door, the thunderous rumble of German Junkers loaded with bombs filled the cold night skies above Bastogne. The overhead drone was so resonant that surrounding buildings shook with the vibration. Within moments German aircraft were unleashing their deadly cargo on the population below. The first wave dropped incendiary munitions, spewing flames as they detonated, igniting and reducing an already-wrecked city to a hellish inferno.

Naftulin procured a large bucket and emptied the bloody contents onto the street before filling it with snow from the sidewalk outside the main entrance. Just then, Renée reappeared at the door and held out her hands to receive the bucket, but Naftulin ordered her in no uncertain terms to get inside. Renée regarded him quizzically as he dropped the bucket and shoved her inside with such force that she fell backwards and landed on a litter patient. As the wounded GI howled in agony, Naftulin stumbled backward, barely maintaining his footing.

Meanwhile, as Jack and the lieutenant exchanged a few pleasantries in the house next door, suddenly their jovial conversation was interrupted by a high-pitched screeching sound. In an instant they all hit the floor as a massive explosion rocked the aid station and the room they were all in lit up as bright as an arc welder's torch.

Naftulin's world went out of focus and it felt as if he'd been hit by a wrecking ball as the percussion from the blast threw him across the street, where he landed on the side of a rubble pile, with flaming debris descending all around. Momentarily dazed and deafened, he raised his head and began to rub his eyes. All he could do was stare in disbelief at the aid station. He attempted to get to his feet, but chunks of broken brick and mortar beneath him rolled under his boots and he slumped back down onto his haunches.

The blast from the five-hundred-pound bomb had blown Augusta clean through a kitchen wall. Jack initially appeared to be in a stupor as he gradually stood upright, dusted himself off, and looked around. He shivered as he cleared the dust from the inside corners of his eyes before slowly sliding his palms down the length of his face. Everything felt intact except for his hearing, but gradually he began to recover his composure.

He couldn't see Augusta. He shouted her name, his hoarse voice almost choking on the pungent smoke. Frantically he clawed at a pile of bricks where the partition wall had been, doing his best to scan for signs of life. When he reached the smoke-filled kitchen area, he discerned a small hand with outstretched fingers extending from beneath a pile of rubble across the room. Jack took it, pulled hard, and in one forceful move he extricated Augusta from beneath the debris. She was dazed but miraculously unscathed, save for a few minor abrasions. Before she had a chance to brush away the broken glass and debris from her uniform, Jack pulled her to him, shouting as loud as he could to be heard above the drone of German aircraft still flying overhead. Augusta was still stunned from the explosion and struggling to recover her senses when she felt Jack's arms envelop her small body.

Jack held her close to him, and for an all-too-brief moment they were lost, holding on to each other against the hideous scene of death and destruction that was slowly being revealed around them.

Jack abruptly turned his attention to the aid station. The three-story building that had been his hospital had been reduced to a flaming ten-foot-high pile of smoldering embers and rubble. Due to the magnesium flares dropped by the German bomber pilots which illuminated the area as if it were daylight, the whole ghastly scene of devastation was clearly visible to all who witnessed it. For a moment Jack stared in disbelief and then he sprang into action.

He quickly gathered some GIs together and raced to the top of the debris where they began flinging burning timbers aside, looking for the wounded. They could hear some of them shrieking for help. At this juncture a low-flying German bomber noticed them and swooped even lower to strafe them with his machine guns. Jack and the other GIs dove under some nearby parked military vehicles while the bomber repeated this maneuver several times before leaving the area.

On Christmas Eve the Luftwaffe managed to conduct two bombing missions. The first went in at 7:45 p.m., and the second, around 10:00 p.m. The first attack lasted approximately thirty minutes. After the attack was over 1st Lt. Eugene Leachman, in charge of the Bastogne detachment, took 1st Sgt. Roy R. Wood and Tech 4 George A. Engle to see if anyone had been injured in the bombing. They discovered that the aid station had been hit and destroyed. Wood formed a bucket brigade directed by Engel and continued to round up men to assist with the rescue work. Two direct hits had impacted the aid station, setting the buildings on fire and causing them to collapse. Despite being slightly concussed and injured by falling debris, Naftulin returned to the burning building and managed to personally extract four wounded men.

Naftulin noted in one letter that Renée had been on the first floor when the bomb hit. Another account states that she was heading toward the kitchen in the house next door, where Jack and Augusta were, when someone pushed her back into the main building. Could that someone have been Naftulin? He'd stuck to Renée from the moment he'd brought her to the aid station. He was besotted with her. Either way, there was something troubling Naf deeply when he went over to the Heintz Barracks to get some treatment.

Located about a block away, the 10th Armored Headquarters was also hit, and soon engulfed in leaping flames. The fire was eventually doused, and the men even managed to save the Christmas tree there and redecorate it later on. A large number of soldiers soon rallied and joined the search for survivors at the shattered aid station. They located a cellar window at the base of the destroyed building, and some men volunteered to be lowered into the smoking cellar on a rope. Two or three injured were pulled out before the entire remains of the building collapsed onto the cellar. Thirty badly wounded men on the first floor had been killed instantly. Those at the back of the building had been blown out into the back garden by percussion from the explosion.

Augusta joined Jack and the soldiers as they sifted through the rubble. After much searching they managed to remove some of the debris and identify most of the casualties that had been incurred by the bombing. While Jack was rummaging around the charred and smoldering timbers he noticed a shock of dark hair protruding from the rubble. Jack dug down a little deeper with his bare hands and brushed the debris from Renée's ashen face. He managed to get his hands under her shoulders and extract her from the carnage. That's when Jack made a shocking and gruesome discovery: The lower half of her body was missing. Renée Lemaire had been blown completely in two. It seems that she had been in the first-floor kitchen of the aid station as the bomb hit, and she either dashed into—or was pushed into—the cellar before the bomb detonated. Ironically enough, all those in the kitchen were blown outdoors to relative safety, since one wall was all glass.

Jack and the soldiers gathered what wounded they could and had them transported to the Riding Hall hospital of the 101st Airborne Division HQ out at the Heintz Barracks. It was the only option at the time, even though conditions there weren't particularly conducive to receiving extra wounded. They were already overcrowded.

Jack then gathered Renée Lemaire's remains together and wrapped them carefully in the silk parachute he'd been planning to give her as a Christmas present. He then solemnly delivered her remains to her father.

Renée was an angel, there's no doubt about that, but she was not the only angel in Bastogne.

———

Renée Bernadette Emilie Lemaire was born in Bastogne on April 10, 1914. Her father, Gustave Joseph, owned a hardware store in the center of Bastogne. Her mother, Bertha Emilie Thérèse Gallee, worked in the shop and looked after three daughters. Renée's elder sister, Gisèle, was born August 4, 1912, and her younger sister, Marguerite (known as "Maggie"), was born July 8, 1916. Renée studied nursing at the Brugmann Hospital in Brussels where she obtained her nursing degree, and then worked as a district nurse at the Ixelles Hospital in Brussels.

Sometime in late 1943 she allegedly met and fell in love with a man named Joseph who was the son of one of Renée's patients. They shared a love of music, and according to Renée she would often sing accompanied by Joseph on piano. At some point Joseph must have told Renée that he was Jewish, but this didn't deter her from making wedding plans, and before long they were discussing their nuptials. Unfortunately these plans were never realized. According to some information, sometime around the end of February 1944, Renée went to Joseph's house after her night shift only to be told by neighbors that the Gestapo had taken Joseph and his father away because they were both Jewish. This was the story she recounted to Naftulin, who was also Jewish.

So who was Joseph? Based on records obtained from the Yad Vashem organization, Dr. Joseph Weinstein is a possible candidate. His story ticks most of the right boxes. He was single and he worked at the Brugmann Hospital, but there is another possibility. Could Renée have fabricated the information about her fiancé? She was, after all, in a very vulnerable position. Maybe she fabricated Joseph to deflect aspersions of being a spinster; in those days she was considered to be already well past marrying age. Thirty years old and unmarried in 1940s Belgium was a disparaging status. It's difficult to corroborate the facts here because there doesn't appear to be any living witnesses to her relationship with Joseph, whoever he was.

After the bombardment Augusta invited Jack to her father's house. He followed her and spent the night on the sofa in her father's living room. Or did he? They were alone there at the time because Henri Chiwy, Mama Caroline, and Charles were in the cellars beneath the Sisters of Notre Dame School, and they wouldn't return until the following morning. Whatever happened between them that night will remain theirs forever, and so it should.

CHAPTER ELEVEN

The Ghost Town

DECEMBER 25, 1944

JACK LEFT BEFORE DAWN ON CHRISTMAS DAY TO SEE WHAT HE COULD salvage from the aid station. Augusta's family returned home around nine in the morning, and she spent the day with them in the cellar of their home on the rue des Écoles. Augusta's father and Mama Caroline were absolutely delighted to see that she had survived the recent bombard-ments relatively unscathed, except for a few cuts and bruises. When her brother Charles descended the steps, he stopped immediately when he saw Augusta and shuffled across the basement floor to give her a hug. Before long he was cleaning his recently acquired Lee-Enfield rifle by candlelight. The small family was reunited for the first time in quite a few days.

Augusta sobbed as she told her father about the recent events at the aid station. At that moment she was unsure about what she was going to do next. She told them that she hadn't slept a wink, and just sat quietly in the corner of the candlelit cellar, contemplating her next move and whether or not she would be able to continue working for the US Army in Bastogne. The bombing had taken its toll on her resilience, but there was another matter on her mind: She was becoming too attached to Jack. She would shake uncontrollably for a few minutes every so often but then it would pass.

It was the saddest Christmas Day that Augusta had ever experienced. At no other time in her young life had she felt as completely desolate as she did at that moment, sitting there in the corner of that putrid cellar.

Her mouth was dry and her body felt as if it hadn't been washed for months, let alone days. Outside she could hear the bombs falling and the occasional agonized cries of the afflicted. She winced when a rat ran over her bare feet. Her father suggested that she should make herself useful and return to the crowded cellars beneath the Notre Dame School, but Augusta wasn't sure if this was a good idea. Either way, whatever her next move, it would be entirely her choice and hers alone.

After a meager breakfast with her family she decided to go and attempt to find Jack. All the remaining wounded had now been moved to the Heintz Barracks, and Augusta would have known about the location because it was a prominent set of buildings that straddled the roadside at the beginning of the Route de La Roche.

— • —

Adolf Hitler himself had given the order to attack Bastogne on Christmas Day. Sometime during the night before Christmas Eve, commander Hasso von Manteuffel of the 5th Army had arrived at Gen. Heinz Kokott's CP to deliver the plans on how the attack was to be organized. At least two regiments of the 15th Panzergrenadier Division would be taken from the reserves and be in position to attack by 3:00 a.m. on Christmas morning. The attacks would be orchestrated from the west and northwest of Bastogne, on Kokott's assumption that the US Army wouldn't expect an attack to come at them from this direction.

In retrospect he had gauged the situation quite erroneously, because the northwest was actually quite well defended, according to 101st records. It was the southwest that was vulnerable. On the other hand, Kokott knew that an approach from the northwest of town would provide him the opportunity to operate his armor in firmer and more open terrain due to the nature of the countryside around there. He now moved his divisional CP from Bras to Gives, and consequently moved most of the units of the 26th Volksgrenadiers into this sector. The attack would come in the area near the junction of the line held by the 327th Glider Infantry Regiment (GIR) and the 502nd Parachute Infantry Regiment (PIR), with units of both 15th Panzergrenadiers and 26th Volksgrenadiers pushing toward Bastogne in a traditional three-pronged attack:

from Givry toward Champs; from Flamizoule, just east of Flamierge, toward Hemroulle; and farther south from Senonchamps in toward the main Bastogne-Marche-en-Famenne road.

Christmas morning in Bastogne was much like the preceding days. In the cellars beneath the Sisters of Notre Dame School, however, some fortunate GIs were treated to a concert of Christmas carols by the school choir. There are few things as emotive to someone far away from home as spending Christmas in unfamiliar surroundings. At about 3:00 a.m. a few German planes droned over the city and dropped bombs indiscriminately. This appears to have been Luftwaffe support that had been promised to General Kokott, who was planning a major attack that day. A couple minutes later the German gunners and mortar crews started to work. Out on the front lines the first barrages crashed against US Army positions, and minutes later, clad in snow camo, the first German grenadiers crept forward against these lines, supported by

Anthony McAuliffe and his staff gathered inside the Heintz Barracks for Christmas.
CREDIT: UNKNOWN

tanks. As the ground shook under the impact of the heavy shelling, the snow-covered battlefield soon became a spectrum of bright flares, deafening explosions, and machine-gun tracers. As mortar rounds exploded in front of and behind the GIs out in the foxholes, enemy activity gathered momentum.

Christmas Day brought no relief to the battered defenders of Bastogne. In fact, the enemy attacks on that day were among the heaviest and most vicious they'd had to endure so far, but the German artillery was now focused on the American units around the perimeter and less on the actual center of Bastogne. The 4th Armored of General Patton's Third Army had suffered heavy losses in men and tanks on its advance north from Neufchâteau, and by Christmas night they were within five miles of Bastogne. General McAuliffe often said that his best Christmas present ever was receiving a message from General Patton informing him that the Third Army was close by.

The bombardment earlier in the day hadn't inflicted much new damage in the already-shattered city, and the ensuing inclement weather had stemmed the shelling considerably. In a paltry attempt to maintain the momentum, the Nazis had been reduced to lobbing random artillery and bombs on Bastogne ad hoc. The defenders and residents were oblivious to the fact that the Germans had been facing stiff resistance all along the Bulge, and to those in the know, it was becoming overtly apparent that Hitler's last offensive in the west was doomed.

With the bombardments abating, the residents of Bastogne were now daring to leave their cellars for short periods in search of food and whatever else they could lay their hands on.

Jack Prior had caught a restless few hours' sleep at Henri Chiwy's house before sluggishly extricating himself from beneath a pile of coats and blankets and stepping outside into the freezing cold. A short while later, on his way to the site of the former 20th AIB aid station, he was approached by an officer from the 10th Armored Division's CCB and given orders to continue his work over at the 101st HQ at the Heintz Barracks, where the remainder of his patients had been rehoused.

Before he headed there he decided to go and have one last look at the site of the former aid station. He sadly scanned the carnage and destruction caused by the previous night's bombing and hung his head in despair. Along the street there were craters in the road, devastated buildings, and the deathly pall of decomposing corpses that sullied the freezing winter air. It was now no more than a pile of smoldering, pungent rubble covered with a layer of fresh snow.

A group of GIs was standing around looking at the still-smoking wreckage of the former aid station when Jack walked over to them and asked if they'd help him clear up so that he could get better access to the cellar beneath the wrecked building. One of the GIs told Jack that he thought he'd heard a voice beneath the rubble. This was all the impetus Jack needed; he grabbed a shovel and began digging furiously in an attempt to locate any further possible survivors.

A colonel in a jeep stopped on the street in front of the debris and asked Jack what he was doing. While Jack explained to him what had happened the previous night, the colonel tried to listen but was distracted by a group of GIs farther along the street horsing around with apparently nothing better to do. The colonel leapt out of the jeep and charged up to them, shouting, "Get your commanding officer out here right now, or so help me, God, I'll have you all on a charge."

A major promptly appeared and received the biggest dressing-down of his career for allowing the soldiers to idly stand by while others were working hard to clear the rubble. Within minutes his men were assisting the other GIs clearing away the remains of the former aid station. They eventually managed to haul two more survivors from the wreckage.

Convinced there were no more survivors, Jack called a halt to the work, sat down beside the road on his haunches, and buried his head in his hands. Then he looked up and in one long sigh he expelled a cloud of frozen breath. A few days previous he'd been watching a thunderstorm from the doorway of his aid station. Jack always enjoyed a good storm, but being a spectator on this occasion damn near killed him. While watching the storm, a shell exploded in the road and Jack was hit by a piece of shrapnel that sent him flying clear to the back of the room on his back. Naftulin was expecting to find a gaping chest wound. After ripping off his flight jacket and many other layers he found a piece of shrapnel the size of a half-dollar on top of Jack's favorite wool sweater that his mother had made for him.

Sitting there outside the demolished aid station, he reexamined the small hole in his overcoat just below the right lapel. Opening his coat for closer inspection he saw again how that small piece of shrapnel had singed right through to the hand-knitted woolen pullover beneath. It was only thanks to the multiple layers of clothing that it hadn't wounded him, but he registered some dismay at the damaged garment.

Augusta had left the relative safety of her the cellar beneath her father's house and walked over to the rue de Neufchâteau. As she arrived she saw that Jack was meticulously inspecting the penny-size scorch mark on his pullover, and offered to fix it for him. Jack gratefully accepted the offer, adding that his mother had knitted the garment and would be furious if she saw that he'd ruined it.

Shortly after, Jack gathered his belongings and prepared to leave the site on the rue de Neufchâteau for good. He wouldn't return there for fifty years, but he kept that small piece of shrapnel in his wallet for the rest of his life. Augusta waved good-bye and returned to her father's house.

She had yet to make up her mind about what to do next. The bomb that had dropped on the aid station had definitely unnerved her, but her emotions appear to have been in suspended animation at that time. She had seen so much suffering in those few days that it drained her. Nevertheless, as a fully qualified nurse Augusta still felt a sense of duty to practice her vocation, even if it was voluntary. Despite all the hardships she'd endured there was one other overriding consideration that she couldn't suppress. She was hopelessly in love with Jack Prior, and she would have followed him to the ends of the earth.

Meanwhile, Lee Naftulin was receiving some basic medical treatment over at the 101st aid station at the Heintz Barracks. He hadn't sustained any serious wounds, just a few minor cuts and bruises, but to avoid the risk of these becoming infected he'd gone over to have them seen to.

Maj. Martin S. Wisely, MC, regimental surgeon of the 327th Glider Infantry Regiment, was in charge of an ad hoc staff there made up of doctors and aid men from the division antiaircraft, engineer, artillery, and tank destroyer units. In an effort to acquire a more spacious location and better protection from artillery and air attack for his patients, Wisely had moved the hospital to the basement garage of the Heintz Barracks. As the hospital population increased, he placed incapacitated patients in the rifle range and Riding Hall, and used another building for trench-foot cases.

These facilities were primitive to say the least; the main ward had a dirt floor, no bathroom facilities, and only a single electric light. A field kitchen set up at one end of the large room fed both staff and patients. The wounded "were laid in rows on sawdust covered with blankets. Each row had a shift of medical assistants, and an attempt was made to segregate incoming cases into specified rows depending upon the seriousness of their wounds." Those deemed unlikely to survive lay nearest the wall. "As they died they were carried out to another building where an impromptu Graves Registration Office was functioning."* Major Wisely and his assistants worked twenty-four-hour shifts trying to keep their patients fed, reasonably warm, and in stable condition; they didn't attempt any major surgery at this time. Morale among the casualties was "extremely high," according to the participants.

Surrounded by pine woods and situated on the road between Champs and Bastogne is the Château de Rolle (Rolley, in French), which was serving at this time as the 502nd Parachute Infantry CP. Just a few hours before the German attack commenced, a midnight Mass had been held there. During the ensuing attacks eighteen tanks lumbered unexpectedly into the vicinity of the château. They were only about 650 yards away when they were spotted.

One regimental surgeon, Maj. Douglas Davidson, MC, of the 502nd Parachute Infantry, who Jack had met on December 23, thought he could do as much for his wounded as the ill-equipped division facility at the Heintz Barracks; therefore, he maintained his own holding hospital in the barn of the château. Davidson was using stables for wards, and had

---

* (From http://history.amedd.army.mil/booksdocs/AMEDDArdennes/ETOArdennes.html.)

coerced the chaplains and a dentist into service as cooks. On Christmas Day, when German tanks and infantry broke through the main line of resistance and momentarily threatened the command post, Davidson gathered all the wounded men who were able to walk and gave them rifles. Then he personally led them to join a scratch force of headquarters personnel in repelling the attack. Not one of the original eighteen German tanks survived the encounter. Tanks from Team Cherry had gone out there to provide armored support to the 502nd.

Despite the setbacks at Champs, the German offensive was now gathering momentum for the ensuing fight; however, it's reasonable to suggest that German general Kokott was painfully aware by then that his plan to capture Bastogne was irretrievably lost. At 12:00 p.m., he asked for permission to halt the attack and reorganize. This request was vehemently denied on the premise that it had become absolutely imperative to capture Bastogne at all costs. Nevertheless, the present fight had almost run its course and was already disintegrating. Kokott reluctantly renewed the attack, knowing that the only result would be an increase in his already-unsustainable losses.

———

Back in Bastogne life had long since lost any semblance of normality. It was now a scene of utter desolation and destruction, a mere shell of its former self. Dead bodies and limbs lay everywhere, some covered, some exposed, their frozen forms accentuated against the unremitting snow and cold. Smoke billowed from the ruins of now-unrecognizable structures. It was difficult to discern which buildings had been shops and which hadn't. Burned-out hulks of abandoned US Army vehicles were scattered intermittently along the entire street. Bastogne felt like a derelict ghost town. Only the occasional thunder flashes of artillery followed by agonized screams gave any indication that there were still people alive there. The scarred and battered ruins appeared to be at the point of total collapse, as if they would shake off what little cement was holding their bricks together and implode in a cloud of choking dust. To the observer it was as if everything within the town's perimeter was dying a wretched and protracted death.

Jack managed to gather what medical supplies he could extricate from the debris and carefully placed them in a canvas bag. A paratrooper from the 327th Glider Infantry Regiment watched him doing this and asked if he knew Doug Davidson. Jack said he had met him over at the Heintz Barracks a few days previous. The paratrooper then said that Davidson could probably use those supplies, so together they agreed to take them out to Davidson's current aid station with the 502nd Airborne, located at the Château de Rolle just a few miles northwest of Bastogne.

They loaded up a Willys jeep and just as a few flakes of snow began to fall, they prepared to set off. Augusta walked up to the jeep and asked Jack where he was going. He told her that he was heading out west but afterwards would go to the Heintz Barracks, and she would be welcome to join him there if she wanted. Augusta said that she'd think about it, when in fact her mind was already made up.

Leaving the center of town heading northwest toward Rolle, Jack and his driver saw satin-smooth snowdrifts piled high on either side of the small country road. With a cigarette jutting aggressively from the front of his mouth, the paratrooper roared forward as they impacted the first drift, causing the vehicle to career dangerously to one side. Then they were on the other side of the road speeding into the next pristine drift. Wheels churning up the snow and engine screaming for mercy, they continued unabated on the virtually impassable road ahead. The paratrooper strategically maneuvered the jeep through every obstruction with grace and expertise while Jack just sat there dumbfounded at the fact they were moving forward at all.

By now Jack was clinging onto the passenger seat for dear life as the jeep lurched and skidded violently along the road at frequently precarious angles. Edging their way toward Rolle, Jack noticed a human shape lying in a nearby field. He mentioned this to the paratrooper and in a split second the vehicle had shuddered to a halt. Jack jumped out and landed feetfirst on the crisp snow. As the blizzard subsided he could clearly see the prostrate shape silhouetted against the snow. He approached and noticed the olive-green uniform of an American soldier—although at that particular time this was no guarantee, seeing that German soldiers had requisitioned a lot of captured US material, including items of clothing.

Over the next hill they could hear a lot of activity. Cannons roaring and mortars exploding interspersed with the rat-a-tat of .30 and .50 caliber machine-gun and rifle fire gave enough indication that the war was close by, and there was absolutely no time to lose.

The paratrooper ran up to him and handed over the canvas medical bag. At first Jack couldn't tell if the figure lying before him was dead or alive. He knelt down beside the body and brushed the snow from its face. "Can you hear me?" he asked to no avail. The soldier didn't respond. Then he checked for a pulse. To Jack's surprise there was a faint pulse, so with the paratrooper's help, he pulled the body from the snow and slapped the face a few times in an attempt to get some circulation going and bring him back to consciousness.

Suddenly the body gave a sharp intake of breath like a cardiac-arrest victim coming back to life with an injection of adrenaline. Then the man breathed heavily, gasping for air. As he reached out his ungloved hands Jack could see that they were blackened by frostbite way past the wrists and way beyond help. There was a bloodstain in the snow beneath him that appeared to have come from a wound just below his belt, at the seat of his pants.

Together Jack and the paratrooper carefully loaded the man onto the back of the jeep and headed along the bumpy snowbound route to Rolle. A few minutes later Jack turned to look at the wounded soldier and asked the driver to pull over. He checked for signs of life and shook his head. The man was dead. Jack closed his eyes and covered the body with a tarpaulin mat before telling the driver to continue.

As they neared the village they saw a deuce-and-a-half towing a 105mm artillery piece setting off in the opposite direction. The truck slowed down when it saw Jack approaching, and its truck driver leaned out as the vehicles stopped almost parallel to each other. "Is that road traversable, sir?" he asked.

"It is with this driver," replied Jack, looking at the paratrooper.

"Strange. Our captain said that it was completely blocked."

Jack discovered sometime later that his chauffeur had been Art Cross, a well-known Indy 500 driver who had enjoyed a lot of success before the war.

There are a number of reasons why the German Christmas Day attacks to the northwest of Bastogne ultimately failed in their objectives. Bad planning and insufficient use of the road network around Bastogne had created calamitous gridlocks for the German vehicles that severely disrupted their timetable. This was exacerbated by inclement weather conditions that had been favorable up until December 23. After that time a mild thaw in some areas had forced German armor to keep to the roads, further restricting their maneuverability. Also their basic intransigence and incapacity to improvise and adapt their plans in accordance with the

American troops in a snow-filled trench during the Battle of the Bulge.
CREDIT: UNKNOWN

prevailing conditions genuinely hampered all their efforts. Occasional clear skies made their columns vulnerable to air attack at a time when the Allies were already enjoying air superiority. This intermittent but effective strafing also had a marked effect on the morale of German soldiers.

The supply depots had failed to move forward as they advanced and also failed to remain operational for sustained periods of time, which overextended supply lines and further emphasized their vulnerability. Another mitigating factor was the time Axis forces allowed the US Army to react and counter each move they made.

General Kokott had repeatedly asked General von Lüttwitz for time to reorganize, but these requests were never acquiesced to. They were answered repeatedly with the same monotonic response: "Bastogne must be taken now." It was that dogged single-mindedness so characteristic of the Germans back then. This only emphasized the German army's inability to operate at anything less than regimental level, whereas the US forces could improvise and operate autonomously right down to squad level if required. Each German move was checked and repulsed at almost every juncture. Persistent and efficient artillery support from the US Army proved to be highly effective at all levels. This meant that a light infantry division supported by good artillery and armor support was infinitely more flexible and able to defeat a numerically superior and heavier-armed opponent. Then there were the morale and luck factors that definitely favored the US Army at Bastogne.

That Christmas Day afternoon Augusta returned again to her father's house, which was surprisingly intact apart from a few broken windows. Jack had already asked her to carry on working with him for the US Army at the Heintz Barracks. She discussed the matter in depth with her father; he concurred that it might be the safest option, but emphasized that it would be her choice, and hers alone. Henri worked his assumptions on the possibility that at least the US Army could offer her some protection if the Germans broke through. Her father also proposed that it could lead to a more-permanent position when they eventually moved out. It all sounded feasible to Augusta, so later that evening she made her decision and went to look for Jack, who had just returned from his mission to see Dr. Davidson.

She had a small altercation with the guards standing at the entrance to the Heintz Barracks because they didn't believe she was a nurse. As she turned to leave, Jack, who was just catching some fresh air, saw her and shouted. Augusta immediately turned around and pressed her small body against the railings of the entrance gates. Jack first sternly berated the guards and then brought Augusta to her new lodgings in a garage basement beneath the barracks. He reminded her how invaluable her services were to him and to the wounded men that she'd tended, but there was more to it than that. He wanted her there where he could see her, protect her, and Augusta had no other desire than to remain by Jack's side.

Sometime around 9:00 p.m. they went to see Dr. Martin Wisely, regimental surgeon of the 327th Glider Infantry Regiment, 101st Airborne, who was only too happy to get extra help. But then Wisely turned his attention to Augusta. He warned her that there could be a problem with some of the wounded, particularly those who came from south of the Mason–Dixon line. He suggested that they play it by ear and avoid any unnecessary confrontations on the premise that it could be potentially bad for morale. Jack protested that this shouldn't apply to Augusta because she was a civilian volunteer and a Belgian citizen. Wisely reminded Jack in no uncertain terms that it wasn't her nationality that had the potential to cause problems; it was her skin color.

<hr>

Maj. Howard F. Sorrel, MC, Third Army, a qualified surgeon, had been flown into Bastogne in a Piper Cub on December 24, 1944. Due to a clerical error he only had provisions for sixty wounded. There were six hundred at the barracks. Sorrel, assisted by the medical personnel, would complete fifteen surgical procedures in just thirty-six hours.

CHAPTER TWELVE

The African Angel

DECEMBER 26, 1944

IT WAS DECEMBER 26, 1944, AND FOR ALL INTENTS AND PURPOSES THIS was going to be a seminal day in the histories of Bastogne and of the Battle of the Bulge.

Early that morning, as the dim light hailed a new dawn beneath the garage of the Heintz Barracks, all was quiet save the occasional smoker's cough. There was almost no light in that basement except for the last flickering glow of some candles placed on an upturned German helmet. The effect in the room was a little stroboscopic as one by one the candles melted into two-inch globules of thick, melted wax and died with rasping fizzles.

Jack hadn't slept well again despite the fact that it had been a long time since he'd rested his weary head on a crisp, white cotton pillowcase. As his whole being begged for respite, he emitted a long, low sigh. This was tiredness like he'd never known before—an aching, gnawing fatigue that consumed his whole being and tormented his soul to distraction. He'd pushed himself to the utmost limits of human endurance and there was still a way to go. That applied to everyone down there on that unforgiving, cold winter's morning.

The day after Christmas brought a little relief for the beleaguered Americans, however, along the southeastern portion of the protective border around Bastogne. They greeted the break and took the time to clean weapons and eat some cold, stale bread. That morning, as work began at the Heintz Barracks, news had filtered through the ranks that

Patton was on the point of breaking through. The ensuing excitement was almost palpable. Dr. Martin Wisely brought some coffee down to Jack and discussed at length what needed to be done. He also told Jack that he'd managed to rig up a shower for those who needed it. This last remark got Augusta's full, undivided attention. There had been no running water and no electricity in Bastogne for over a week.

Within minutes she was standing in what had been a small windowless storeroom, now functioning as an improvised shower cubicle, holding a fresh bar of soap and looking up at a large oil drum full of water suspended precariously above her head. She stood there in anticipation for a moment and then braced herself as the first freezing drops of water cascaded down onto her diminutive frame. The first contact momentarily took her breath but she soon overcame the initial shock and began working the soap into a lather as she doggedly scrubbed her whole body. As the last drops emptied from the oil drum she began to dry herself off and put on the crisp new US Army uniform that Jack had provided for her. She felt lighter, almost light-headed, after finally discarding days of accumulated grime that had clung to her body. The shower had reinvigorated her, and although she was still tired, she was now ready to start again.

Dr. Wisely's warning about possible racist reactions was realized as soon as Augusta entered the former Riding Hall. She would have understood some of the vitriol that was poured out in her direction from the soldiers who were recalcitrant when it came to being treated by the black nurse. Augusta asked if there were any wounded black soldiers. Wisely replied that there were about forty from the 969th Field Artillery Regiment, and further assured Augusta that she would have plenty to keep her occupied. The 969th, along with the 333rd, were African-American field artillery battalions that sustained heavy casualties assisting the 101st Airborne in the defense of Bastogne. The 969th would later be awarded a Distinguished Unit Citation, the first ever presented to an African-American unit. Undeterred by Wisely's remarks, Augusta would treat both regardless.

With Augusta by his side Jack began the triage process in the Riding Hall. Naftulin arrived there sometime later and greeted Jack warmly. He said that he was still a little woozy from the anesthetic, but nonetheless capable of working if they could use the help.

As a further bonus to the medical team, they could now count on the expertise of renowned surgeon Dr. Sorrel, who had daringly flown into Bastogne in his Piper Cub. When he saw the Riding Hall for the first time and observed the mass of patients needing surgery, Dr. Sorrel was overwhelmed. Nevertheless, he took command of the situation and suggested attending to the GAS-infected extremities first. He said that more lives could be saved this way as opposed to spending too much time on stomach, chest, and head wounds. Jack and Augusta assisted him in this gargantuan task.

Naftulin had already had one altercation with a patient who had cast aspersions on his ability to change a wound dressing. The same patient had later seen Augusta walking around and remarked that he didn't want to be touched by no "nigger wenches or Jew boys." Naftulin had seemingly ignored the remark, but, according to his diary, that evening—armed with a can of ether and a pair of dental forceps—he skillfully removed the patient's front teeth.

Although some of the buildings at the Heintz Barracks were being utilized as hospital wards, they were still under constant artillery fire, periodic bombing, and strafing. The medical personnel continued to work untiringly and devotedly until the siege was lifted. A total of 943 American, and 125 German, casualties were collected and taken care of at the temporary second-echelon medical clearing unit and at the 501st Parachute Infantry Regimental aid station.

By mid-afternoon, General McAuliffe had received word that elements of the 326th Airborne Engineers were reporting contact with "three light tanks believed friendly." Along the ice-covered road from Assenois (the Anglicized pronunciation of this town raised a few eyebrows), just a few miles southeast of the Bastogne perimeter, three American Sherman tanks and a half-track rumbled forward followed by two more Shermans sweeping the rear.

The three Sherman tanks were commanded by Lt. Charles P. Boggess; the half-track had become inadvertently attached to the tank column. Boggess moved fast, and as they rolled forward the commander

M4 Sherman tank during the Battle of the Bulge. CREDIT: UNKNOWN

ordered covering fire to spray into the tree line. The offensive move met little enemy resistance, but in the melee a three-hundred-yard gap had developed between the first three vehicles and the last three, giving the enemy just enough time to throw a few mines out on the road before the half-track. The vehicle rolled over the first mine and exploded, throwing burning metal, shrapnel, and body parts into the gray skies and across the fresh snow. Gunfire from turret-mounted .30 caliber machine guns saturated enemy positions with devastating speed, and after a short while, the two rear tank crews hastily disembarked, cleared the remaining mines, and then radioed for more elements of their column to follow them.

At 4:50 p.m. (the time is indelibly recorded in 4th Armored Division dispatches) Boggess saw some engineers in friendly uniform preparing to assault a pillbox near the highway. These were men of the 326th Airborne Engineer Battalion. Gen. George Patton had finally broken through the Nazi lines.

Unbeknownst to the occupants of the Heintz Barracks, contact between the Bastogne garrison and Patton's Third Army had been established. Patton's Third Army had finally reached the perimeter of Bastogne and breached the German lines that had managed to hold the city under siege for over a week. The 4th Armored Division had bravely run the

Gen. George S. Patton before an address to Third Army troops.
CREDIT: UNKNOWN

gauntlet and beaten a narrow but precarious corridor. Despite ensuing strenuous German efforts to close it, the corridor remained open.

The staunch defense of Bastogne had impeded the Fifth Panzer Army's drive to the west and, late in the afternoon of December 26, Lt. Col. Creighton Abrams's tanks finally broke through. Accompanied by an aide, McAuliffe had driven a Willys jeep out to see Patton's troops for himself. Capt. William Dwight, the second soldier to arrive with his tank after 1st Lt. Boggess, scrambled out, saluted, and asked, "How are you, General?"

"Gee, I'm mighty glad to see you," said McAuliffe, happy to be reconnected with the outside world. Only twenty minutes later Colonel Abrams was shaking hands with the general. The 101st's greeting party, by McAuliffe's order, was well-dressed and clean-shaven in an effort to display that they had everything under control.

The siege of Bastogne was over.

On December 26, 1944, at 4:00 p.m., a surgical team consisting of Maj. Laman Soutter, MC, Third Army; Capt. Stanley Wesolowski, MC, Third Army; Capt. Foy H. Moody, MC, Third Army; Capt. Edward N. Zinschlag, MC, Third Army; Capt. Henri M. Mills, MC, Third Army; and four enlisted surgical assistants were flown in to assist the medics at the Heintz Barracks.

The narrow corridor hammered through the German lines by Patton's Third Army was only a few miles wide in some places. Nevertheless, that was enough to bring in fresh supplies and ferry out the badly wounded to safer areas down south, away from Bastogne, even if they did have to run the gauntlet.

General Kokott's last concerted attempt to capture Bastogne had failed. His intention had been to circle through the village of Savy into Bastogne. Though they'd managed to edge in between two companies of the 327th, they were caught in the open by howitzers which literally blew the infantry assault to smithereens. Four armored tank destroyers continued toward Hemroulle, but were finally brought to a halt by a large ditch. While they were in the process of maneuvering, all four were destroyed by close-range artillery and tank-destroyer fire. Seventeen men from the 327th defending a roadblock on the western perimeter were attacked by two Mark IV tanks, a few half-tracks, and infantry. Near Hemroulle, Companies A and B of the 327th GIR defended against an attack by five tanks and a company of German infantry. The infantry were turned back and the tanks destroyed by artillery fire. By mid-afternoon, Kokott learned that the German 5th Parachute Division at Assenois, as well as the 39th Regiment, were under attack from Patton's 4th Armored Division. In the late afternoon, the commander of the 39th radioed the unwelcome information to the German commander that Patton had broken through.

At the Heintz Barracks Dr. Martin Wisely was authorized to negotiate a truce to evacuate his wounded to the 42nd Field Hospital near Wiltz, about seven miles away. Using a captured German medical officer, he contacted the Germans, who responded that they were willing to allow such an evacuation, even though they had some reservations. They were planning to arrange the transfer on the following day, but by that time the 4th Armored Division had broken through to Bastogne and all bets were off.

Meanwhile, six medical officers and four enlisted technicians, all volunteers, from the 4th Auxiliary Surgical Group and the 12th Evacuation Hospital arrived by glider during the afternoon of December 26. Using an operating lamp and an autoclave provided by the 42nd Field Hospital, the surgeons and technicians set up a four-table theater in a small tool room adjoining the garage. They assessed and categorized those needing surgery, and by nightfall had the first men on the temporary operating tables. They were assisted by Augusta, two other Belgian nurse volunteers—Andrée Giroux and Blanche Dombier-Hardy—and Dr. Jack Prior, who was also a qualified anesthetist. They operated throughout the long night until around noon the following day, all in an attempt to clear the backlog of wounded that had been waiting for up to eight days for surgical intervention. They also performed many necessary amputations. After a short rest they continued to work for a further twenty hours straight, completing in total fifty operations and incurring three postoperative deaths.

The afternoon of December 26, the Heintz Barracks was a hub of activity as GIs began celebrating. Augusta noticed the commotion being made by a small group of soldiers and started walking over to see what it was all about. Before she could reach them a GI appeared at the entrance to the hospital and shouted excitedly, "Patton—it's General Patton! He's finally made it! He's here. We're saved!" The news was greeted with yet another loud cheer and a round of rapturous applause from inside the hospital.

That same day, as a hazy orange sun was dipping low in the west, a hushed silence descended on the hospital building. A fresh-faced General McAuliffe entered the hall accompanied by his aide. Taking up position near the entrance, he folded his arms as his aide said, "I'd like your attention for a moment, please."

The general stepped forward and cleared his throat. "I'm pleased and grateful to report that the Third Army has finally arrived in Bastogne."

Spontaneous cheering and applause erupted around the whole place. Walking wounded shook hands and congratulated each other. Augusta unexpectedly found herself in a group hug with four African-American GIs who whooped and whistled with all the strength they could muster. One of them threw his arms around Augusta and jubilantly shouted, "Patton has broken through!"

Augusta forced a smile, ducked out of the hug, and looked around for Jack. She didn't entirely understand the implications of this latest development, but instinctively knew that it could mean Jack would eventually leave Bastogne. This prospect filled her heart with foreboding. He was the reason she had volunteered to go out to the battlefield to retrieve wounded soldiers. He was the reason she had gone to the Heintz Barracks. And although she would be powerless to delay the inevitable, she just hoped that his departure wouldn't happen anytime soon.

As Jack shook hands and laughed with his fellow soldiers, she spotted him at the far side of the Riding Hall. She walked over, tapped him on the shoulder, and asked, "Who is this Patton, and what has he broken?"

CHAPTER THIRTEEN

Speechless

DECEMBER 27–29, 1944

ON DECEMBER 27, MAJ. LEWIS A. CURTIS, CO OF THE 75TH TROOP
Carrier Squadron, led the final combat resupply mission to Bastogne.
During the night German bombers had managed to hit the place on
two separate occasions, but it hadn't prevented the US Third Army from
expanding its corridor to Bastogne and allowing American reinforcements to flock to the city. The road was now open from Assenois to Bastogne, and military vehicles were moving along it bumper to bumper in
both directions. For the moment the Germans in this sector were apparently too demoralized by the speed and sharpness of the blow to react in
any aggressive manner. Although the enemy troops around Assenois had
been broken and scattered by the lightning thrust on December 26, the
Third Army was still facing some strong opposition. As supply trucks and
replacements for the 101st and 10th Armored Division rolled through
the shell-razed streets of Bastogne, a medical company had arrived to
move the casualties back to corps hospitals in the south.

Also on December 27, a glider surgical team arrived. This was a
highly organized and specialized unit that worked as teams on the abdomen and chest wounds. It was their role to prepare as many casualties as
possible for evacuation to the rear. This was a welcome relief for Jack and
the other medical staff out at the Heintz Barracks.

Fighting continued around the perimeter as more reinforcements
arrived and more German divisions were thrown into the fray. The
Führer-Begleit-Brigade was ordered to stop their advance west and head

to Bastogne immediately. This particular command had come directly from Adolf Hitler, who had been informed of Patton's breakthrough. Due to a lack of fuel the tanks of the Führer-Begleit-Brigade ground to a halt one after the other, and most of them would never even reach Bastogne. The intention was to use the Brigade for the purpose of closing the gap in the encirclement around Bastogne by means of an attack in a southerly direction. To precipitate this they would need to protect their flanks.

They discovered to their dismay that the 26th Volksgrenadiers were no longer in a position to offer effective support because they had been severely weakened by the preceding battles, and didn't have the capacity to field any serious armor at that stage in the battle. Further reconnaissance revealed that the high ground south of Chenogne would have to be captured and held in order for the attack conditions to remain favorable for the Axis forces. Gradually an air of desperation began to permeate the ranks of the attacking Germans, and as the temperature plummeted yet again, it was beginning to severely affect the morale of these troops.

Early on the morning of December 27, 1944, ambulances drove along the liberated corridor toward Bastogne. Around noon the ambulances returned loaded with a cargo of wounded soldiers and civilians heading in the direction of Arlon. As reinforcements and food supplies entered the city, ambulances, trucks full of POWs, and civilians left.

Despite the freezing-cold misty weather and blizzard conditions on December 27, around seventy ambulances managed to transport 964 wounded personnel away from Bastogne. Many of those casualties were suffering from hypothermia. The convoy was accompanied by light tanks from the D company 37th Tank Battalion. Throughout the course of the day 130 C-47s and 32 gliders flew resupply missions to Bastogne. German antiaircraft fire and Luftwaffe managed to bring down 9 C-47s, but miraculously, no gliders were hit that day.

As Augusta went about her work at the Heintz Barracks, she still had to contend with occasional racist remarks by wounded men unused to being treated by a black nurse. She got a verbal roasting from a rare Cajun speaker on one occasion, but his accent was so alien to Augusta that

A downed C-47 on the outskirts of Bastogne. CREDIT: UNKNOWN

the effect on her was minimal. She learned all the names of the surgical instruments in English, and although she wasn't considered fluent in the language, she never failed to communicate effectively. Her knowledge of the English language improved tremendously during those days. She also picked up a few rather descriptive expletives that were often used by the GIs at the time.

With each day that passed her affection for Jack grew. Due to the demands of the work they wouldn't have had much time alone together, but working in close proximity for a number of days, they had become very close. He was her friend, guardian angel, and counsel for the duration. Most evenings Augusta remained at the barracks, but occasionally she returned to her father's house, roughly a mile away, just to check up on her family.

Because Augusta was a civilian volunteer, she wasn't paid for the work she performed for the US Army. As the fighting moved away from Bastogne, Jack compensated for this by arranging much-needed provisions for her family. On more than one occasion he drove over to her father's house to personally deliver these supplies. He even organized some supplies to be delivered to the Notre Dame School.

Naftulin was back on the scene and proving himself useful to the crew, working full out to tend the wounded and get them evacuated south as soon as possible.

Then something peculiar occurred that was to change everything.

Late in the afternoon of December 29, Jack ordered Naf to get some rest after he'd been on duty since two o'clock that morning. Naftulin eagerly concurred with the request and removed his formerly white but now heavily bloodstained doctor's coat. First he went over to the mess to get something to eat, and then he retired to the room he shared with about ten other staff. He lay on his bed and within minutes he'd succumbed to extreme fatigue and fallen asleep.

About four hours later he awoke in a panic, screaming, "My God, I'm blind!" By this time other members of the medical staff were on hand to assist. They led him out of his room and over to where Jack was just finishing an operation. Jack shone a penlight on Naftulin's pupils in an attempt to ascertain what the problem was. He couldn't see any exterior damage.

"I'm blind!" screamed Naftulin as he tried to rub his eyes with his fingers. Jack waved them away and continued with his examination. He concluded that he couldn't see anything physically wrong. The only feasible explanation Jack could provide was that this loss of sight was probably the result of delayed shock from the bombing at the aid station.

On January 2, on Jack's orders, Dr. Irving Lee Naftulin was repatriated to the United States. He never entirely recovered from his wartime experiences, and lived with the consequences of these for many years. Precisely what caused him to lose his sight remains a mystery, the most likely cause being post-traumatic stress disorder. Although his sight returned a few weeks later, his army service was effectively over. He would spend the rest of his life suppressing flashbacks and struggling with alcoholism in an attempt to deal with his condition. Jack and Naf stayed in contact with one another, and met again years later when Naftulin visited Jack at his home in Syracuse.

Although many were evacuated through Patton's Third Army corridor, there were still plenty of new arrivals to contend with due to the ferocity of fighting that continued around the widening perimeter. There was a lot of praying done during those dark days in and around Bastogne.

The 10th Armored Division's Combat Command B was entering the last phase of their engagement in Bastogne. Fresh units and other reinforcements were pouring into the city, and Jack Prior and his medical staff expected to be relieved any day. While the 101st Airborne Division was assigned to advance with the Third Army to assist in driving the enemy farther eastward from Bastogne, the bruised and battered tankers of the 10th Armored, with their bullet- and shrapnel-riddled vehicles, would get some relief from the constant fighting they had endured throughout the previous days.

The bitter struggles of the previous week produced some of the worst carnage of the war and had tested the nerve of even the most resilient,

Third Army Dodge WC54 3⁄4 Ton Ambulances taking wounded GI's away from Bastogne, December 27, 1944. CREDIT: UNKNOWN

but for everyone the end was now clearly in sight. Meanwhile, there had been a welcome development: Jack and his staff were relocated to better accommodations within the barracks, and for the first time in weeks they would sleep in real beds with crisp, clean cotton sheets.

Jack was promoted to captain on New Year's Day, 1945, and his new silver bars were pinned on by Doug Davidson in an informal ceremony that Augusta attended. Not only was it validation for his service (especially in recent weeks), but he could also send home an additional $75 per month. He couldn't wait to write to his mother.

As most of Jack's division prepared to move out, he and his team were ordered to remain at Heintz Barracks for just a little while longer. Heavy casualties continued to pour in as fresh US divisions moved forward to close the bulge in the Allied line. The Siege of Bastogne may have been broken, but fighting was far from over.

For Jack, there was one final mission.

—◦—

General Patton's relief of Bastogne has long since become one of the legendary feats of the Battle of the Bulge, but even when he'd relieved Bastogne he still harbored doubts about the eventual outcome of the battle. He was heard to say at one juncture, "We can still lose this war." Although he had effectively carved a corridor through German lines, the fighting was still far from over. The corridor was only one mile wide in places, and those transports in and out remained vulnerable to German shelling.

General Maxwell Taylor, commander of the 101st Airborne, had arrived back in Paris from the United States on the afternoon of December 26. He had initially asked to be parachuted into Bastogne, but this request was rebuffed by his superiors. On December 27, he left France and headed to Bastogne in a Willys jeep. Traversing the narrow corridor he reached the town at 4:00 p.m., about twenty-four hours after it had been relieved by the Third Army.

Arriving at the Heintz Barracks, General Taylor met acting 101st Commander General McAuliffe, and inquired about the situation concerning the 101st Airborne. At that particular time the division still numbered 711 officers and 9,516 men.

Around this time, Augusta's brother Charles used the Third Army corridor to travel south and link up with other members of the Resistance in Luxembourg. Her father and Mama Caroline remained in Bastogne for the duration. Henri was still hoping that the US Army would offer permanent employment to Augusta, but hadn't yet broached the subject with anyone. That was still to come. The uppermost consideration on the minds of those civilians who had remained in Bastogne was survival, and those civilians unwittingly caught up in the conflict often went to extraordinary lengths to survive. Tragically many lost their livelihoods, their homes, and their families.

Augusta was beginning to display further signs of physical afflic- tion brought on by her many recent ordeals. She had difficulty verbally responding to people around her, and would become unexpectedly mute for hours on end. Although she still communicated with Jack, her expe- riences had left a marked effect on her ability to be spontaneous and talk to others there at the Heintz Barracks. There were occasions when she would find herself simply at a loss for words, unable to describe or articu- late the horrors that she'd seen and endured during her time in Bastogne. She could still speak when she had to, but she kept her questions and responses to short, staccato monosyllabic sentences.

Having spent weeks among dead and dying young men, internalizing her feelings and presenting a stoic exterior had begun to leave her literally speechless. Her situation was exacerbated by being the constant target of cutting insults and terrible aspersions against her character by some of the wounded GIs as she went about her daily chores. Despite all of this adversity she labored on, maintaining her dignity and fortitude through- out. But there was only so much a person in her precarious position could withstand. She was reaching her breaking point.

Although the accommodations at the Heintz Barracks were better now, constantly interrupted sleep due to shelling was enough to grind down even the strongest. Henri had noticed a stark change in Augusta's character. She had gradually become very subdued and timid over the past weeks, and her usual effervescence was gone. More than once he had advised her to quit working for the US Army, but she steadfastly refused to abandon her work and carried on regardless, for one reason and one reason alone: She wanted to remain close to Jack.

At least now the end was in sight, but precisely what that "end" would entail filled Augusta with apprehension and dread. She wanted the fighting to stop so that no more young men or civilians would have to suffer further. And yet, at the same time, she knew that her life had been irretrievably changed. After this was all over, and it would be soon, there was no going back to the way things had been. She was convinced that Jack loved her, but simultaneously she worried about their future, and that uncertainty was hard to bear. She'd noticed that Jack rarely if ever displayed his feelings for her around others. There were days when her heart was so full that she felt as if it would explode, and then there were other days when being around the dead and dying almost drove her to distraction. Deep down she knew that she would have to face the inevitable and whatever that entailed.

CHAPTER FOURTEEN

A Great Leveler

LATE DECEMBER 1944

DESPITE THE FOG THE ALLIES HAD TO CONTEND WITH THE THREAT OF additional surprise air attacks by German forces still in the vicinity. The US Army sent out regular patrols to closely monitor the situation, and on December 28 Allied commanders began planning a coordinated counter-offensive. Wounded men continued to arrive at the Heintz Barracks, but by now the staff there were in a better position to deal with them.

In one way Augusta benefited from her experiences with the US Army. Because drugs such as sulfa powder (sulfanilamide) and penicillin had been discovered during World War II, she had the opportunity to observe advanced surgical techniques. The primary reason for the improving mortality rate was the speed with which wounded men were now being treated.

The whole process began with the front-line combat medics, the first to assess and treat specific injuries. Depending on the severity of the injury the decision would be made whether or not to evacuate the wounded person back to the Heintz Barracks. The main objective of the front-line medic was to get the patient away from there as soon as possible. Many times this involved the medic climbing out from the protection of his foxhole during shelling or into no-man's-land to help a fallen comrade. Once with the wounded soldier, the medic would do a brief examination, apply a tourniquet if necessary, sometimes inject a vial of morphine, clean up the wound as best as possible, and then sprinkle sulfa powder on it, followed by a bandage. Then he would drag or carry the patient out of harm's way and to the rear. On many occasions this was achieved under enemy fire or artillery shelling.

This is one of the many reasons why combat medics like Jack Prior earned such high regard and respect from the soldiers. In most cases, the Germans respected the Red Cross armband, but there had been exceptions, particularly among the SS.

⁓

Augusta continued her work at the Heintz Barracks under Jack's auspices. Despite the increasing number of wounded arriving there, with the current arrangement at least she could take small breaks between shifts. Once new supply routes were established it meant that all staff members were now well provisioned. Clean uniforms, clean bedding, and fresh food made all the difference to the working practices there.

Jack intervened on Augusta's behalf on more than one occasion when she was being lambasted with racist remarks. One particular patient from Alabama strongly protested against being treated by a black nurse. He was cursing Augusta and vigorously resisting her attempts to change his wound dressing when Jack got involved. He told the intractable GI in no uncertain terms that he would inevitably die if his wound became infected. He gave the wounded man a stark choice: "Either Augusta treats you or you die—your call." The GI became very compliant and allowed Augusta to change his dressing without another complaint. When push comes to shove, death is a great leveler.

The following day Jack wrote in his diary about a half-track that had taken a direct hit on a bridge four miles away in Assenois. Jack actually knew one of the medics on board this vehicle. When he received the request for assistance he turned to one of his own medics who had recently been given a citation for bravery and said, "Take a vehicle and bring them home."

The GI replied, "No, Doc, they are still under heavy fire. That would be a suicide mission." Jack was shocked that someone in his unit would actually refuse a direct order, and he never forgot that night. Although he didn't court-martial the medic, he never wrote him up for another citation and refused to give him a positive reference. In his autumn years Jack often spoke of this medic, and even attempted to locate him because he was having nightmares. The problem was that he couldn't recall the medic's name. He wanted to apologize for his poor decision, and he prayed that he hadn't prevented the man from becoming an excellent doctor. Jack knew all too well that courage was a quantifiable and limited resource, particularly among those who had faced the prospect of imminent death on more than one occasion.

Having no alternative, Jack decided to go himself. It was just a few days before the remaining 10th Armored were due to pull out of Bastogne, and Augusta once again bravely volunteered to go with Jack and two paratroopers out to the perimeter of Assenois to collect any wounded. It was going to be another subzero foray as Augusta climbed into the front passenger seat while Jack and the paratroopers loaded up the deuce-and-a-half with medical supplies. As they traveled south they passed the seemingly endless columns of reinforcements and supplies snaking their way into Bastogne from the south and west.

Progress was labored due to dense fog and frequent stops to allow vehicles flowing in the opposite direction to pass by. The day after Patton broke through, the first fresh units into Bastogne had gone down the main street with bulldozers and cleared a large swathe of traversable road through the rubble to make way for the incoming vehicles. When they finally reached their destination two miles southeast of Bastogne they saw the upturned M3 half-track lying about twenty yards from the side of the main road in a still-smoldering field. Jack counted eight bodies lying in the immediate vicinity of the half-track, and deduced that there were probably some soldiers trapped underneath the vehicle, as well.

He jumped out of the truck and then turned to help diminutive Augusta climb down from the high passenger seat. The two Airborne soldiers took shovels out of the back of the truck and wasted no time in attempting to dig underneath the M3 while Jack and Augusta walked among the bodies, checking for signs of life. The bodies were mostly frozen solid and had been badly mutilated by the powerful blast that had taken out the half-track. Severed limbs and pieces of torsos were scattered around the area.

One of the paratroopers saw an arm protruding from under the vehicle and noticed that the hand was moving ever so slightly. After a few minutes of frenetic digging they managed to extricate the survivor and drag him a few feet away from the vehicle. It was only when they'd pulled him free that they noticed that both of his legs had been blown off, one above the knee and one below. The wounded GI tried to speak but failed to make any audible noises as Jack stuck a vial of morphine into the man's thigh and Augusta applied dressings to his shredded, bloodied stumps. The paratroopers loaded the man onto a stretcher and placed him carefully in the back of the truck before returning to the upturned half-track.

Suddenly, about thirty yards away, the ground erupted as 88s and mortar shells began to explode around the small group. Jack, Augusta, and the paratroopers began to run for cover and were only a few paces away from the half-track when the percussion from an explosion behind them forced everyone to dive into a nearby ditch. The half-track had been hit by an 88mm and literally blown to pieces. Burning debris from the blast had caused the canvas cover on Jack's deuce-and-a-half to catch fire, but the small team was helpless to prevent it spreading. He looked down at Augusta who was cowering next to him. She'd grabbed his shoulder and buried her head in it, covering her ears with her hands. They watched in horror as the flames rose higher and their wounded man was slowly incinerated where he lay. Black smoke and the repellent smell of charred flesh filled the air as the shelling began to dissipate. The Germans simply didn't have enough ammunition for a sustained bombardment and it was all over in minutes.

A passing quad with its 50mm machine guns and a half-track with a 105 howitzer were returning fire across the field, but as the bombing subsided they stopped firing and everyone tenuously got to their feet. Jack, realizing that their mission had been fruitless, gave the order to hitch a lift on one of the passing vehicles and return to Bastogne. With the firing temporarily abated they all left the ditch and walked toward the road. One of the paratroopers walking a few paces in front heard a resonant click from beneath the sole of his boot.

He'd inadvertently stepped on the release mechanism of a land mine. The other paratrooper immediately dove over and pushed his comrade to the ground while he took the full force of the ensuing explosion and disintegrated in a cloud of blood, smoke, and disembodied flesh. Twenty yards away from the explosion, Jack and Augusta recoiled as pieces of his body flew in all directions and splattered their uniforms. They dove to the ground as Jack threw his sizable frame over Augusta's to provide her with some protection from the blast. She cowered there beneath him on the frozen hard soil, not daring to move. A few inches from her fingertips she could see one of the paratrooper's blue eyes with the bloody sinew still attached. She tried to scream but the sound dissolved between her larynx and the protracted strands of saliva. No sound emanated from her mouth. She tried again but the result was the same.

A passing team of engineers surveyed the scene and immediately began using mine detectors to secure a path back to the road for Jack, Augusta, and the surviving paratrooper. All of them appeared to be badly shaken, but Jack was the most coherent. He'd already been in the proximity of a few blasts since he'd arrived in Europe and quickly regained his faculties. The paratrooper hadn't escaped entirely unscathed, although his wounds weren't life-threatening, and he appeared more concerned with the recent fate of his comrade than his own well-being.

When they finally arrived back at the Heintz Barracks, Augusta was in shock. This time Jack's efforts to comfort her were to no avail. She simply couldn't speak. She wanted to, but the words wouldn't form in her mouth properly, and try as she might, she couldn't get them out. A few hours later she was cleaned up, but there were still some dried spots of blood congealed in her eyelashes and eyebrows. She looked up when Jack entered the cellar room and didn't say anything to him. Jack confined her to her room for the duration and closely monitored her condition.

Within a few days she was up and about again, yet there was something markedly different about her now. She didn't say much anymore, and when she tried all she could manage was a suppressed whisper. None of Jack's attempts at levity could raise a smile on her pursed lips.

As the days passed the fighting began to move away from Bastogne, but the scarred buildings and devastated lives remained. Augusta appeared to be working on autopilot. She still attended her duties, but the spring in her step had become a tiresome, laborious trudge as she mechanically responded to requests and hardly displayed any emotion at all. It was as if her lifeblood was slowly ebbing away. Her senses had been dramatically assaulted; she'd seen too much death, and there were only so many depredations her tormented soul could weather.

She remained polite and attentive but she wasn't herself anymore. At night, in her room at the barracks, she sobbed uncontrollably, emptying her heart and cursing the world for all her woes. It felt good to cry, to release the anger, the hurt, the heartache she'd suffered after seeing so many young men die so far from home, so far from their loved ones.

Jack had also sustained hidden wounds, but therein lay his key to survival. Just like Augusta he also internalized the pain and suffering he'd witnessed. He kept it to himself, kept up a brave front, but deep inside he knew that these days were going to follow him for the rest of his natural life.

The time was soon approaching when he would be forced to move out. He was dreading that day, but he knew he would have to get through it somehow; after all, that's what soldiers did when their mission was accomplished. The hardest thing would be saying good-bye to his Augusta, his African angel. Late at night after the long day was done, this thought alone would cause him to well up.

CHAPTER FIFTEEN

The Last Dying Gasps

JANUARY 1945

JACK'S UNIT—COMBAT COMMAND B OF THE 20TH AIB, 10TH ARMORED Division—had performed well and exceeded all expectations. They had cleared most of the roads north while CCA and the 35th Division had pounded away against the German remnants that were clinging doggedly to the Arlon-Bastogne highway in the south. The battle wasn't over yet, but the proverbial tide had turned and the US Army was sweeping in, witnessing the last dying gasps of a broken, dispirited enemy.

Patton may have forced a corridor through to Bastogne, but now German divisions had begun to descend on it like flies around the muzzle of a snorting bull. The east side of the corridor managed to deflect the repeated blows of an attack by two Volksgrenadier divisions supported by elements of the 5th German paratrooper division. Through the dense fog the Germans had stormed into Lutrebois just about four miles south of Bastogne, and only about 1,300 yards from the main highway.

The confrontation that followed was the result of a carefully executed ambush orchestrated by six medium Sherman tanks. Using the cover of fog they positioned themselves on the edge of the woods at Lutrebois. As German Mark Vs moved forward in twos and threes, the Shermans opened fire, destroying all the German tanks without sustaining a single loss to their own armor. Throughout the rest of that day the 35th Infantry Division, supported by low-flying Thunderbolts, would incapacitate fifty-five German tanks.

The German offensive was grinding to a gasping, spluttering halt as the order from OKW began to filter through to the German ranks to pull back behind the Siegfried Line along the German border. In some parts of the Ardennes the retreat was becoming more of a rout. Hitler was exasperated and bitterly disappointed by this defeat, but in a rare moment of lucidity he decided to cut his losses and prepare for the final battle.

In a vain and desperate act the Germans attempted one more offensive farther south in the Alsace region of France. Operation Nordwind was an abortive attempt to destroy a thinly held line of US forces there. Eisenhower hurriedly brought in battered divisions that had fought in the Ardennes to strengthen the US position. The offensive began on January 1 and had petered out by January 25. Hitler's abortive Operation Nordwind offensive effectively removed all Axis forces from France. Fighting continued in the Luxembourg area for another few weeks, but the Battle of the Bulge and the battle for Bastogne were effectively over. Hitler's last gamble in the west had failed, and now within a few weeks Germany was itself going to be under siege as Russian armies drove west toward Berlin and the Allies continued their march east.

Just one day before Jack left Bastogne, the First Army and the Third Army met a few miles north of Bastogne in the ruined city of Houffalize. The mighty pincer was now closed and the remaining German divisions were being driven all along the front. A once-beautiful region had been devastated by the largest land battle in United States military history.

On January 17, 1945, the moment had come for the remaining elements of the 10th Armored Division to ship out and say good-bye to Bastogne. Jack had been dreading this day. He carefully folded and packed his kit and walked toward the parade ground of the Heintz Barracks. Most of the division had left the previous day. It was then that he saw Henri Chiwy walking purposefully out of the morning mist in his direction.

According to his diary Jack didn't recognize Henri at first through the haze, but then realized who it was as he got closer. He had seen Henri briefly when he'd first met Augusta some weeks previous, and had visited him at his home a few times after that to give him provisions. He hadn't expected to see Henri that day, and Augusta had no idea that her father had planned to pay a visit to the barracks. The two men shook hands on the parade ground and then Henri asked Jack straight out if he had any plans for his daughter.

Jack misconstrued the question initially and went on to explain that he had been extremely grateful for Augusta's assistance, but his job in Bastogne was over and he didn't have any specific plans for her. He also went to some lengths to explain that there had been absolutely no impropriety between him and Augusta. Then Henri interjected and said that he wanted Augusta to remain with the US Army. He asked Jack to take Augusta with him when he left Bastogne. Henri Chiwy's motives were not entirely clear at this point, but it's apparent that some of this exchange was labored due to his lack of knowledge of the English language. In all fairness he probably just wanted Augusta to be safe. She didn't need a job, as she already had one at the St. Elizabeth Hospital in Louvain, and had every intention of returning there when the situation allowed.

Jack later wrote in his diary that Augusta was "willed" to him by her father. He probably meant that Henri was insisting that Jack should take responsibility for her well-being. There's no doubt that Henri wanted to know if the US Army had any plans for his daughter, and although he was an intelligent man, he couldn't sufficiently articulate his request because Jack appeared quite indignant at the proposal.

When Augusta's father had returned to Belgium after his service in the Congo, he had given up his two children to his childless sister-in-law, Caroline, who adopted them. This was probably just a technicality for administration purposes, because he worked extremely long hours and his veterinary services were constantly in demand. Nevertheless, they all lived in the same house so he saw his children almost every day, regardless. He always maintained that he was their father and was always there for them both.

On this occasion Henri and Jack didn't part on friendly terms. Jack ended the conversation quite abruptly, exhaled sharply, and turned to go, leaving nothing behind but a small cloud of condensed breath dissolving into the freezing air around Henri Chiwy's solitary figure.

Jack then visited Augusta in the Riding Hall and asked if she'd follow him to one of the adjacent offices. It was there that he told her that her father had been to see him. She clenched her fists and rolled her eyes and appeared quite annoyed, but didn't say anything. Then Jack explained that he had received orders to move out and rejoin his unit out east. He felt awkward as he thanked her profusely for all her work and gave her an affectionate hug. Augusta tried to look into his eyes but couldn't. She didn't want Jack to see that she was hurting.

Jack then gave Augusta an address to write to him and promised to keep in touch. As he gently handed her the slip of paper Augusta tried to hold back her tears, and failed. She put her head on his chest and wept, but her tears weren't just for Jack. They were for all the misery and hardship they'd endured together over the past four weeks. The indelible bond they had nurtured was stronger and deeper than love. They had been there for each other throughout, and now it was over. Augusta had thought about this moment, but despite its inevitability, it still shredded her heart to pieces.

Jack cupped her small face in his hands and told her to be strong. Augusta pushed his hands away because she had been strong—very strong. Now that strength was all used up and she couldn't muster any more. She couldn't bring herself to watch him leave for good. She just stood alone and stared at the floor as Jack left the office.

After he'd closed the door Augusta dried her face and composed herself. When she finally emerged into a fresh, freezing-cold winter's day with almost clear azure skies, she scanned the parade ground to try and catch one last glimpse of the man who had changed her life.

Before climbing into the back of a deuce-and-a-half Jack looked back, but with the sun in his eyes at first there was no sign of Augusta. She was just in time to see Jack's transport leaving the Heintz Barracks for the last time. Jack spotted her and waved energetically, but Augusta didn't reciprocate; she just stood there with tears coursing down her face, shaking her head and feeling as if her whole life had just been emptied into an enormous, bottomless abyss. She walked slowly back to her room and collected what few possessions she had before going over to the Riding Hall to bid farewell to the remaining staff.

With a heavy heart she walked back to her father's house. When she arrived there she confronted Henri about visiting the barracks and talking to Jack. This caused some commotion in the Chiwy household, but not for long.

Bastogne would never be the same again. Augusta would attempt to pick up her life and move on as Jack did, but the tethers of her experiences and the inner turmoil that these caused would never leave her.

———

Jack Prior was a great doctor. He received various medals for serving with the 10th Armored Division in the European Theater during World War II. His decorations included the Bronze Star, the Silver Star, the Legion of Merit, the Belgian Croix de Guerre, and the medals of the cities of Bastogne and Metz. Following World War II he became a member of the Army Reserve and commanded the 376th Combat Support Reserve Hospital, from which he retired in 1977 with the rank of colonel.

As for Augusta, she was not recognized for her service to the US Army, and she resigned from her position as a nurse at the St. Elizabeth Hospital in Louvain. After the battle her life would be devastated for a long time to come, and she would carry the suffering in her heart forever. She couldn't face nursing again and needed time to convalesce, so she stayed with her father and Mama Caroline in Bastogne.

As the days passed Augusta wrote to Jack every day at the address he had given her, but she never received a reply. Every morning she would follow the same routine, racing downstairs to see if the postman had brought anything for her, but it remained a fruitless hope.

Then in late February 1945 a letter arrived from the US War Office. She eagerly ripped it open and read the contents. The War Office informed Augusta that Capt. John Prior had been killed in action. She ripped the letter to shreds and threw it into the open hearth.

Chapter Sixteen

Broken Town, Broken Heart

In the months that followed Jack's departure Augusta mentally withdrew from the world and spent her days alone in her room, gazing out the window in quiet contemplation. She rarely ventured out or saw friends and became very distant. Henri and Caroline tried to get her some professional help, but she refused to cooperate and they didn't insist. Something inside her had died in Bastogne alongside the victims of the fighting.

She couldn't talk about her experiences or recount any of the suffering she and others had undergone. It had all been too much to bear, and she closed down completely, refusing to talk to anyone at all about the war. As winter gave way to spring Augusta appeared to show some signs of recovery, but it was a slow and emotionally excruciating process. The rule in the Chiwy household was, "Don't mention the war when Augusta is around." Any mention of it would cause Augusta to become completely uncommunicative and to wholly retreat into herself.

When she eventually went to see a doctor she was referred to a hospital in Namur where they took a series of X-rays. It was there that they discovered the blast from the explosion on Christmas Eve had shattered two vertebrae at the base of her spine. There was no psychiatric diagnosis at this time. Many years later it was revealed that she was suffering from a form of PTSD that manifested itself as selective mutism. Whenever Augusta heard a reference to the war she would recoil into her shell and refuse to speak for days, weeks, sometimes months on end.

The war was almost over, and it was time to rebuild—rebuild houses, rebuild businesses, and, most importantly, rebuild lives.

The city of Bastogne was a mere shell of its former self. Refugees returning to the area discovered that most of their homes and farms had been reduced to rubble. Even though the fighting had long since moved on, the area in and around Bastogne was still riddled with explosive remnants of war. As the weeks passed, refugees risked being blown apart by mines that had been placed on roads, paths, hillsides, and in the woods and fields, ready to explode at the slightest touch.

The Germans had rigged booby traps inside some of the derelict houses, and for many years following the war there were still casualties. In the perimeter of Bastogne forty people were killed in the first five months of 1945 by unexploded ordnance. Half of the victims were children under fifteen years old.

Belgian army minesweeping units cleared away no less than 114,000 mines. Despite their efforts hardly a week passed without someone inadvertently stepping on or driving over a mine. Army engineers did what they could to remove all of this ordnance, but there were inevitably places that they overlooked, places that they missed with their mine detectors and probing bayonets.

In 1950, Augusta married one of these Belgian minesweepers, a soldier named Jacques Cornet. When they went to the town hall to get a marriage certificate the officials there steadfastly attempted to dissuade Jacques from marrying Augusta, on the premise that their mixed-race children would be ostracized by the community. Jacques ignored their impudent advice and went ahead with their plans. They married and eventually had two children, both light-skinned—not that it mattered to Augusta.

Augusta had absolutely no idea at the time that Jack was not really dead. The KIA message from the US War Office was merely a ruse to dissuade former European girlfriends and mistresses of GIs from trying to pursue them. Jack had gone to Germany with the 10th Armored Division, who, among other things, provided transport for the survivors of Dachau as the Allies began to uncover the extent of Hitler's malevolence and destructive hatred.

After the war, as GIs boarded ships to begin their journeys back home to their cities and farmsteads, the inhabitants of Bastogne delved among the ruins for reminders of their former lives before the battle. Some US Army officials remained on-site as the Red Cross moved in and began assembling temporary shelter for those who had lost their homes. The derelict high streets and alleyways were still shrouded in the repellent smell of rotting corpses and fuming, pungent wreckage, but now the big cleanup could get under way. Sherman tanks were fitted with bulldozer attachments and cranes to move and hoist the smoldering timbers from the remains of this ancient market town.

Some officials from the Red Cross visited Augusta at her father's home to ask what she had done during the battle for Bastogne. They knew that she had volunteered but didn't have any precise details, and Augusta couldn't give them any. She couldn't bring herself to speak about her experiences. After the war she was just another casualty, a young girl in a broken town with a broken heart.

Years later, Augusta was watching a documentary about the Battle of the Bulge with her husband when he asked, "How come you were never recognized for your service to the US Army?" Augusta responded that she had no idea, and didn't care. Then her husband said, "It's probably because you're black," and left it at that. The question was never asked again.

Augusta accepted her husband's explanation and never pursued the matter further. She just wanted to put it all behind her and get on with her life, even though she still had to deal with her recurrent ghosts and the terrifying nightmares that continued to blight her life.

On Christmas Eve, 1958, Augusta received a peculiar package. The stamp and postmark indicated that it had been posted in America. She carefully opened the package to find a box of candy inside, along with a card that read: *Remember Christmas Eve. Love, Jack.*

———

After the war ended Dr. Jack Prior returned to the United States. He married Elizabeth Troy and became a respected pathologist. He once said that pathology was the only medical activity he could think of where the patients didn't scream. He too had been severely affected by his experiences in Bastogne.

Although Augusta worked sporadically as an independent nurse, she didn't return to full-time nursing until 1964, when she became a night nurse at the Traumatology Center of the Brugmann Hospital in Brussels. This was the same hospital where Renée Lemaire had worked before returning to Bastogne during that fateful winter of 1944–1945.

In 1994 Augusta unexpectedly received a letter informing her of the forthcoming fiftieth-anniversary commemoration of the Battle of the Bulge to be held in Bastogne. By that time, she had been corresponding with Jack for a few years and knew that he was going to be there, so after giving the matter some serious thought, she decided to attend. Augusta's husband chose not to go with her.

When she arrived in Bastogne with US general Charles Hewitt and her close friend Elizabeth Dugaillez, there was already a sizable crowd assembled on what was formerly known as the Route du Neufchâteau, now the rue de Neufchâteau.

As Jack waited beside Maggie Lemaire, Renée's sister, in front of the plaque that was due to be unveiled at the site of the former aid station, they scanned the crowd that was amassing in preparation for the ensuing ceremony. Suddenly Augusta tapped Jack on the shoulder and he turned around, surprised to see a small, bespectacled, well-dressed lady before him. They embraced, and the first thing he said to her was, "Oh my God, Augusta, you're so small."

"And you're so big," she retorted, laughing.

A lot of the time they just stared at each other, silent, lost in mutual memories, sharing the things that only veterans can share. Over the next few days they attended the ceremonies together before parting company at the Mardasson Hill, where the largest US memorial outside America is located. That was to be their final meeting.

Jack was born in St. Albans, Vermont, and on November 23, 2007, at the age of ninety, he died at home in Manlius, New York. During his lifetime Jack was awarded many medals and accolades for his service, but for sixty-five long years, nurse Augusta Chiwy remained unrecognized for her contribution to the Allied war effort.

That's where I came in.

Chapter Seventeen

Searching for Augusta

2007

IN MY HUMBLE OPINION THERE IS NO BETTER PLACE TO BE EARLY ON A Sunday morning than in my car driving around the quiet, winding lanes of the Belgian Ardennes while the morning mist is still clinging to the multitudinous pines and hovering above those effervescent trout streams. I know there are more dramatic landscapes around the world, but the balance of field, forest, and river in the Ardennes always feels just right to me. It's a beautiful place, and so peaceful now. So different to what it was in the winter of 1944–1945 when Augusta and Jack were there.

Finding information on nurse Augusta Chiwy was going to take a lot of time. Augusta was a civilian, and this was the very first time that I'd attempted to trace one. I quickly discovered that it wasn't going to be an easy ride. The biggest problem was the country where I live, Belgium. There are three national languages here; it's a country that gives you three for the price of one, but on this occasion this wasn't going to be a bargain—it was to be an administrative nightmare.

Almost every lead on my journey to discover who this nurse was became a cul-de-sac. Attempting to procure information in Belgium can be an administrative nightmare—like swimming in mud. Although everything is based on precise appointments, they are often not kept, and it can take weeks to get a response to an e-mail or letter.

After a few laborious months I contacted my friend Mike Collins in New York State and asked him if he was planning to visit the archives in Washington, DC, anytime in the near future. He was. We had already written a fairly successful book together, and I liked his style. Mike was the consummate researcher who almost always managed to get the information I needed. Thanks to him I discovered that in December of 1944, the 20th Armored Infantry Battalion of the 10th Armored Division was the unit that ran the aid station in Bastogne. That was a good start.

I took this information to the former HQ of the 101st Airborne Division in Bastogne, to a place called the Heintz Barracks. I went there because Mike had sent me a DVD titled *Tigers on the Loose* about the 10th Armored Division. The acting commander of the 101st Airborne Division, Gen. Anthony McAuliffe, appeared in the documentary, praising the efforts of the 10th Armored Division. Moreover, there were some amateur historians at the barracks who were always willing to help with research.

As soon as I arrived at the barracks I met my respected friend, adjutant Eric "Rony" Lemoine. Our conversation soon turned to the subject of the Siege of Bastogne. Rony, whom I regard as an authority on the Battle of the Bulge, told me that there were a few medical teams operating in the city during the siege. Guiding our discussion in this direction was the recently added display of World War II medical equipment there. He went on to tell me about a US aid station that was bombed on the rue de Neufchâteau, and showed me a small shrine dedicated to the memory of nurse Renée Lemaire. Below the photograph was a copy of the commendation that she had received from the Belgian government.

"Renée was an amazing lady," I said to Rony, who nodded in agreement.

"She was indeed," he replied. "We call her the 'Angel of Bastogne.'"

"Ah, but according to my information she wasn't the only angel who worked in Bastogne during the battle, was she?" I said, tapping the side of my nose.

"No, you're right," said Rony, nodding. "There was another one—a black nurse called Augusta Chiwy."

"That's actually why I'm here. I was wondering if you could shed some light on that story for me."

Rony lit a cigarette and took a draw before exhaling and coughing loudly.

"Well," he said, "all I know is that her uncle was a local doctor who must have done something important, because he had a street in Bastogne named after him. It's called rue du Docteur Chiwy."

"Do you know anyone who might be able to tell me more?"

Rony grimaced and shook his head. He must have registered the dismay creeping over my face because suddenly he put his finger to his lips and said, "Hang on a minute. There is one man in town that might be able to help. He's a local artist who knows everyone and everything about this town."

You know how you always notice a few drops of water before a pipe bursts? Well, that's what happened then, because as I returned to my battered Ford Galaxy my cell phone rang. It was my dear friend, Mike Collins. I could tell from the tone of his voice that he was excited about something; in fact, I could hardly understand a word of what he was saying.

"Have you got a paper bag handy, Mike?" I said. "Take a few deep breaths and start again from the top."

Mike told me that he'd discovered the name of the chief medic who had worked for the 20th AIB at the aid station in Bastogne.

"That's fantastic, mate," I shouted, trying to suppress my rising enthusiasm. "Where is he?"

"He just died."

"Oh, dear. Give me some good news, will you?"

He would, but it wouldn't be till later on. At that moment I was drowning in disappointment.

⌁

A few hours later I went to a cafe to meet with the local artist Rony had mentioned. Over a beer (or three) he told me that he knew something about Augusta Chiwy. According to him she had an uncle who had a street named after him. "It's called rue du Docteur Chiwy," imparted the artist in a somewhat sage manner. I knew that bit already, but then he went on to tell me that Augusta had been visiting her adopted mother and father in Bastogne when the battle started.

Armed with this information I went to the town hall in Bastogne. The person at the reception desk didn't speak much English, and my knowledge of French left something to be desired, but we managed. She advised me to speak to the person responsible for tourism and gave me directions to the appropriate office.

Minutes later I was knocking on the door. A woman answered, wearing a green dress that could have doubled as a six-man tent. She was eating a croissant while frowning, clearly not in a good mood. I was a little bemused because I didn't think it was possible to eat those things sideways on.

I enquired politely, "I'm trying to get some information about Augusta Chiwy, a former resident of Bastogne."

The woman looked at me and appeared to say something that sounded like, "I want muffleys." She repeated the opening statement, this time after chewing a bit more of the croissant, so I understood it.

"I'm from Houffalize," she said.

"You're from Houffalize? What's that got to do with anything?" I asked.

"I don't know anything about Bastogne. I think there is a street here called rue du Docteur Chiwy," she said, smiling. At least I think it was a smile—could have been trapped wind.

"I know that bit, but you're the manager for tourism in Bastogne," I interjected. "Doesn't that title alone imply that you must know something about the place?"

"So what? Go to Arlon," she harrumphed before slamming the door in my face.

This was not going to be the sole encounter of this nature—just the first of many uncivil civil servants I was going to have to deal with on my journey.

I returned home from the tourism office and decided to drive down to Arlon the next day. The two-hour drive to visit the archives there, just next to the Luxembourg border of Belgium, was worthwhile because it revealed more information about the composition of the Chiwy family, including their professions in 1944, and so forth.

On the way back from Arlon I decided to stop off at a geriatric nursing home in Bastogne. It was just a hunch, but it turned out to be quite a good one. I walked in bold as brass and explained to the receptionist that I was trying to find out information about a former resident of Bastogne. She took me to the director's office where I had to explain everything again.

The portly director didn't say anything, just rose sluggishly from his chair and beckoned me to follow him down a long corridor to a kind of dayroom where the residents were sitting around the place in various stages of disinterest and disintegration. Then he put his hands in his pockets and bellowed something in French about Augusta Chiwy. Some of the residents were cupping their ears while others were drinking various beverages.

Suddenly, over in the far corner, one old dear put her hand up.

"That lady knew Mrs. Chiwy," he said, pointing. "You may talk to her, but don't stay long. They get very tired very quickly." And with that he turned and walked away.

I thanked the director and watched him leave before making a bee-line for the lady who had responded. I sat down beside her and she stared at me through watery eyes before saying in English, "I'm Andrée Giroux, and yes, I knew Augusta. She was lovely. I knew her because I lived here in Bastogne and I was a nurse too."

"Excellent," I replied. "Tell me about her."

Andrée gazed toward the window, deep in thought, and smiled benignly before saying, "I remember Augusta telling me that nursing was the only profession where a black woman could shout at a white man without getting hurt." She ended this statement with a slight giggle. Andrée told me that Augusta had graduated a year before her. They hadn't attended the same nursing school, but Andrée had also volunteered to help wounded American soldiers at the 101st HQ.

My research was going well and I'd already begun to build a profile of the type of person Augusta Chiwy was, but there was still one major niggling doubt that pervaded my thoughts at the time: Was she still alive?

Knowing that married women in Belgium retain their maiden names, I'd scoured multiple phone books looking for the name "Chiwy" and hadn't had much success, so I started visiting the town halls. Belgium is a small country of around ten and a half million inhabitants, but it has 589 separate municipalities. That meant 589 town halls, each with their own administration. I began making phone calls to the various departments, but this quickly proved fruitless. It would usually go something like this:

> *"Hello. I'm sorry to disturb you, but my name is Martin King, and I'm trying to locate a Belgian person."*
>
> *"So, what has that got to do with me?" was more often than not the curt reply from both genders, and in all languages (although rarely in English).*
>
> *"Well, I thought you might be able to connect me with the right department."*
>
> *"I don't know what you want."*
>
> *"I want to find someone who may have lived, or may still be living, in your area."*
>
> *"Are they missing? If they're missing, you should call the police."*
>
> *"No, that won't be necessary; can you put me through to civilian registration, please?"*
>
> *"They won't be able to help."*
>
> *"Why not?"*

What followed was usually one of three responses:

1. *They're all out to lunch.*
2. *They're on holiday.*
3. *There's nobody there at the moment. See above.*

Most of the people who worked in these places were notoriously uncooperative, so I printed out a list and decided to start visiting them one by one. I couldn't for the life of me understand why people were so unhelpful here in Belgium. It was as if some of them had a grudge against the world and everybody in it. Despite this, I refused to give up. Every setback made me even more determined to find out if Augusta Chiwy was still alive.

Despite its small size as a country, Belgium is frighteningly big on bureaucracy. Belgians are by nature nice people, but give them any position of authority and they transform, or rather mutate, into sentinels from hell. All town hall clerks and minor officials are armed with an extensive battery of Victorian stamps and a rulebook as obtuse as it is thick, with which they do their utmost to make the life of the ordinary citizen a living nightmare. For a country that has three official languages and multiple administrative departments, it is glaringly lacking in any cohesion. Switzerland is often accused of having more rules than cows, but Belgium is not far behind, and for its bureaucrats the devil really is in the detail. The mentality of officialdom in Belgium is not for the fainthearted or those of a nervous disposition. (Incidentally, more tranquilizers are prescribed in Belgium than in any other European country and it's not hard to figure out why.)

When approached or questioned, the perpetrators and protagonists of administration and bureaucracy in Belgium appear to suffer from some kind of cerebral infarction that causes them to lose all sense of reason and humanity. The victims are the population. This administrative malice isn't just confined to the indigenous population, either. Far from it. It extends and becomes even more malicious when dealing with foreign nationals, as I discovered to my chagrin.

Around nine months after I'd started, I struck gold in my search to discover more about Augusta and Jack. I received a phone call out of the blue from a gentleman claiming to be Jack Prior's son, Jeff. Mike had located him during his research, and made the initial contact. Jeff and I made plans to meet up in New York during an upcoming trip I would be taking for a book-signing tour, with Mike.

Some weeks later, when Mike and I were at Siena College in Albany on our tour, I noticed a bearded man enter the auditorium and sit down way at the back. When we'd finished our lecture and Q&A session, he walked up to the front and introduced himself as Jeff Prior. He told me that his father had been a meticulous diarist and letter writer and that he had all of these documents in his possession. He would be happy to pass them on to me for my perusal if I wished.

I very much wished to have a look at them, and about a month after my return to Europe a huge heavy box arrived via FedEx. Without wasting a moment I went to my man cave with a box cutter and tore into it. This was it! Precisely what I needed to fill in the blanks. It was *all* here.

I gazed transfixed at Augusta's letters to Jack, his diaries, personal correspondence—everything.

Among Jack's photographs was one of him and Augusta standing together beside the American memorial in Bastogne. On the back is written, "50th Anniversary, Bastogne, 1994." So she was still alive in 1994. But was she still alive now? I had no idea, but I was determined to find out.

Late one night, while I was delving through the box of goodies from Jeff Prior, I noticed a handwritten letter. The last paragraph read, *I will never forget Bastogne, I will never forget you, and I will never reveal our little secret.* The letter was signed, *With a fond embrace, Augusta Chiwy.*

Were they in love? I asked myself. No, that wouldn't have been possible back then. When I read more letters, however, it became clear that a very strong bond had existed between these two people. Later on I would discover the foundation for this bond, but at the time I just wanted to find out if she was still alive.

There were times when I really began to lose hope of ever finding out what had become of this courageous woman whom history had disregarded and forgotten. During those times my wife would go with me to the town halls and let them know her opinion on the matter of noncooperation. She was incredibly supportive and encouraging throughout, and equally astonished by the misanthropic attitudes of town hall employees. Although I'd always start each day with the thought, "Somebody here knows something," the day would usually end with, "What the hell is wrong with these people?" My wife would encourage me with three little words: "Don't give up."

— ⁓ —

"Hello—are you Mr. King?" said a voice with a Flemish accent.

It was early, and I was still wandering bleary-eyed around the kitchen, trying to make a cup of tea. I dropped the teabag when the person said, "I have some news about Augusta Chiwy."

"Yes, please. I'm Mr. King. Tell me."

"Stop looking for her. She's dead." Then the nameless, faceless person hung up.

I was beginning to lose focus. I hadn't been diagnosed as obsessive-compulsive, but there was definitely another agenda here. I had become obsessed with wanting to know more about this Congolese/Belgian nurse. I dismissed the person that called as a crank. Maybe it was true; maybe she was dead. If she were still alive then she would be in her late eighties. Then there was the other possibility: If she were still alive, maybe she was no longer compos mentis.

These thoughts and a thousand others pervaded my every waking moment and even infiltrated my dreams. I needed a holiday but that was definitely not possible due to the amount of time and money I'd been pouring into this research. Apart from my wife, no one was offering any support or encouragement, and even hers was showing signs of strain.

I knew something important—that Augusta Chiwy was a genuine heroine, a war hero, and I felt that surely the Belgians would want to know more about her; after all, they didn't have that many war heroes to choose from. In fact, a significant number hadn't even signed up for the Allies.

The days began to fuse into one another. Another day, another town hall, another dead end. I wasn't getting any closer to finding out where she was, or if she was still alive. I couldn't quit while I was ahead because I wasn't ahead. I was getting nowhere. Maybe it was time to cut my losses and give up.

I wasn't thinking straight. If Augusta were still alive she would probably be located in the French-speaking part of Belgium, but I decided to try one last part of Flanders before hitting the south. She'd qualified to become a nurse in Louvain, which was known as Leuven to the Dutch speakers, and was located in the predominantly Dutch-speaking part of Belgium. Dutch and Flemish are more or less the same language, with a few grammatical and phonetic differences, so it was possible that she may have learned to speak Dutch. I'd checked all the town halls in and around Louvain, so now I decided to drive down to the heart of Flanders, to the town of Ypres.

My first impression was that the people there could speak relatively good English and they appeared friendly—until I got to the town hall.

There it was the same old story, with one added complication: Nobody used any consonants in their vernacular. What on earth were they speaking? It didn't sound like any Dutch that I'd heard before, and by that time I had accrued a relatively good knowledge of the language. I even thought I heard a few Bantu-style clicks and pops in their delivery. The town hall officials were completely unhelpful, and they may have even been insulting; I don't know since I couldn't understand a word.

I returned home deflated once again, and went to my man cave to see if there were any e-mails. There was a very interesting message from Rony Lemoine. He said that he'd had a visit from someone who claimed that Augusta was still alive. He'd included the e-mail address and telephone number, so I immediately called.

"Hello. I got your number from Adjutant Lemoine. He mentioned that you know something about Augusta Chiwy," I said. I actually almost shouted, I was so eager to hear his response.

"Yes, I know about her. She is still alive. My name is Pol, and I work for the Belgian army." The voice was the usual lackluster Flemish monotone.

"Great! So where is she?"

He hesitated before saying, "I don't know. A friend of mine said that he'd seen her. Very sorry that I cannot help you more. Bye-bye."

I decided to call Rony and tell him about the "contact." Rony was upbeat as always when he told me that Pol's friend had been with him when they had visited the barracks, and that they had both signed the visitors' book.

"Maybe he is the one who knows where Augusta is?" he said, before promising to send me the details of this other person. Five minutes after I'd put the phone down the e-mail arrived with the name and address copied straight from the visitors' book. A quick search on the Net and I had the phone number written down.

"Wait, I'll get my husband Carl for you," said the woman who answered the phone.

Seconds later a light male voice spoke. "Hello, what can I do for you?"

I told him that I'd spoken to Pol and that he'd mentioned a certain friend of his. Was he that friend? He was.

"I'm trying to find out some information about a woman called Augusta Chiwy."

He acknowledged that he knew her, but added, "She never talks about the war."

"Where is she?"

He went on to tell me that he'd met her and her son in 1994 at the fiftieth anniversary of the Battle of the Bulge. Her son was a professor at the University of Louvain la Neuve. This was the best lead I'd had so far. Carl promised to call me a few days later with some additional information.

When he did, it wasn't the information I wanted.

The phone rang at an ungodly hour that morning. I rolled over lethargically and picked up the receiver while emitting a jaw-dislocating yawn.

"Yeah, who is it?" I groaned.

"It's Carl. We spoke the other day about Mrs. Chiwy."

I sat up in bed and pulled the receiver close to my ear.

"Yes, we did. Do you know anything about where she is?" I asked.

"No, I don't know where she is, but I think you should stop looking. We have enough dirty niggers in Belgium."

"No chance," I said. I literally threw the phone to the other side of the bedroom and woke up my wife in the process. This only served to intensify my desire to discover Augusta's whereabouts, because I knew that somebody somewhere knew where she was.

I was going to find her.

My obsessive search was starting to consume all my waking hours. Why were people so discouraging and uncooperative? Surely they would be proud to know that there was a genuine heroine here? I walked out to my car that morning clutching a liter bottle of water and a lunchbox. Suddenly my legs felt like lead and my vision began to blur before I passed out.

The next thing I knew I was lying in a hospital bed and being told by a doctor that I was a diabetic. I promised to lay off the booze if they would let me out. It took a few days, but armed with an insulin pen and a lot of instructions, I walked out of the place and continued my search.

It was late October 2008, and I remember feeling good that morning, almost bouncing over to my battered Ford Galaxy with a pronounced spring in my step.

My wife shouted to me before I got in the car: There was a letter for me, from the archives in Arlon. One of the lovely ladies who worked there had found some information for me that she thought I would appreciate.

I most certainly did. The letter said that Augusta Chiwy had married a Belgian soldier called Jacques Cornet in 1950, and that Augusta's father Henri Chiwy had died in 1948.

Now I had another name to find: Jacques Cornet. Her husband had been a soldier; surely he would be easier to find. At least I'd be back in my comfort zone. I immediately drove down to the Belgian Ministry of Defense and was turned away at the door.

"Please write us a letter and we will get back to you," said a uniformed receptionist rather haughtily. That wasn't particularly reassuring, as I'd come to know firsthand that Belgian administration was a nightmare. The reply could take weeks, months. That wasn't good enough. I attempted to appeal to the man's better nature only to discover that he didn't have one. I considered pleading with him but decided to maintain some semblance of dignity. In my desperation I stopped a passing officer and dropped the dignity thing by begging for some assistance. The officer gently patted me on the shoulder and moved the receptionist aside while he entered some details into the computer.

"I've got him here," he said after a couple of minutes. "Jacques Cornet, Belgian Army, first sergeant, discharged April 1949. Elsenborn Barracks. Hometown Brussels. Does that help, sir?"

I thanked the officer warmly and left feeling that I was finally narrowing down the search.

Everybody knows that Brussels is the capital city of Belgium, but it's also a province comprised of nineteen separate municipalities, including the municipality of the City of Brussels, where the administrative staff had absolutely no time at all for potential time-wasters like me. They told me so in that obnoxious manner that I had become accustomed to. The center is predominantly francophone, but most of the surrounding areas are Dutch-speaking. That had been the case for over two hundred years, since Napoleon had first entered the city with his Grand Armée in 1803. From that moment on the Dutch speakers had dispersed to the suburbs and the francophones had ruled the city. My plan was to visit each town hall separately, one every day, until I'd found what I was looking for.

I was becoming immune to the ignorance and unfriendliness of town hall admins. I walked automaton-like to the reception desk of one particular town hall in a run-down Brussels suburb and delivered my well-rehearsed speech.

"Wait a moment. I'll just have a look in our register," said a bespectacled, round-faced woman whose magnified eyes appeared to dominate at least half of her visage.

"Yes, please have a look, would you; that's very kind of you," I said, raising my hands to the counter of her kiosk in anticipation. I didn't notice at first that my fingers were drumming a march on the counter but the volume increased as I waited and waited.

"Yes, here we are. Mrs. Augusta Chiwy and Jacques Cornet, Avenue Notre Dame du Lourdes."

"What! You've found her?"

"No, mister, you have," she replied, giggling.

I drove as fast as I could (without accumulating another speeding ticket for my collection) to the address that the nice woman had given me at the town hall. After parking the car badly, I jumped out and ran to the apartment building.

There on the left-hand side of the main entrance was a list of names and doorbells. I scanned down until I reached Chiwy–Cornet. I pressed that bell so hard I think I broke it. No one answered. I pressed again and again. Still no response. I heaved a deep sigh and sat down on the curbside to smoke a cigarette.

Suddenly a voice came from above me. "*Bonjour, monsieur—allô!*"

I looked up, almost expecting to be the recipient of a bucket of water on the head.

"Hello there, *madame.*"

"You speak English. Can I help you?" said the lady, hanging half of her torso over a fourth-story balcony.

This was the first time in my search, nearly a full year by this point, that anyone had said that to me. I could feel my eyes welling up.

"Yes, you can help me. Where is Mrs. Chiwy?"

"Ah, yes, poor Mrs. Chiwy."

I expected to get some bad news and braced myself for it.

"She had a bad fall." *Here it comes*, I thought. "But she's all right. You can find her at the care home not far from here. Wait, I will come down and give you the address."

My heart was in my mouth. Could it be true? Could it really be true?

I drove to the care home like a maniac. My haste definitely caused two bikers to dismount and I think that I may have run over something hairy. Then there it was. The care home looked like a relatively new building. I walked up to the entrance and took a deep breath before entering. The receptionist was a pretty young girl in her late teens or early twenties. She was filing her nails when I approached. I was pleased that she was young because this meant that she'd probably speak some English.

"Excuse me, *mademoiselle*, but do you have a woman called Augusta Chiwy living here?"

"Now let me see." She typed the name into her computer and smiled. "Yes. She's on the second floor. Would you like to visit her?" she asked. I just nodded dumbly as I tried to absorb the information and the directions. All I could think was "She's here—she's really here."

I've never trusted elevators, so I searched frantically for the fire-escape stairway and walked up to the second floor. To help one get around easier all the wings of the home were named after flowers: Dahlia, Begonia, Freesia, and Rose. This particular one didn't smell of flowers, and I suspect the others probably didn't either.

I hesitantly approached a nurse in the corridor and politely asked, "Excuse me, *madame*, could you tell me where I can find Augusta Chiwy, please?"

"Ah, you're here to see our Augusta, are you?"

"I am, indeed."

She pointed to a long corridor and said, "She's down there."

I carefully maneuvered my way past empty wheelchairs, a portable scale, and a chairlift. In my hurry to get there I'd forgotten the room number, so I tried every door. When I got to the one at the end I knocked and waited. A tiny voice said "Hello" as I stood there, wishing that I'd brought something with me like flowers or grapes, or something appropriate. I was really nervous, so it was with some trepidation that I prepared to enter the room.

I walked in and there, lying on her bed, fully dressed in a blue cardigan and brown slacks, was an old lady with a very high forehead and a receding hairline. My first impression was, *My God, she's tiny.* Her diminutive, fragile frame couldn't have been much more than five feet, but there she was, the legend of Bastogne, in person—and contrary to what I'd heard, very much alive.

"*Oui, monsieur; je peux vous aider?*" she asked, slightly inclining her small head toward me.

"Yes, you can help me. Are you Augusta Chiwy?" I asked hesitantly. She smiled a huge beaming smile that appeared to illuminate her face. She asked if I was Jack Prior (with "Prior" pronounced as *PREE-or*).

"No, I'm not Jack Prior," I said, "but I know who he is. I've read his diaries, and he talks a lot about you. You are Augusta Chiwy."

She stared at me for a while. Finally, after what seemed like an age, she looked toward the window. The distant, wistful look in her eyes seemed to indicate that her mind had moved into another place.

"Ah, Jack," she said in English. "I miss him very much, you know. I miss him so much."

With that her eyelids closed. I waited, hoping she'd open her eyes again and keep talking. Several minutes went by, but when she took a deep breath I realized the visit was probably over. With that I backed up slowly to the door.

Once in the hallway, I navigated toward the stairs. I felt like I was floating on a cushion of air as I made my way to the exit. As soon as I got outside I fist-punched the air and yelled an almighty, "Yes!"

I'd really found her! I'd found Augusta Chiwy.

I began visiting the geriatric care home quite frequently. It became a routine. In those first three months or so, Augusta would say very little, or wouldn't speak to me at all. She'd smile at me benignly but refuse to say anything. I'd sit patiently beside her bed, turn on my handheld recorder, and ask a question or two. Initially it was fruitless. I had to be patient, very patient. Some days she would barely acknowledge my presence, but whatever the reception I always knew that I was in the presence of a living legend.

After a while we became good friends and I gained her trust. Whenever she saw me approaching she would put her arms in the air and shout at the top of her shrill voice, "Martin, *mon ami!*" She kept my phone number beside her bed next to a telephone with large numbers, and photographs of her immediate family on each speed-dial digit (although she never did call me).

I soon discovered that Augusta did not like to talk about the war. She never said as much, but there were times when one could see it in her eyes. She would not be coerced. She'd sing you an old song, talk about her recent maladies in great detail, comment on the social divide between the north and the south of Belgium, or complain about how bland the food was there in the home. She even spoke about her relationship to the Egyptian queen, Nefertiti. She was in many ways just like any other resident, but she wasn't just another resident; Augusta was much more than that.

Every so often when she was happily chatting away she would interrupt her own speech flow and gaze silently, contemplatively, toward the window of her small room that looked out onto a busy street. That was the time to listen, and listen well. This was her cue that she was ready to talk. There was no self-pity or displays of extreme emotion in the oratory, just hard-line, honest observations from someone who was there, someone who survived Bastogne.

To the privileged observer, her inner turmoil was more than apparent when she relayed these stories. Questions were superfluous because she would say what she had to say and then conclude, "It was all so very long ago. Let's leave the past where it belongs, my friend." Then she'd return to her inner sanctuary. This was the sign that it was time to go and leave her there in her twilight world, fluctuating between memories and present events.

Augusta always denied ever having known anything about either General Patton or General McAuliffe. She must have heard the names repeatedly while she was in Bastogne, but they were never in her immediate vicinity, apart from when she worked at the Heintz Barracks. I've met literally hundreds of World War II veterans over the years, and it's often the case that they can't tell you what they had for lunch, but they retain a remarkable capacity to recall some things from the distant past in minute, meticulous detail.

Augusta could be very vague when it came to her personal knowledge of Renée Lemaire, and she often dismissed questions by saying, "She was very popular with the soldiers." When I first asked her about Renée, she denied ever having known her, and later inquiries about Renée's character seldom yielded information. She had no recollection of the "parachute silk for a wedding dress" story that Jack Prior wrote about. All Augusta would say was that Renée was very kind and friendly.

In a later interview she remarked that Renée was never a friend of hers and never treated her like a colleague. Although they would have worked in relatively close proximity to each other for those days, it's possible that Renée was too preoccupied with comforting the soldiers to acknowledge Augusta.

Augusta would often begin or conclude my visits with the same question. She would always ask, "Do you know Jack?" I would always reply "Yes, and he knows you." Then she would inevitably augment the conversation with, "He was in love me with me, you know."

When I informed her of the recognition and awards I was attempting to get for her, she would clasp her hands to her mouth and her eyes would shine with almost childlike excitement. While we talked she would be seated on her bed, legs dangling, and then with one rather energetic heave-ho she would say, "Look—I can still do this," and she would throw herself from being seated to lying down on her bunk with one swift move.

Once I'd gotten to know her she would reel off events, dates, and times with alarming clarity, like a machine; other times she would simply revert to her mutism. As the months passed this flawed military historian began to piece together a remarkable story of a flawed, unwilling heroine who displayed extreme courage and tenacity in the face of great adversity.

She had returned to her Congolese roots in the 1970s to visit her brother Charles for one last time, and never went back again. Charles had returned to the Congo in the 1950s and died sometime in the early 1980s. His family was murdered during the Rwandan genocide, but Augusta never talked about it, except on one occasion when she was wearing a silk scarf that one of her nieces had given her.

Relating her experiences proved to be quite cathartic in the long run. She became much more lighthearted and jolly, although there were still times when she would recede into herself and go completely mute. The mutism could last for hours, days, even weeks, and during that time it was pointless to ask her anything.

Sometimes quite unexpectedly she would put her hands together and pray to God. When this occurred she prayed for her mother, her father, her children and grandchildren, Jack Prior, Renée Lemaire, and all the young men who had died in her arms. At the very end she would open one eye, look at me, and then pray for the author of this volume. When she did this, one was not witnessing the incoherent rantings of an unstable mind. No, no; far from it. The prayers were purposeful, genuine, and precise.

From what I had read about Jack, I'd deduced that he was a man of great integrity and intelligence. He was someone whose presence would have given one great reassurance in the heat of battle. He was a man's man who didn't suffer fools gladly. His character encompassed all the attributes of a real war hero, albeit a reluctant one. When I read personal accounts of his exploits during the battles at Noville and Bastogne, I was both moved and inspired by the exceptional humanity he maintained throughout.

Jack and Augusta were dedicated professionals who applied themselves heart and soul to the job they had to do. They wouldn't have had much time for anything else. That said, it became obvious during my research that they had both nurtured deep and profound regard, even love, for each other. I still find it nothing short of astonishing that so much unadulterated affection and respect between two very different but equally remarkable individuals could flourish in the midst of something as evil and debased as warfare. Throughout the ensuing decades after the war they exchanged many affectionate letters and gifts. From 1958 until his passing in 2007, Jack sent Augusta a box of chocolates every Christmas. Augusta often reciprocated by sending him Belgian pralines.

The most absorbing aspect of this very human story for me was the relationship between Jack and Augusta, which remained unequivocally pure and innocent. As the story unfolded in their personal letters and diaries, I often felt like an uninvited intruder. There's something inherently uncomfortable about reading someone's personal papers even when that person is deceased. At the same time it aroused an insatiable thirst in me to discover more. The more I read, the more compelling the story became. I had spent more than eighteen months visiting various town halls in the south of Belgium, wearing out lots of shoe leather and running up an extortionate phone bill attempting to get a lead on Augusta's whereabouts.

Over the years I have interviewed many British, American, and German veterans of World War II. They all have imparted memories, both good and bad, about their experiences. All were modest, humble men and women whom I've admired and supported for decades, but I have never encountered a story as emotive and powerful as that of Congolese/Belgian nurse Augusta Chiwy. According to some history books, she was killed along with nurse Renée Lemaire during the fateful Luftwaffe bombardment that occurred in Bastogne on Christmas Eve. Thankfully, I learned the truth.

When I eventually established that she was alive, I began a campaign to get her the official recognition she so richly deserved. Both national TV stations here, north and south, ignored my requests completely, and not one single newspaper or weekly magazine would run the story about this Belgian/Congolese nurse who had saved so many American lives in World War II. According to them it simply wasn't news, and at her age, she wouldn't last much longer anyway, so what was the point?

I remember being completely exasperated by the Belgian media's reluctance as a whole to acknowledge a war hero, and a Belgian one at that. When I contacted the US Army's 10th Armored Division veterans association, they designed a special certificate for Augusta. Some weeks later I personally delivered this certificate to her, signed by every surviving 10th Armored Division veteran of the Battle of the Bulge. They thanked her for all the excellent work that she had done for them and made her an honorary life member of their organization.

Some good friends in the United States also rallied to the call and published her story on various websites. Over a period of about three years the story gathered momentum, until early in 2011 when I sent a registered letter to the reigning King of Belgium, Albert II. God bless the man, he responded almost immediately, writing to tell me that he fully supported my campaign. You can say what you want about royalty, but when they show their colors so effusively, I for one have no complaints.

In a response to His Majesty's official letter supporting my campaign for Augusta in April 2011, I submitted a comprehensive dossier to him, detailing her exploits and achievements during World War II. Mike, my researcher in the United States, had been down to the archives in Washington, DC, to cross-reference a few details, and consequently confirmed the information we needed. The King wholeheartedly approved and supported the submission, and on June 24, 2011, Augusta Chiwy was made a Knight in the Order of the Crown at the Ministry of Defense in Brussels. I attended the ceremony with my wife and son. It was a proud day indeed. This was the equivalent of a knighthood here in mainland Europe, and we were reliably informed that Augusta Chiwy is the first black person to ever receive this accolade here.

About a month later I got a call from someone representing the 101st Airborne, informing me that Augusta Chiwy would receive their Civilian Humanitarian Award. Result! On December 15, 2011, in the presence of the US ambassador to Belgium and various high-ranking US Army officials, I wheeled Augusta into the Royal Military Museum in Brussels.

I recall the look of incredulity that registered on Augusta's face when press corps cameras started flashing away. We smiled at each other and I whispered in her ear, "We did it, Augusta."

She looked ponderingly at me and said, "They took their time, didn't they?" and laughed.

A few days before the award ceremony I'd passed the story onto the Associated Press representative in Brussels, and as a result every major American news organization sent film crews and reporters to Brussels to get the inside story. The very next day she made headlines all over the world. Augusta's smiling face was on so many front pages and television screens that we lost count. Gen. David Petraeus, former commander of US and ISAF forces in Afghanistan, and now a retired military officer and public official, personally wrote to Augusta to thank

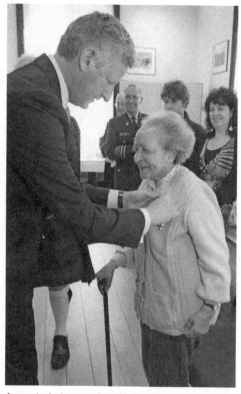

Augusta being made a Knight in the Order of the Crown. CREDIT: AUTHOR'S PERSONAL ARCHIVE

her for all her work. Of course the Belgian media, who had initially ignored the story, were now all over us like a rash. Augusta was pleasantly bemused by all the attention, and took it all in her stride.

I enjoyed every minute. This was what I'd been working for. Finally the world was hearing about this remarkable woman and her contribution to the war effort. Shortly after that I began writing about her.

When I found Augusta, I began finding myself. She gave me a sense of purpose in my life that I'd never really felt before, and I'm grateful to her for that. Thanks to her I began to understand the old adage that it is better to give than to receive, because in giving there is fulfillment and vindication of what it really means to be human.

Augusta with author and fellow historian Mike Collins. COURTESY OF MIKE COLLINS

My local municipality made me an honorary citizen, and I was given the title of "Cultural Ambassador." It wasn't all roses, though. Not one Belgian TV station agreed to screen the documentary *Searching for Augusta*. It is available on Netflix throughout the world except in Belgium. VRT, the Belgian Dutch speaking channel, said that the documentary was, and I quote, "Too bombastic." Furthermore, when I wrote to complain and explained that it was being screened from coast to coast in the United States on PBS, one of the VRT news producers said, "PBS is not important in America." I refused to argue with this ill-informed, base opinion.

So now Augusta is a Knight of the Realm; an Honorary Member of the 327th Regiment, 101st Airborne Division; a recipient of the US Humanitarian Civilian Award; an Honorary Citizen of Bastogne—the list goes on. I firmly believe that the story of Augusta Chiwy has even greater relevance today.

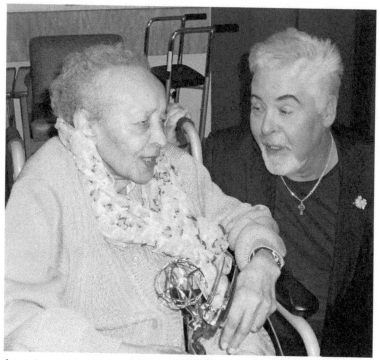

Augusta receiving her Emmy Award and having a good sing song with the author. CREDIT: AUTHOR'S PERSONAL ARCHIVE

In August of 2015 the documentary about Augusta's wartime experiences and my quest to find and campaign for her, titled *Searching for Augusta: The Forgotten Angel of Bastogne*, was recognized by the Academy of Television Arts and Sciences. It received the Emmy Award for Best Historical Documentary. When my Emmy arrived by FedEx I immediately took it down to the care home and gave it to Augusta.

"This isn't mine, Augusta. It's yours," I said, and handed it over. She eyed the object with great interest and then insisted on having me wheel her around the care home while she displayed it to all the other residents. She was very proud of the award, and knew precisely what it was.

Twenty-four hours later, she died.

Augusta Marie Chiwy died on August 23, 2015, and was buried with full military honors in Bastogne, not far from the grave of Renée

Ambassador Denise Campbell Bauer, Augusta Chiwy and Martin King at the US Embassy reception and screening of the documentary *Searching for Augusta*. Augusta received a commemoration flag of the United States of America from the wonderful ambassador. My wife, Freya, also attended this auspicious ceremony. CREDIT: AUTHOR'S PERSONAL ARCHIVE

Lemaire. Her coffin was carried by three American soldiers on one side and three Belgian soldiers on the other. I read the eulogy at the ceremony. The world's media zeroed in on the story, and it received global attention.

As society becomes more fractious and divisive, we need to be reminded of Augusta's deeds so we can reassert the fact that caring has no boundaries; even in the direst of circumstances love can prevail, irrespective of conflict, color, and national identity. Nurse Augusta Chiwy was my friend, and the most modest, unassuming heroine I ever met.

Epilogue

Jack returned to Bastogne for one final visit in 1994. He would see Augusta Chiwy for the last time. There's something poignant and deeply moving about an old soldier returning to the battlefields that he experienced during the war. What inspires them to want to go back? Is it a longing to recall those tumultuous days of uncertainty and devastation, or is it something stronger? Some veterans say that they return to lay the ghosts to rest, but I think it's something more than that. A personal, subdued celebration of endurance and survival and the return to those fields of fire is the ultimate pilgrimage that a veteran can make. It's as if they want to justify their lives by acknowledging their sacrifice, and that of their comrades in arms.

The 10th Armored Division's CCB incurred 500 casualties during the siege of Bastogne. That's almost a fifth of CCB who entered Bastogne on December 18, 1944. Additional casualties were attributed to the other fragmented units that found themselves in Bastogne. It is estimated that the casualties of the 101st Airborne Division totaled 189 officers and men killed, 1,040 wounded, 407 sick and injured, and 412 reported MIA.

A temporary cemetery was established at Foy in 1945 that contained 2,701 corpses of American soldiers killed during the Battle of the Bulge. Soon after the war in 1948 the bodies there were exhumed, and some were placed in the US cemetery at Hamm. The rest were transported to Antwerp and repatriated in accordance with the wishes of the next of kin. During the exhumation specialists examined some 267 unknown remains and positively identified all but 101 of them.

Belgium is no stranger to conflict, having experienced it before. After World War II Belgians were hoping that this would be the last time they would have to start over from scratch. Even though construction techniques had modernized and become more effective, it was going to take a long time to rebuild Bastogne. The people of the Ardennes are tough and resilient; they've had to be, because the area has been fought over for literally thousands of years. They have weathered many a storm and recovered, as they would recover from this latest episode in their history.

Belgium is only a small country, but its strategic location has often been acknowledged by commanders from Julius Caesar to Napoleon. It's the only country in Europe that has four European borders. To be more specific, if you draw a line from Scotland to Greece and then another from Denmark to Portugal, you will find Belgium right in the very center. Napoleon once said, "Brussels is the first rung on the ladder to taking Europe." Adolf Hitler had tried to enact the most antiquated military thinking with his "divide et impera," Caesarian strategy, and it had failed.

Within a few months Hitler would take his own life and the United States would begin the Marshall Plan, officially known as the European Recovery Program (ERP). All over Europe refugees were returning to or leaving their homes. All the roads were gridlocked with every kind of transport imaginable, from trucks to hand-drawn carts, cars, and bicycles. To the itinerant observer it would have appeared as if the whole of humanity was in transit.

During the siege itself, the medical units and attached facilities had to contend with a few major problems. First, there was the problem of limited supplies; and second, the inability to provide emergency surgery for the badly wounded. The afflicted soldiers and civilians faced the same deprivations throughout the siege. By the third day, supplies of penicillin, plasma, morphine, dressings, litters, and blankets were running dangerously low. To compensate for the lack of warm bedding the medics organized foraging parties that scoured ruined dwellings for blankets and duvets.

The air resupply missions that began on December 23, 1944, eased most of the medical supply issues. In little more than four hours, nearly 250 planes had reached Bastogne. Each carried 1,200 pounds of material, but not everything reached the intended drop zones, nor did everything fall where Americans could recover it. By the end of the day, however, fresh food and medical supplies were arriving at the aid station, allowing Jack's team to administer anesthetics and other medications for the first time in days. Penicillin and other medicines, plasma, Vaseline gauze, anesthetics, morphine, distilled water, syringes, sterilizers, litters, and blankets arrived in the parachuted bundles. Even the parachute cloth was used as additional warm coverings for patients. Whole blood was also among the air-delivered supplies, but the bottles broke on landing or were destroyed when a German shell blew up the room where they were stored.

As the days passed and casualties increased, it became apparent to the division surgeons that those awaiting surgery would die unless operations could be arranged. The field army, corps, and division medical services displayed a high degree of ingenuity and adaptability during the defense and eventual relief of Bastogne. After the initial disaster of the loss of an entire auxiliary surgical team, 11 officers and 119 men of the 326 Medical Company at Barrière Hinck, combat medics, established an alternative second-echelon facility inside the perimeter and used what human and materiel resources were on hand. Remarkably enough, they kept most of the casualties alive until the evacuation that began on December 27, 1944.

When Team Desobry entered Noville they were equipped with fifteen tanks. As they returned to Bastogne, only four of these tanks were still operative, and one of them looked like it had escaped from a junkyard. Furthermore, the 1st Battalion of the 506th Parachute Infantry was a full-strength unit when it went to assist Team Desobry; throughout the course of the fighting at Noville, it lost 13 officers and 199 enlisted men.

By their combined efforts they destroyed or immobilized somewhere between twenty and thirty known enemy tanks of all types, including three Mark Vs. There's every possibility that they probably damaged or destroyed many more. Headquarters of the 506th estimated that the assaults of the German infantry had cost the enemy the equivalent of half a regiment. The men who fought in Noville had held their ground for a decisive forty-eight hours—sufficient time in which to organize the defense of Bastogne.

The stand at Noville made by Team Desobry was one of the most significant and vicious encounters of the whole battle. Capt. Irving Lee Naftulin, who, up until the retreat from Noville, had displayed neither aptitude nor enthusiasm for being in a war zone, earned himself a Silver Star for his courageous rescue of wounded men from a burning half-track.

When Jack applied for two Bronze Stars to honor his soldiers who fought in Noville, he was informed by one of his superiors that no more Bronze Stars would be given, because they had all been allocated to the 101st Airborne. Jack was so annoyed that he crossed out "Bronze" and wrote "Silver" on the application. Both soldiers received their Silver Star medals.

The Siege of Bastogne was a battle that deeply affected both civilians and military alike. It was unlike any other battle before, but more importantly, it forged bonds of lasting friendship that have survived for generations. There are many reasons for this, but the main one is the problem-shared-is-a-problem-halved aspect. This shared adversity and the unity that developed because of the incredible hardship and deprivations they endured together remains the most poignant aspect of this battle, even to this day.

Looking at the photographs of Jack and Augusta taken during their brief reunion in 1994, one can clearly see the deep affection between these two remarkable people. In one particular photograph Jack has his arm around Augusta. She maintained till the day she died that he loved her, and even though Jack wasn't known for wearing his heart on his sleeve, for all intents and purposes, this was probably true.

EXCERPTS FROM INTERVIEWS, DIARIES, LETTERS, AND REPORTS

ARTICLES IN *DETROIT FREE PRESS*, DECEMBER 30, 1945

Marjory Avery was a *Detroit Free Press* war correspondent in Bastogne, known to her friends as "Dot." Before working for the *Free Press* she'd been at the *New York Herald Tribune*. She was one of the few women correspondents who witnessed the linkup between US and Russian soldiers at the Elbe River in 1945. After the war she went on to teach journalism at the University of Pittsburgh.

BASTOGNE DESOLATE AFTER LIBERATION

SURVIVORS TELL OF BLOOD AND FIRE OF HOSPITAL BOMBED CHRISTMAS EVE

by Marjorie Avery, *Detroit Free Press* War Correspondent

BASTOGNE—With three other reporters, I reached Bastogne the day after the relief column had forced its way into the city to make contact with American forces which had been cut off for a week. How we got here and what we saw on the way a number of times when we detoured to avoid German pockets doesn't enter into this story. The town is still burning from German bombing. There are the usual scenes of wreckage and desolation. Civilians are digging themselves out, picking up bits of junk and trying to salvage their homes. Bulldozers crashing along the streets are trying to clear passageways. There is constant jolting from passing heavy artillery, tanks, and trucks. In a pile of rubble which had been an improvised hospital before bombs hit it on Christmas Eve, German prisoners and medical corpsmen are searching for bodies.

American troops stand or stroll along the street, grinning and asking the outsiders for news about the war.

"The Germans said Luxembourg had fallen," a Yank said, "but we didn't believe it."

I was struck by remarks made by a soldier who looked like a character from a Maudlin cartoon—unshaven, grimy, and hollow-eyed.

"How do you like the town?" he asked me.

"It's horrible," I said.

He looked around him for a minute.

"It was real pretty before we dug in."

"Come in, let us tell you about our Christmas."

Some soldiers from an armored unit called, "Ever heard of C rations?"

I went into their home where they had a fire and were boiling water. I was very grateful for a few sips of coffee. It was bitterly cold and white mist penetrated right through the clothing to the bone.

"Aw, we weren't so bad off," said one soldier. "We got pretty low, but then planes came and dropped us ammunition and food. We could have held out indefinitely."

Later we talked with Capt. Jack Prior of St. Albans, Vermont, a medical officer attached to a unit who was directing a search for the bodies of soldiers and Belgian nurses who were killed when the hospital was hit.

Captain Prior told the epic story of the retreat of his unit from Noxville [sic] to Bastogne. The armored unit to which he was attached was trapped by German tanks and ringed with German artillery fire.

"We had only ten minutes to clear out," Prior said. "We had no litters, so we tore down doors and strapped the patients to them. There were no ambulances, so we tied the doors to anything we could find—jeeps and tanks.

"We had only got a short distance down the road when the column stopped. We were zeroed in by German artillery. There was fire also from small arms and bazookas.

"I didn't see how anyone could get out alive. We all jumped into ditches. We had to leave the wounded strapped to the vehicles. If we would have taken them off it would have been the end for them. Because we never could have got them strapped on again."

FREED BASTOGNE IS CITY OF DEATH AND DESOLATION

"I lay in a ditch wondering what would happen if we had casualties and I had to go to their aid. I prayed for courage, because we all felt that it would be sure death to go back to that road.

"Then just thirty yards away a tank was hit by a shell and burst into flames. I could hear the wounded screaming for help.

"Before I could go to them one of my litter bearers and the bravest man I have ever known got up and said, 'I'll go, Doc.' He is Pvt. Bernard F. Morrissey of Providence, Rhode Island, and we call him The Man with a Thousand Lives.

"Another litter bearer, Pvt. Ignacious Vaznon, from Chicago, volunteered to go with him and the two walked down the road of death to the burning tank. A jeep driver whose name I have never known helped them. He was the smallest of the three so they lowered him into the burning tank and he started pulling out men. We got out three and my litter bearers loaded them and brought them back to where we were. Every one of us was inspired by their bravery. We forgot fear and set up an aid station around that jeep, treating the wounded who were brought to us.

"All the time snipers were potting at us and burp guns, machine guns, and artillery were hitting the road. In all we were two and half hours in that place before the column would move. All the time we were under murderous fire.

"Finally word came that it was safe for the column to take a side road that would get us to Bastogne. We drove slowly along, the patients still in the jeep and tanks. Tanks and heavy artillery got

through, but the light jeep bogged in mud. Several artillerymen got down and pushed the jeep through the mud.

"We gave the wounded plasma all through the journey. We got to Bastogne where I thought there was a completely equipped hospital waiting. We didn't lose any lives."

Captain Prior didn't find a hospital waiting for the wounded. He found nothing, and he was almost out of medical supplies. He said if it hadn't been for Lt. Robert Talbot Carlisle (Kentucky), medical advance officer, they would have been in a bad way. Lieutenant Talbot went around Bastogne begging supplies. He charged into drugstores, went to doctors, and canvassed private homes. He gathered enough to fix up a couple of rooms where the wounded could be treated.

Then they learned that they were cut off and Bastogne was a besieged city.

"We weren't doing badly," Captain Prior said. "We had a few corpsmen, so we trained our litter bearers to be nurses. They did a grand job. They gave tetanus shots, injections, and sulfa drugs, gave plasma and changed dressings. They even set bones and irrigated wounds."

Germans came over every night and bombed the group. Artillery shells landed in the city. But the worst day of all was Christmas Eve when a group of six German planes, knowing the defenders had little ack-ack, came over early in the evening and dive-bombed. One bomb hit Captain Prior's hospital, collapsed one floor, and set the building afire.

"We rescued all we could," he said. "Men not too badly wounded got out themselves. Some threw away splints and walked out on broken and fractured legs. Lost five corpsmen and thirty wounded."

A soldier came and reported to the captain that more bodies had been found. "Bring them here," he said. He turned to me again. He said, "To me there is not much joy in our rescue."

In the defense and relief of Bastogne the field army, corps, and division medical services displayed a high degree of resourcefulness and adaptability. After the initial disaster of losing the 326th Medical Co. at Barrière Hinck, medics inside the perimeter assembled a new second-echelon facility in the midst of combat, using what human and materiel resources were available at the time. They managed to keep most of the casualties alive until evacuation. Medics outside the perimeter made every effort to send in needed supplies and to reestablish forward surgical support for the besieged troops, and they lost no time in evacuating the Bastogne hospitals after the relief.

It's difficult to determine exactly how many wounded died there due to a lack of early surgery or as the result of other deficiencies, but one thing is sure: The resilience and commitment to duty of both enlisted medical staff and volunteers alike can never be underestimated. The Siege of Bastogne brought out the best and the worst in people who experienced it firsthand. It showed the world that in the midst of all that violence and misery the human spirit still had the capacity to transcend all the adversity placed before it and shine through.

THE HOTTEST TEN DAYS

With the American forces in Bastogne, Dec. 30 (Delayed)

The boys of Maj. C. L. Hustead's unit of the 10th Armored Division are eating a dinner of hot C rations today after tins of cold meat and paste biscuits, and they are calling this their New Year's dinner.

This unit which still is fighting after ten days, in which "everything happened that can happen," is one of those that was relieved when reinforcements and supplies smashed through the German ring around this town. But the big fight of this particular unit began long before it found itself trapped here with the 101st Airborne Division.

Even on the defensive this unit took a terrific toll of German tanks, which today are lying smashed and burned a few miles outside Bastogne. The hottest ten days in the unit's history was related today by Major Hustead, who comes from Falls River, Nebraska, and Maj. James V. Duncan Jr. of Jefferson City, Missouri, his executive officer.

"We were just moving into position at Noville, six miles northeast of Bastogne, on the morning of December 19," said Major Hustead, "when the Germans hit us. At the time we had only the men of headquarters and one mortar platoon, and every man was shooting rifles as the German infantry moved in. We managed to hold until a few of our tanks got into position, but the German tanks moved up, too, and two of our tanks were knocked out, but we broke up the attack.

"An hour or two later the first elements of the 101st infantry arrived, and though short on ammunition, we nevertheless planned a joint attack. We jumped off at 2:30 and by a strange freak the Germans attacked at the same instant and we met them head-on. After an hour of furious battle both sides retired to regroup. Between tanks on each side of our position they hammered us from both sides. But we managed to beat them off and hold our position.

"At five o'clock the next morning they hit us again, this time with a column of ten tanks. However, our tank destroyers were ready for them on the brow of a hill and knocked out five, the rest retiring. The following morning we found ourselves surrounded but we were told another unit was counterattacking in the direction of Foy, between us and Bastogne, at 11:20, and we were given orders to withdraw to Foy. Thirty-four wounded were strapped to the doors and were tied to the tops of tanks, jeeps, and trucks. We left one man to blow up an ammunition dump across the street from our command post and ordered every vehicle burned as a smoke pot to cover our movement."

Major Hustead, with his infantrymen, joined the counterattack on Foy, captured the village, and took twenty prisoners. Major Duncan, meanwhile, was moving up with a column of vehicles, but didn't move far before trouble hit.

"We were barely outside our position, said Duncan, "when the lead vehicles were fired upon by tanks at the top of the hill. It was impossible to turn back, so we had to stand there and take it while we got word back to our tank destroyers. We knew the available tank destroyers couldn't clear the road, but only hold off the attack, so we had to find a new route. With thirty men I made a reconnaissance and found a route through a swamp and went back to lead the column through."

All this time the men in the column were taking the fire from German tanks, artillery, and bazookas. Capt. Jack T. Prior of St. Albans, Vermont, a medical officer, called the scene the most terrifying in his experience.

"The hardest part was that we were unable to get the wounded off the vehicles," [Prior] said.

"We had to lie in a ditch while the wounded on tanks and jeeps begged us to take them down, even if we had to leave them behind when the column started to move. Many others in the column were wounded, so we set up an aid station in the ditch and found places on the vehicles for them. Several were given plasma on the spot."

The route through the swamp led finally to Bastogne, where Major Hustead and other officers thought the worst was over. But they had been here only two days when they found Bastogne also was cut off, and they joined the 101st Airborne Division in the defense which had just ended.

Correspondence between Jack Prior and George E. Koskimaki

Notable military historian and author George E. Koskimaki corresponded with Jack Prior. This is an excerpt from a letter Koskimaki sent to Jack on July 26, 2006:

Considering fifty years had passed since I started writing the Bastogne book, it was amazing how stories from the 10th and the 101st blended together. I don't know if you were ever aware of our account, but if you do not have a copy I'd like to send you one of the rare copies still available (although Random House is coming out with a paperback next year). I was aware of the nurse Renée Lemaire and her Congolese partner from previous research, but after reading your description I wanted her memorialized. The producers of Band of Brothers consulted with me several times, and one suggestion that I made was that they fit in a scene featuring [Renée], and of course they "Hollywooded" the whole thing by having an E Company medic [Roe] have a crush on her, though he never even got to meet her. She was at your aid station and not at the dirt-floor facility.

We can only respect and honor their deeds because in our ignorance we cannot begin to imagine the horrors that nurse Augusta Chiwy, Dr. Jack Prior, and our other veterans witnessed and experienced during that unforgiving winter of 1944–1945. They survived when many others perished. Although researcher Mike Collins interviewed many of the veterans that appear in this volume, I never personally met Dr. Jack Prior, but having read his letters and diaries and having spoken to those who knew him, I am sure without a doubt that I would have liked him a lot. He was a truly remarkable human being, and according to all who knew him he was the gentlest of gentleman.

Interview with *Post Standard* Columnist Dick Case

When Case interviewed Jack Prior, the doctor said that he was in awe of the two Belgian nurses who risked death from a German firing squad, the penalty for suspected collaborators. That's why he saw to that memorial for Renée Lemaire, and why he nurtured his sixty-year long-distance friendship with Augusta. "We write and exchange Christmas cards and gifts [each year]," Jack said. "I got a package of candy from her this morning."

Edited Transcripts of Recordings and Interviews with Augusta Chiwy

What follows are excerpts from edited transcripts of recordings I made of my conversations with Augusta, along with other notes made during interviews, from 2009 through 2013.

Audio File No. 1 (recorded August 18, 2009)

I got an invitation from my father to spend Christmas with him and my Mama [Caroline] in Bastogne. I was happy to be going back there. Although I thought of Bastogne as my home, I hadn't lived there for a long while. Louvain had been my temporary home and the place where I had studied until I graduated in 1943. I worked there as nurse at the St. Elizabeth Hospital. I was a very good nurse.

Interviews with Augusta (2013)

My father's [sister-in-law] was Caroline. As soon as I arrived it was she who took care of me. Before leaving the Congo my father had confided everything to the governor of the Congo. The governor left with my father, and I stayed with Caroline. Caroline said to me, "If your Papa doesn't take you, I will take you."

——◦——

When I finished my nursing studies, the director of the school told me I could not return to Bastogne because there were too many Germans around. If the Germans found out I was a nurse they might oblige me to work for them. At Louvain they paid me to replace nurses that left on vacation around Brussels and other nearby places.

——◦——

Author's note: During my visits to the care home, Augusta often related the story of how she was once accosted by a Flemish racist whom she berated fiercely by insisting to him that she was definitely his superior because she was in fact a direct descendant of Queen Nefertiti. She probably based this on having seen an image of the notorious Egyptian queen; back in those days Augusta had a high, back-combed hairstyle that in silhouette probably resembled the notorious depiction of the queen.

Augusta can be a witty, sardonic, sarcastic, and ultimately entertaining individual, but there are ghosts in her attic and she does have demons. Whenever she spoke about Bastogne and her wartime experiences, she could become very melancholic and subdued to the point of being uncommunicative. She would talk when she wanted to, and on her terms. This gave me the impression that she was incredibly resolute and determined; there was never room for negotiation. I believe that these characteristics were probably the core essentials that helped her survive throughout the war and after.

───

My father took a bike and went to get potatoes to make me french fries. About a half-hour later he comes back. He had taken a bad fall so we had to find a doctor. Because there were Germans all around, a lot of people had left; doctors, lawyers, priests. There was only one doctor left on the other side of the square. He took X-rays and nothing was broken. He had a dislocated shoulder. So, the doctor and I made a makeshift sling to keep his shoulder in place.

───

I arrived home, taking a small street that went directly to my house. Papa asked me how I was doing. As soon as I could I went directly to the basement and stayed there the rest of the morning. I shook uncontrollably for a half-hour. Everybody says that I knew Renée Lemaire, but I didn't really know her. We said hello when we saw each other in the street but we were not friends. The first bomb fell at the place where there were forty Americans, and Renée Lemaire died; she was crushed. I was nearby with Jack Prior.

Audio File No. 2 (recorded August 27, 2009)
Do you know how difficult it was for me to get back to Bastogne that day? I used every form of transport possible to get home to my mother and father. The morning that I left the tram was standing-room-only. It took a whole day to go from Louvain to Bastogne.

Audio File No. 3 (recorded September 21, 2009)
I spent one night in Noville at the church and then I had to go back to Bastogne. The Germans started bombing Bastogne, and the only safe places in town were the cellars. The fog was so thick that you could cut it with a knife.

Audio File No. 4 (recorded September 28, 2009)
The situation in Bastogne was getting worse by the hour. I really thought that the Germans were going to walk up the main street any minute. The noise of the battle was getting closer and some bombs were even hitting the town.

Audio File No. 5 (recorded October 2, 2009)
The bombing just got worse, and everybody in the center of town was living in their cellars. Even I was living in a cellar. Dr. Prior came around to my house to ask if I could help him with their wounded. My father thought that somehow I would be safer with the US Army, so I said yes and volunteered, of course. I thought the whole debacle would be over faster if I was busy doing something useful.

Audio File No. 6 (recorded October 8, 2009
That was the day that I met Dr. Prior. I'll never forget his face, because when we first met he stared at me for a long time. He had a kind face, and you could tell that all the soldiers liked him very much. I was very nervous about working for the Americans because some of them didn't want a black nurse touching them. Those were strange times indeed, very strange and very hard. I had almost nothing to work with; neither did Renée. She didn't say much to me apart from giving orders, because we were both very busy. The smell inside the army hospital was terrible, and if I close my eyes I can still smell it. I didn't smell that great either because I hadn't had a bath for four days.

Audio File No. 7 (recorded October 20, 2009)
I think Jack said something about the "Nuts" thing, but I'm not sure. You could tell on the faces of the soldiers that things were getting worse, though. I saw the famous American general McAuliffe, but I'm not sure when that was. The town square in Bastogne is named after him, you know. The street named after my uncle, rue du Docteur Chiwy, is right next to it. It means something to me that the [former] "[Place du] Carré" square is called "McAuliffe Square" these days. Once, [McAuliffe] came there. Only soldiers were allowed to meet him, but I was able to approach him and I saw him. As for Patton, I've no memory of ever having seen him. When I had begun working at the house [aid station],

my own clothes became so soiled so quickly that I had to change into a military [uniform]. Now I looked like an American soldier.

Audio File No. 8 (recorded November 12, 2009)

I went out to Marvie with Dr. Prior to pick up some wounded soldiers. It was very dangerous and we were nearly captured. The snow came down very hard, I remember. I don't really remember seeing the big supply drop, probably because I was in the center of town and it happened outside somewhere. Someone told me later that Renée was very excited about getting a silk parachute to make a wedding dress with, but I don't remember that. We weren't friends at all, and she was very different in the way she talked to me and the way she talked to the Americans. Her English must have been a lot better than mine.

Audio File No. 9 (recorded December 5, 2009)

I remember Christmas Eve 1944, but I often wish I could forget it. It was a terrible day for all of us. The loudest explosion I had ever heard happened on that day. BOOM, it went, and knocked me off my feet. Dr. Prior was amazing. He helped me a lot, but some [people] couldn't be helped anymore. I was very lucky, I suppose.

Audio File No. 10 (recorded December 17, 2009)

Patton, Patton—who was that? I don't think that I ever saw the big general. I just wanted the war and all that to be over so that things could be like they were before. That was the problem. Things were never going to be the same again. Did Patton save Bastogne? Everybody said he did. I don't know.

Author's note: In 2011 Mike Collins and I visited Augusta at the care home where she was living at the time. She became particularly animated that afternoon when I told her that Mike was from America. She asked the inevitable "Do you know Jack Prior" question, and then when we were comfortably seated, she told us the most amazing story about her experience out east of the Mardasson Hill during the worst of the fighting. My French is only marginally better than Mike's, but we both got the gist of the story. She recounted in incredible detail what had occurred on the morning of December 22, 1944. We both listened attentively, never daring to interpolate or disrupt this remarkable flow of information. She sat on her bed, legs dangling, and told us in great detail how the Germans almost got her that morning.

As our visit concluded both Mike Collins and I were deeply moved by this story. Augusta looked intently at me, then at Mike; she held her index finger to her lips as she said, "He was in love with me, you know." Then she just stood bolt upright and said, "Look, I can still do this!" And with a devilish smile she performed her "throwing myself up onto the bed in one move" trick, and lay there to attention. "Those Germans really were bad shots, you know," she repeated, smiling up at the ceiling.

Audio File No. 11 (recorded January 12, 2010)

Oh my God, what a day that was! I'll never forget it as long as I live. I'd eaten my first hot meal in over a week and slept in a clean bed. The fog came down again. There was still a lot of fighting going on, but at least now we had fresh medical supplies, and some of the wounded were being evacuated down south to Luxembourg somewhere.

Interviews with Augusta (2013)

I had an armband around my arm. This was because if you were a doctor or medical person you had to wear an armband. I showed them my armband, and then they told me that at the seminary there were a lot more armbands. So I went to the seminary. And what do I see? A long hall, and someone was standing at the very end. The person asked me what I wanted. So I responded. They told me that everyone had been evacuated, but maybe there would still be someone here at the seminary. This person told me that everyone at the seminary had been evacuated as well. So, I said I would go back home. He asked me where I lived and I said I lived at the end of the town. So, he told me to come and look at something. I approached him and he told me to look at the Germans that were right outside. The town had just been fired upon and [we] were going to fire back. I went toward the door and waited and suddenly, "Bang!" Gunfire on Bastogne. Everything started to tremble. I saw these cellar steps, and saw people I knew. I followed them just to be with them. Then a nun who saw me said, "Hail Mary, full of grace," and told me I could not stay there. There was no room for me. So, I left.

During our trip back they asked me if we were taken prisoner, what would I say my job was. I said, "I would say nothing and put myself in the hands of the Lord." In the evening, when it was finished, I returned home. Jack Prior asked me to come back the following day at 9:00 a.m. [So the next day] I put on my uniform; the snow was quite deep by then. I wore an armband. All the city officials—the doctors, the lawyers, and some of the priests—had left Bastogne because there were Germans everywhere around the town. I walked to the barracks. Yes, I went on foot, alone. I wore my Red Cross armband for safety, just in case.

So, we arrived at the barracks. I asked myself what I was doing there. The first day, I took care of the people in the room next door. I did not say anything, I just helped. Otherwise I just waited, saying nothing, and they told me to do this or that. I had to stay in that one room. Jack Prior was there and told me to stay in the one place. There was sand on the ground because this was a horse stable [the Riding Hall]. The horses were in another place. They were calling me left and right, so I would go see what they needed me for.

My father held Jack in high regard. One day after we had been working together, Capt. Jack Prior came home with me. He was very tired. He had worked until midnight and hadn't had any sleep. He asked me if he could stay at my home. There were a lot of local people staying there because they were afraid of the bombs, and we had a large-enough house to accommodate them all. Jack thought that it would be okay to go up to one of the bedrooms, but I told him, "My God, no, that's not possible." All the mattresses were in the cellar. So I told him that he could settle himself on the divan in the dining room.

When he lay down there I brought him a handmade quilt. My grandmother had made it. She kept some animals [probably ducks or chickens]. The quilt was stuffed with feathers. It was a very warm quilt and I tucked him in with it. I filled a hot water bottle for him, too. My father was watching from the serving hatch that was between the kitchen and the dining room. He told me to warm up a glass of mulled wine and give Jack something to eat, so I did. Then when he fell fast asleep I closed the door and left him to sleep in peace.

❧

Author's note: The US Army Nurse Corps accepted only a very small number of black nurses during World War II. By the end of the war in September, 1945, there were still only 479 black nurses within the Corps, out of some 50,000, due to the quota system of the then-segregated army. As an example, in 1943, the army allowed only 160 black nurses into the Corps. The duty assignments for black nurses were limited to the care of black troops only, in black wards or hospitals. Although there was no written rule governing the treatment of white wounded by black nurses, it was generally considered inappropriate.

❧

I asked him [Jack] to give me his address before he left. Jack Prior took me in his arms and told me to stay right there. He was my friend and doctor. My father thought that Jack was protective toward me, too. My father trusted Jack Prior to look after me; he would not have done that with somebody else.

❧

Papa just wanted me to be safe, and he thought the best way to achieve my safety was for the US Army medics to take me with them. I cried when Jack left Bastogne; it broke my heart, but I knew he had to go. He spoke a little bit of French and a little bit of English. Eventually we managed to understand each other. And when he left Bastogne, I said to him, "Give me your address and I'll be your marraine de guerre." [**Author's note:** This expression, which translates as "war godmother," means that Augusta wanted to correspond with Jack—be his confidante and friend, someone who would be there for him, and to whom he could write during the war.] *He gave me his address, and fifteen days later, during lunch, my letter was returned with a 'Deceased' stamp on it. My father and Mama Caroline were there. Can you imagine my reaction? When they told me Jack Prior was dead, I was very sad. I was so disappointed to see this that I threw the letter and its contents on the fire.*

After that I met my future husband and we were married. I had two children, a boy and a girl. When I heard people say, "You are going to have a black baby," I would say whether it is black, green, or red, it's my child. There was no maternity [wing], so I don't remember what floor I was on in the hospital. There was a doctor and a midwife who helped with the delivery. When my son was born, they said, "Oh! It's a boy, and he is all white!"

EXCERPTS FROM JACK PRIOR'S LETTERS

To his mother: *Dear Ma, I guess they gave us a good write-up and I have some real exciting personal experiences to relate when I can, and yes, I was one of those sweating it out in Bastogne. Don't believe those who say they caught us asleep, 'cause when the whole story is out you will know they didn't.*

She [Augusta] was "willed" to me by her father, and when we eventually left Bastogne he was most distraught with me for refusing to take her along.

I spent the next few days assisting Major Sorrell in surgery, and, on December 27, a Glider Surgical Team arrived. This was a highly organized unit, and they worked as teams on the abdomen, chest, etc. It was their role to prepare as many casualties as possible for evacuation to the rear.

EXCERPTS FROM JACK PRIOR'S DIARY

When my oldest son was a youngster he periodically posed the question, "Dad, what's the most exciting thing that ever happened to you?" It was a question I never remember asking my dad, and I wonder today what his answer would have been. (He did not serve in World War I.) At any rate, my answer to my son, John, was always the same: recounting episodes of the Battle of the Bulge, with particular emphasis on Bastogne, since I was "[a] resident" there from December 20, 1944, until January 17, 1945. I would often tell the children the depressing story of [the Christmas of] 1944, just after I had finished reading The Night Before Christmas to them on Christmas Eve, emphasizing that this particular Christmas was neither happy nor merry for many people. For a long time I had promised myself to put this Christmas story on paper, and it is some twenty-eight years later that it is occurring.

Much of the detail of this particular period remains surprisingly fresh in my mind, and the dates and sequences I had recorded daily in my diary which I carefully kept (contrary to my army directives) and still possess. I have always chuckled over the years to see general after general (one being a past president) publish his [memoirs], which had to have had origin in a carefully kept record—maybe this rule did not apply to generals! On December 14 I was detached to the 20th Armored Infantry Battalion as their surgeon to replace their regular officer who had been evacuated with pneumonia. I had assigned to me a dentist, and about thirty enlisted men who were trained as litter bearers and first-aid men. Our detachment had armored half-track ambulances and two jeeps and was a well-trained unit. The 20th Armored Infantry was part of a combat team, the latter composed of a tank battalion, an engineer platoon, and a reconnaissance squadron.

This team, called "Team Desobry," after its infantry commanding officer, moved through Luxembourg on December 17 on what we believed was an administrative march, with eventual quartering of the unit in Luxembourg. I have always been impressed with how little information in the army filters down to personnel at my level from the Army and Corps Headquarters. Perhaps there was some virtue in this, for our assignment actually was to move into the town of Noville (about four miles northeast of Bastogne). Field Marshal Gerd von Rundstedt could have told us our assignment. As the West Front Commander, he had struck a blow in the Ardennes. He was on his way to override Belgium, Luxembourg, [and] Northern France, and penetrate to the Channel coast. The little village of Bastogne was in his way since it was the hub of a network of seven spoke-like highways and would need to be taken on the way to his capturing Antwerp, [the] largest supply point for Allied troops on the [Western] Front. Soldiers of the 9th Armored Division, [and] 4th and 28th Infantry Divisions could also have made our assignment clear, since their ninety-five-mile sector was being overrun by the German onslaught at that moment.

Arriving in Noville we found a sleepy little crossroads. My aid station was located in the pub. I found this type of building always best for our purposes since the large drinking area accommodated many litter patients. Within two hours of our arrival the little town had turned into a shooting gallery featuring small-arms, machine-gun, and tank fire on the main thoroughfare. The large front window of the pub was an early casualty, and it was necessary to crawl on the floor to avoid being hit as we treated our increasing number of casualties. Someone had selected our backyard as the "ammo" dump, and this did not boost our equanimity. Team Desobry was ordered to hold Noville at all cost, and it was not until the Battalion Command Post was hit and Major Desobry was wounded that we were ordered to withdraw to Bastogne.

Evacuation of the scores of injured had been virtually impossible. We did load four patients into a half-track at one point and just as it lumbered off, it received a direct hit from a tank and burst into flames. The four patients were unloaded and returned to the aid station, this under the gaze of the German tank commander.

Upon receipt of the withdrawal order we were given ten minutes to move out. Since I had no functioning vehicular transportation and no litters, I decided I would stay and surrender my patients to the Germans. I asked for volunteers to stay with me but the silence was deafening! It looked as if only myself and the tavern owners (an old lady and her husband who, said their rosaries aloud for two days in their cellar) would remain behind. At this point my first sergeant seized the initiative and ran into the street, shouting at the departing tanks to swing by the aid station. The tankers ran into our building after ripping off all the doors from the walls, strapped our patients to the doors, and tied them to their vehicles. The column then moved down the road to Bastogne where I assumed there was a hospital and fresh defenders!

It was not until after the war that we learned that Team Desobry had stopped the entire Second German Panzer Division which had assumed it was opposing a much stronger force. Outnumbered by ten to one, the Noville defenders knocked out thirty-one enemy tanks in two days.

Even the trip back to Bastogne turned into another firefight. In a later-afternoon fog the column was stopped by the enemy, who knocked out our tanks and harassed us with small-arms fire from the flanks. We treated serious injuries in the ditches as we waited three hours for the column to move again.

Lying in the ditch and having sniper fire chip away at a fence post beside me was a terrifying experience. I was head to head in the ditch with my dental officer. He did not wear a helmet with the bright red cross, and suggested mine was a sniper target and should be shed—a suggestion I resisted.

Many of our enlisted men demonstrated great bravery on the road, pulling tankers from their blazing tanks, driving jeeps with the injured on the hood to our aid station. Many of these airmen were soldiers whose reputations in the unit would have given no clue to the fact that under stress they could meet this challenge. This observation was to be pounded home again, time after time, in the months ahead. I have never learned who to predict will be a hero! I have often thought I'd still be in that ditch on the Bastogne road if it had not been for the arrival of a Parachute Battalion from the 101st Airborne Division. This division had been hastily summoned from a rest area and was rushed to Bastogne without sufficient weapons and suitable warm clothing. They were instrumental in getting the remnants of Team Desobry back to Bastogne on December 20 by routing the enemy.

On December 22 a German commander sent a major, captain, and two enlisted men into the town with a white flag; it was quickly rumored that they had come to arrange our surrender. Many of our defenders took this lull to shave, wash, to visit the straddle trenches. What followed is well known: We were given two hours to surrender the garrison or face complete destruction. The German commander, Lt. Gen. von Luttwitz, listed one Artillery Corps and six heavy A.A. Battalions as ready to annihilate us. General McAuliffe's reply of "Nuts!" posed a problem for their interpreters. The best they could do with the translation was: "Go to hell." We were advised that a heavy shelling would occur; it did, but I cannot recall it being any different from the usual.

Living in a city without electricity, water, food, and medical supplies was a challenge. My men scrounged port steaks, ham, and jam from the vegetable cellars of deserted homes. The combat units sent whatever food they found to the aid station, and any medical supplies in deserted doctors' offices found their way to us. Civilian physicians were always scarce in towns we took. I never remember seeing a civilian physician in all of Germany. The only explanation for this I can offer was that many physicians were members of the Nazi party, and that they took to the road before we arrived. Jewish physicians had either left the country or were in concentration camps. This, of course, had serious implications in that the civilian population descended upon our aid station as soon as the Red Cross flag was hoisted; I even [delivered a baby]! The water problem was serious; melted snow was some help, but champagne filled a big gap. Very few people have shaved and bathed in champagne as I did!

December 24 was another day of constant shelling. General McAuliffe sent his famous Christmas message to the troops, asking them, "What's merry about this Christmas?" He added that they were cold and hungry and not at home, but that they had stopped four Panzer divisions, two infantry divisions, and one Parachute division. He concluded his message [by] saying that we were giving our loved ones at home a Merry Christmas, and that we were all privileged to take part in this gallant feat of arms.

At 8:30 p.m. on Christmas Eve, I was in a building next to my hospital, preparing to go next door and write a letter for a young lieutenant to his wife. The lieutenant was dying of a chest wound. As I was about to step out the door for the hospital, one of my men asked if I knew what day it was, pointing out that on Christmas Eve we should open a champagne bottle. As the two of us filled our cups, the room, which was well blackened out, became as bright as an arc welder's torch. Within a second or two we heard the screeching sound of the first bomb we had ever heard. Every bomb as it descends seems to be pointed right at you. We hit the floor as a terrible explosion next door rocked our building. I ran outside to discover that the three-story apartment serving as my hospital was a flaming pile of debris about six feet high. The night was brighter than day from the magnesium flares the German bomber pilot had dropped.

My men and I raced to the top of the debris and began flinging burning timber aside, looking for the wounded, some of whom were shrieking for help. At this juncture the German bomber, seeing the action, dropped down to strafe us with his machine guns. We slid under some vehicles and he repeated this maneuver several times before leaving the area. Our team headquarters about a block away also received a direct hit and was soon in flames.

A large number of men soon joined us, and we located a cellar window [they were marked by white arrows on most European buildings]. Some men volunteered to be lowered into the smoking cellar on a rope, and two or three injured were pulled out before the entire building fell into the cellar. I estimated that about twenty injured were killed in this bombing, along with Renée Lemaire. It seems that Renée had been in the kitchen as the bomb came down and she either dashed into, or was pushed into, the cellar before the bomb hit. Ironically enough, all those in the kitchen were blown outdoors since one wall was all glass.

I gathered what patients I still had and transported them to the Riding Hall hospital of the Airborne Division. At about 2:00 a.m. Christmas morning the bomber returned and totally destroyed a vacant building next to the smoldering hospital. I have often wondered how the pilot picked this hospital as a target. There were no external markings, but, as some of the men said, the bomb must have come down the chimney. Many tanks and half-tracks were parked bumper to bumper in the street in front of the hospital, so it seems probable he simply picked an area of high troop concentration.

Before our unit left Bastogne we dissected the hospital rubble and identified the majority of the bodies, including Renée Lemaire. I brought her remains to her parents, encased in the white parachute she so dearly wanted. I also wrote the following commendation for her and forwarded it to our commanding general:

From: Capt. John "Jack" Prior, MD
SUBJECT: Commendation for Renée Bernadette Emilie Lemaire (deceased)
To: Commanding General
10th Armored Division
APO 260, US Army
(Attn: Division Surgeon)
Thru Channels:

As Battalion Surgeon, 20th Armored Infantry Battalion, I am commending a commendation for Renée Lemaire on the following evidence:

This girl, a registered nurse in the country of Belgium, volunteered her services at the aid station, 20th Armored Infantry Battalion in Bastogne, Belgium, December 21, 1944. At this time the station was holding about 150 patients since the city was encircled by enemy forces and evacuation was impossible. Many of these patients were seriously injured and in great need of immediate nursing attention. This girl cheerfully accepted the herculean task and worked without adequate rest or food until the night of her untimely death on December 24, 1944. She changed dressings, fed patients unable to feed themselves, gave out medications, bathed and made the patients more comfortable, and was of great assistance in the administration of plasma and other professional duties. Her very presence among those wounded men seemed to be an inspiration to those whose morale had declined from prolonged suffering.

On the night of December 24 the building in which Renée Lemaire was working was scored with a direct hit by an enemy bomber. She, together with those whom she was caring for so diligently, were instantly killed.

It is on these grounds that I recommend the highest award possible to one, who though not a member of the armed forces of the United States, was of invaluable assistance to us.

Jack T. Prior
Captain, M.C.
Commanding
Renée Bernadette Emilie Lemaire
Place du Carré 30
Bastogne, Belgium

I have never heard what action was taken on this commendation.

It was at this point that I visited the acting Division Surgeon of the 101st Airborne Division and requested he make an effort to bring medical help to us.

I had not visited the Airborne area up until this time, December 23. Their headquarters and hospital area was in a former Belgian barracks compound. Major Davison, their surgeon, listened as I detailed our hopeless situation, and he assured me it was impossible to bring a glider surgical team into the area because of the weather, and because the Germans would knock down anything that tried to fly in. He also stressed the fact that his paratroopers were used to being cut off (Normandy and Holland), and this situation was the expected.

Davison then brought me to a Riding Hall where I saw the unbelievable! There on the dirt riding floor were six hundred paratroop litter cases; I cannot recall the number of walking wounded or psychiatric casualties. These patients were only being sustained, as were mine. I did see a paratroop chaplain (armed with a pistol and shoulder holster) moving among the dying. While I was there someone announced that General Patton was only a few miles out and that the road in would be opened momentarily. This evoked loud cheers and whistles from all those in the Riding Hall. GAS gangrene was rampant there, aided and abetted, I'm sure, by the flora on the dirt floor.

Major Davison did drive into the German lines later with a white flag in an attempt to arrange a truce for medical evacuation. He proposed to take out one German wounded to two American, but this was refused by the ranking German medical officer. I returned to my aid station very depressed. It is ironic, but surgical help did arrive in the person of a Major Sorell on December 26. He came in via a Piper Cub to care for sixty patients; a mistake in decoding from the Airborne headquarters had occurred, and the figure of six hundred surgical patients was interpreted as sixty. Major Sorrell had a basic instrument kit and a few cans of ether. When he saw the Riding Hall and the mass of patients needing surgery, he was overwhelmed. His decision was to take care of the GAS-infected extremities first, feeling that he could save more lives this way, as against the time it would take to do one belly, one chest, or one head case.

[**Author's note:** The chaplain was Father Francis Sampson, who was later taken as a POW near Bastogne. I think that Jack was referring to Maj. Douglas T. Davidson.]

On December 23 hundreds of C-47s droned over Bastogne and multicolored parachutes fell to earth, each color representing a [certain] category of supplies. Food, ammunition, blankets, and medical items were eagerly gathered. There was no attempt at control collection, and each unit corralled whatever fell in their vicinity. Many parachutes fell in German territory, and we later learned that they relished the famed "C" rations. Even the parachutes were utilized as bedding in our hospital. I can recall Renée Lemaire leaving her duties and rushing into the backyard to get a chute. She wanted the silk for a wedding dress. She invariably was beaten out by a soldier and always returned empty-handed.

From Jack Prior's Last Diary Entry:

I recently discovered a battered old molding shoebox in our storage area. It contained letters I had written to my parents during my army time in Europe. The box survived undisturbed for over sixty years, and had been transported from my family home in Vermont through various apartments and households over the years here in Syracuse. The envelopes were carefully dated by my father; some letters were short "V" mails, while others went on for several pages. While censorship precluded information that could be of use to the enemy, they did contain my thoughts and vignettes encountered as a battalion surgeon with a rapidly moving armored division as it went through France, Belgium, and Germany. I commanded a medical detachment of thirty men, litter bearers and vehicle drivers, and we were responsible for the medical care in and out of action for an armored infantry battalion of 1,500 personnel. We ran a sick call when in bivouac and were first on the scene for the care and transportation of the wounded in combat. Try as I might, I could not remember clearly many of the incidents I wrote about so long ago.

My detachment with its six vehicles was invariably at the tail end of the infantry and tank column. I was a notoriously poor map reader, although I had gone through map school at least three times. To further complicate the situation most of our movement was at night with blackout conditions. One night riding in my lead jeep vehicle we got far behind and lost the column. I came to a T crossroads at about 3:00 a.m. and there was no road guide posted to direct our group. I carefully examined both road possibilities, hoping that the tank tracks would make my decision for me to go right or left. This was of no help, so I made a random choice. We drove all night, never finding our unit, and stopped at dawn on a hill overlooking a tiny German village below.

Believing that my column had most likely bivouacked in the village, my driver and I went into the small town. It was 6:00 a.m., very quiet and not a soul to be seen. We circled the center where a small water fountain was operating and my driver said, "Captain, we'd better get the hell out of here." I concurred, and as we drove back out the road we encountered an infantry unit (not ours) minesweeping the road we had just traversed. A full colonel swore at me, saying the road we had just traversed had not been cleared. I assured him that there were no mines and the village contained no enemy. Later I learned that the colonel and his unit spent several hours in a firefight in the village, and I suspect that he is still looking for me.

I did find my unit several hours later. As our column sped through village after village I was intrigued to study the reaction of the human population. They hung white sheets over their doors and watched stone-faced as we passed. The children waved and cheered as their parents looked on disapprovingly. Rarely we were offered a bottle of Schnapps which we didn't dare drink. Occasionally we saw boys in their spotless Hitler youth uniforms and wondered how they would be controlled when the army of occupation became in charge. At nightfall we bedded down in civilian homes for some needed slumber. The homeowners were hurriedly displaced despite angry protests as we allowed fifteen minutes for them to evacuate. It was obvious, however, that they were prepared since they emerged with packed suitcases. I spent the night elsewhere with friends.

Since our battalion mess section rarely caught up with us, my thirty-man detachment became responsible for procuring and preparing whatever food we could find. Living off the land dictated a diet of eggs and chickens we gathered from nearby farms. One day our search party returned with seventy eggs and two chickens. Later that week we were treated to a goose and a turkey. One day some vegetables purported to be onions turned out to be tulip bulbs which had very little taste. Canned C rations and chocolate D bars were always on the menu. One of our men created an "ice-cream parlor," mixing D bars with fresh snow.

One house we liberated contained a new shiny small motorcycle. I thought we should appropriate this and I put it in my half-track ambulance, [to] use it for sport when the war ended. The problem presented was who was going to kick-start it because we had encountered booby traps many times when trophies like this presented themselves. We solved the dilemma by ordering a German civilian to turn the cycle over. After a prolonged investigation for hidden wires he turned it over on the first try and it worked perfectly. I allowed my sergeant to ride it when there was a lull in the fighting; in return he was responsible for the cycle's maintenance. One day he was stopped by a full colonel who asked who owned it; when he said Captain Prior, the cycle was promptly placed in the column trailer, never to be seen again (rank has its privileges).

Letters from home were our number-one priority, and the chief charac-teristic [of mail delivery] was that it was sporadic. One private was assigned as the unit mail clerk. Each day he drove back many miles to the division headquarters where the incoming letters were sorted. Often he traveled thirty to forty miles only to return empty-handed. When this occurred he would be ostracized, cursed, and relegated to the last place in the mess line. There were times when we received no letters for a month. Rumor had it that all European mail had been misdirected to the CBI [China Burma India Theater]. There were said to be three million letters involved. I recall receiving seventeen letters in one day and then none for several weeks.

Time really had little meaning to us. I recall arguing with my dental offi-cer over what day of the week it was. He maintained that it was Wednesday, and I was certain that it was Tuesday. When the dust settled we brought in a referee who settled the argument, advising us that it was actually Thursday.

I describe one incident when our detachment set up in an abandoned schoolhouse. The many windows were blown out and it seemed we would be [there] for a while, so as shelter from the cold wind we elected to plug up the windows. We found multiple, tightly bound large packages in the basement which we carried up and used to close the windows very nicely. It wasn't until a German civilian wandered by and interpreted the underside labeling that we were informed that the packages contained TNT. The school was promptly abandoned and we found new shelter very quickly.

My children often ask me if I was ever injured by enemy fire, and I have to admit to one embarrassing episode. When there was a lull in the fighting medical officers were ordered to lecture to their troops on a variety of subjects. We were mandated to cover venereal disease and the uses of their first-aid pack immediately after being infected, and before medical help arrived. We stressed that rather than shouting "Medic, medic," they should evaluate their injury and possibly save their life by using the tourniquet the pack provided.

As a youngster I had a fascination for watching lightning, and one day during the continuous shelling in Bastogne I stood in the open door of my aid station, watching the incoming artillery display, which recalled my childhood lightning interest. One shell landed in front of me and I was blown twenty yards back into the building against the back wall. My chest burned and I shouted to my dental officer that I was hit, and did nothing to evaluate my *injury. When the officer started cutting into my fleece jacket I rallied enough to protest and ask to simply uncover the area. It proved to be a 50-cent piece of shrapnel which was hot but had rested on my skin without the slightest laceration. I kept the souvenir for some time but decided to eliminate my keepsake from my lectures to the troops.*

Paul Prior's Recollections of His Brother Jack

Jack's son Jeff Prior suggested that I contact his uncle Paul to get more information about his father, and graciously provided phone numbers and contact details. I sent these on to Mike Collins, who expertly conducted the interview and collated the following information from Paul Prior.

Childhood

When Jack was in school he was quiet and never really played any sports; even when he got into high school, he only played a little bit of tennis. He was sort of a good student—not superior, but very adequate. During his high school years, Jack joined CMTC (Citizens' Military Training Camp), which was federally funded throughout the United State so that high school students could learn military drilling and training during the summer. Jack was at Fort Devens in Massachusetts for a month and a half or so, and when he came back from there he was gung-ho. He'd put on some weight; he was stronger, and was interested in boxing. When he was back from CMTC he became a man. At that time he wanted to go to the Golden Gloves boxing tournament. My mother almost burned down the house when she heard that. He even had a punching bag. He almost had his head knocked off down there at CMTC.

He finished high school and attended the University of Vermont, where he went out for football. He never played a down in high school, but he made the freshman team. While at University of Vermont his first year, he got involved with the ROTC, and he got very gung-ho with that too. When he graduated in 1938 he got the highest honors in ROTC at UVM. All he wanted to do was join the army. He would have been a second lieutenant, but my mother was going to go crazy; she wanted him to go to medical school. He applied and was accepted. He was going to turn down the acceptance to medical school to join the army, but my mother won that battle, and he went to medical school.

He obtained high honors at medical school and he graduated in 1943. He trained in New York State and was inducted into the army as a medical officer. He got engaged to a beautiful young nurse during his internship in New York, but he left to go overseas. My mother and father were enthusiastic about him going to war, and they were proud to see him in the uniform. When he came home from leave before he left for Europe, he was a first lieutenant. We were all glad to see him, and we just thought, He is going to war, and that's the way it is. During Jack's time overseas my mother was much more guarded and my father was enthusiastic; she wanted him to come home and start a medical practice in St. Albans.

Wartime

He would write letters periodically, but there were gaps in the writing, apparently because of where he was located. He never told too much in the letters, just that he was with the division. My parents were totally surprised that in the Sunday New York Times *he was mentioned as the only surgeon in Bastogne, and that he received the Silver and Bronze awards too. Someone called them to tell them that Jack was located there.*

Postwar

When he got home from the war he was pretty depressed. It took a few years for Jack to open up about the war. He did not want to talk about things. When the war was over, he became the ski doctor in Germany; then when he got discharged and he came home, my mother said he would go to his room and stay there. Basically she was very worried about him. It was the combination of the Dear John letter and his experiences overseas that [made him] depressed.

He also felt he was not trained well enough, and he wanted to gain a medical specialty, so he decided to take a year of pathology at Binghamton City Hospital in Binghamton, New York. He became a pathologist later on after passing his boards.

When he would come home on weekends he would go for a walk or hike up different trails around St. Albans with me [brother Paul], and he really enjoyed being outside.

He met this girl who was a stenographer over in Binghampton during that first year of his pathology residency, who had lost her husband during the war. He ended up marrying her.

He told me later about how a German officer was captured and the boys wanted to shoot him, but Jack took care of him. Somehow the German took Jack's name down, and later on when Jack returned to Bastogne, the officer met him there.

He repeatedly told me about two nurses in Belgium; he could not say enough good about these two people. All he did was talk about the two nurses.

DEATH NOTICE FOR JOHN T. "JACK" PRIOR

November 23, 2007

Dr. John T. "Jack" Prior, 90, of Manlius, died Friday at home. Born in St. Albans, Vermont.

(Published in the Syracuse Post Standard on November 25, 2007)

SILVER STAR CITATION: CAPTAIN IRVING L. NAFTULIN

Dental Corps, Medical Detachment 20th Armored Infantry Battalion, United States Army, for gallantry in action at Noville, Belgium, on December 19, 1944. Subjected to intense enemy fire and the danger of exploding gasoline, Captain Naftulin, battalion dental surgeon, assisted in the rescue of three wounded men from a blazing ambulance. His gallant achievement reflects great credit upon himself and the military forces of the United States. Entered the military service from Ohio.

Dr. Irving Lee Naftulin said at the time: *"There is no use for a dentist at an aid station unless they want him to do only first-aid work. He doesn't do any dentistry whatever there."*

Dr. Irving Lee Naftulin, acting as a medical superintendent at the time, was also in charge of rescue efforts and miraculously escaped serious wounds. He said, *"We had thirty-four wounded in the building at the time and seven were in the basement. They were screaming with pain as the fire started there. Sgt. Kenneth Souder, an engineer from Michigan, found a tiny hole at the rear of the basement. While the rest of us fought the fire he tied a rope around himself and went in and got out two of the wounded men before he was overcome himself. He was pulled out by Tech 5th Grade Osborne Wayner of Stanardsville, Georgia. Another engineer named Riordan got out four more, and Corp. Bernard Morrissey of East Providence, [Rhode Island] got out the last man."*

Obituary, Irving L. Naftulin (died February, 1984)

Palm Springs, California: Irving L. Naftulin, DDS, 76, a former Freemont dentist who lived the last eighteen years in Palm Springs, died after a lengthy illness. Surviving are his wife, Jean; a daughter, Joyce Fisher, of Madison, Wisconsin; a son, Dr. Don Naftulin, also of Palm Springs; five grandchildren; and a brother, Louis Naftulin, of Phoenix, Arizona. Dr. Naftulin was a Freemont dentist for thirty-five years, and during his time in Freemont he was very active with the Beth Israel Temple. Known as the most decorated dentist in World War II, he had served in the Armored Division. He was buried at sea with full military rites. It was suggested that any memorial contributions be to the Cancer Society in his name. Information was received locally by the Keller-Ochs-Koch Funeral Home.

Letter to Jack Prior from Maj. William R. Desobry

The following is a letter to Jack Prior from his commanding officer, Maj. William R. Desobry, who was still in the US Army, US Army Center and Fort Knox, dated January 15, 1973.

Many thanks for your kind letter of December 20 and the very interesting article. Please excuse my delay in answering, but I was subjected to one of the so-called minor operations over the holidays. By the way, the first since I was wounded at Noville.
I might be able to answer some questions for you.
*   **First:** *The 20th AIB had been in a training situation for about a week. I was a relatively new commander, having come over from the 54th AIB. The battalion surgeon was evacuated really for imbibing a little too much from his medical stocks, plus others. The battalion was preparing to attack through a small bridgehead over the Saar River*

through the Siegfried Line and on to the river Rhine in the vicinity of Mainz.

Second: *Shortly after midnight on December 16, 1944, we received orders to move at first light to Luxembourg to go into First Army Reserve. We did this and moved out in combat formation, which was our SOP. Our route took us across the Moselle River and on to Luxembourg city, where we bivouacked that night in the villa of a Shell Oil representative on the edge of the city. We had absolutely no information of a German attack in Belgium.*

After we had been in position about two or three hours, the Germans ran into our outpost in the east and were stopped. We could hear them moving around us to attack from the north, which they did just before daylight. Later I learned this was the entire 2nd Panzer division, which had the mission of seizing Bastogne from the north. When the fog lifted in the morning it was a shock to us to learn that we were in the low ground with the Germans on the high ridges on our east and north. These are the consequences of not having maps. We were ordered to seize and hold Noville because it was at the extreme range of our supporting artillery.

We held on all morning, repelling numerous German tank attacks. At one time German tanks made it into the town but were destroyed. It was obvious that we were in a difficult position, so permission was asked to withdraw to high ground about one mile to our rear. This was denied.

About noon we received word that a reinforcing parachute infantry battalion from the 101st Airborne Division would join us. Their battalion commander agreed to attack at 2:00 p.m. in order to seize the high ground, from which the Germans were giving us fits. So at 2:00 p.m. we attacked. The Germans chose identically the same hour to launch another attack. The result was quite hectic and resulted in losses on both sides. We were able to seize part of our objective but couldn't hang on, so we pulled back into Noville.

The rest of the day consisted of numerous attacks from all sides with little gained or lost. I was wounded early in the evening, was fixed up, and evacuated to the Parachute Regimental aid station in

Bastogne by one of their jeep ambulances, and further evacuated to the
101st Airborne Division Mobile Surgical Hospital and operated on.
Shortly thereafter I was captured in an ambulance on the way back to
an evacuation hospital.

Some interesting facts about the battle of Noville are:

1. We were attacked by the entire 2nd Panzer division and
   stopped them. This division was then diverted to attack west.
   It spearheaded the entire German attack and got the Moselle
   River [probably the Meuse River], the farthest advance by any
   German division. The remnant of this division pulled back
   into Germany after the Bulge was over. But every armored
   vehicle in the division was lost. We counted over thirty-two
   German tanks destroyed at Noville at the end of the day.
2. When you withdrew to Bastogne the next day you had to fight
   through the 26th Volksgrenadier Division ,which had cut the
   highway. Had we withdrawn the day before this would not
   have happened.
3. Our little force held the northern approaches long enough for
   the 101st Airborne Division to secure Bastogne. If we hadn't,
   Bastogne could never have been defended because the Germans
   would have beaten the division into the city.

Third: On the morning of December 18 we moved out once again
for Belgium. We had been given a route to follow but had no maps
or destination. We navigated by sending our cavalry out in advance
and they marked the route and guided us at crossroads. Early in the
day we were ordered to send billeting parties to Belgium, all of which
were later rescinded. In the middle of the afternoon I moved up front
to Task Force Cherry to see if he knew more than I did. I found him in
a Belgian gasthaus [a German-style inn or tavern]. By chance there
was a civilian radio giving out the daily news. Since I spoke some
French, I learned of the big German attack in the Ardennes. This was
the first Cherry and I knew of the situation we were getting into.

Fourth: *Later in the afternoon I was ordered to Bastogne to receive directions. I arrived there after dark after having worked my way through TF Cherry and O'Hara. It was then that I first learned of the big fight, the German breakthrough in the area, and of our orders to defend Noville.*

Fifth: *We moved through Bastogne and onto the road to Noville under MP guides from VII Corps, which was evacuating Bastogne, as we still had no maps. We proceeded up the road to Noville with a small cavalry screen to the front and occupied Noville shortly after midnight. We immediately took up defensive positions, sending cavalry units to the east and north to contact friendly or enemy units and give us warning. We had little information because this is the nature of a breakthrough of this magnitude. Our cavalry made it all the way to Houffalize, the town where Patton on the south and Montgomery on the north eventually sealed off the Bulge later in January. There we contacted large German forces moving west, not south, to Noville. We heard nothing from the east, but small friendly units and some individuals reported Germans coming from that direction.*

This has been a little long-winded, but I thought you might be interested. As you say, information at the time was scarce, but that is the nature of war.

Once again, many thanks for your thoughtfulness in writing. I found your article to be one of the best. I have sent it to the Armored School Archives to be kept as reference material.

My very best wishes,
William R. Desobry
Major General USA
Commanding

Recollections from Veterans
of the Battle of the Bulge

Author's note: The following recollections come from other veterans who were in Bastogne during the Battle of the Bulge. Mike Collins and I interviewed some of them for our other books, *The Tigers of Bastogne* and

Voices of the Bulge. Others appeared in the documentary about Augusta Chiwy, *Searching for Augusta: The Forgotten Angel of Bastogne* (2014). They provide the reader with a broader picture of the situation there at the time.

Leon A. Jedziniak, Medic Co. A, 501st Parachute Infantry Regiment, 101st Airborne Division

TRIP UP

We had just gotten back from the Netherlands, and we were still getting new equipment when we were told to get on the trucks to go up to Bastogne.

I walked through the city when we arrived and they told us to go to Neffe, and we ran into the Germans pretty soon after we left Bastogne. The first night I was with ten guys and we were with the 705 Tank Destroyers. That was the only time I was warm during my time in Bastogne. They took me out and I was with a different unit for two days, but I do not remember the number. Most of the time we did not have enough men for a full platoon, especially once guys were getting wounded or frozen feet.

THE "NUTS!" RESPONSE FROM GENERAL MCAULIFFE

It was a real good booster; the guys like hearing that one.

ZEROED IN

The Germans knew where we were, even in the foxholes. I had one man get killed next to me by a shell. Later on, I had two young kids, sixteen or seventeen years old, who surrendered to me when I had a guy on my back, bringing him back to the aid station. I used them to carry the guy on my back. I found a rifle and I had one of the guys hold the muzzle and the other the stock until I found an MP to take the prisoners and the wounded to an aid station.

WHAT A MEDIC HAD

The medical kits had been returned back to supply and we never got new ones. I wound up with an officer's aid kit; the morphine was frozen, and there were sulfa pills and other drugs. I carried the morphine under my armpit to keep it warm. Trench foot was rampant. Treating the wounded, you did the best that you could. The second day we had snow, the temperature was down to zero, and a lot of the men had summer uniforms. I took clothes of dead soldiers to treat the wounded, and we did not have many litter bearers to help get wounded men.

CHRISTMAS EVE

I was at Mass in seminary with the priest there, and we gave some money that we had to the church.

BREAKTHROUGH

We started to get some stuff, like the ten-in-one rations from those guys who came in with the tanks. We got the wounded out as quickly as we could when the road opened. The civilians came out finally; they had been hiding.

AIRDROP

I happened to be in a farmhouse the day before, and I had a Coleman stove, and the other guys had a crock of oleo and potatoes, and we had french-fried potatoes. For a long time we did not have food. That day the airdrop was the most beautiful [sight] you could see. A hundred goddamn C-47s coming and dropping parachutes; they even dropped in doctors for the hospital. We were using [part of] the seminary for our aid station. The P-47s coming in [knocked] out the tanks too.

Author's note: Some of the German veterans that I interviewed made frequent references to the "Jabos" (pronounced *yabows*—Allied fighter bombers). They told me how demoralizing it was to see columns of German armor blown to pieces from these highly effective machines.

Recollections from William Kerby, 20th Armored Infantry Battalion

BASTOGNE

I saw [Naftulin and Renée] walking around town together a few times that week. I saw the black girl too.

CHRISTMAS EVE

On Christmas Eve, we were told that the Germans had parachuted men in white uniforms around Bastogne. I posted guards at each corner of the building. My post was facing the aid station about thirty-five or forty yards away. All of a sudden the night sky was brighter than the Las Vegas strip from the magnesium flares that the German bomber pilots had dropped. A few seconds later, the first German bomber dropped his first bomb on the aid station, a direct hit. The second bomb landed in our backyard and wiped out all our empty foxholes, leaving only the latrine . . . Thank God!!

The second German bomber dropped down to strafe us with machine-gun fire. All the GIs started to shoot at the plane with machine guns, rifles, and carbines. He dropped a bomb that was a direct hit on a building two doors from ours. That building just happened to be a distillery. The bottles flew all over, and some were found two weeks later in the snowbanks.

I faced toward the aid station and Renée Lemaire was helping some wounded GIs out of the building. She went back in the building and came out helping more wounded, yelling, "Help, help, water, water!" The flames from the fire were intensifying. She was safe and sound out of the building but decided to go back in and help. Renée Lemaire never returned. The woman was a heroine and a saint. I am an eyewitness to these above facts.

Recollections from George Waters, Battery B, 796th Antiaircraft Battalion

We arrive, assemble, and park our vehicles in the town square. We enter a building midway in the block on the north side. It is about the the third building from the west end of the corner. It appears to be a kind of bar, or hotel or cafe. Tables and chairs, a brick floor, and has a stairway at the rear that leads to the basement or cellar. We enter the cellar from the main floor by way of the back stairs. We move to the front of the basement where we use candles for light, but no blankets. We seem to be playing a waiting game of one sort or another. Ed, Sam "Blackie" Zipparo, Al Knocky, Clyde Stevens, Red Busato, Joe Bengal, Tom Penny, and I are among those present at the front of the cellar. We find a large barrel of beer, find that it is warm and decide against further consumption. It's dark and we are attempting to get settled for the night when we receive our first "Bedcheck Charlie" who flies over and starts the most unforgettable night of our lives.

As the sound of the plane drones overhead, the fact that we can hear it from our sub-level catacomb substantiates the thesis that he is indeed very low. Immediately after passing over we hear a thunderous explosion. The brick floor over our heads visibly trembles up and down numerous times like ripples over water. The changes in air pressure do the same thing to the ears of each man. If one cups the hands over the ears and alternately presses and releases the pressure on the eardrum, one can understand the feelings we experience here.

To say that we are frightened would be to put it mildly. We look at each other wondering if another blast will follow and if it will be even closer. This kind of defenseless onslaught with no escape or ability to divert the attack leaves us with the feeling of abject helplessness, and totally terrified. Some knees knock so loudly that someone calls out, "Come in." One nerveless fellow, however, calmly rolls over and sleeps, Sam "Blackie" Zipparo. Suddenly a voice screeching with excitement sounds above all the chatter. "Hurry up and give us a hand; the hospital across the square has been hit!"

Some look at one another, some ignore the plea. Clyde Stevens, Albert Knocky, and I, along with two other GIs I don't know, ascend the stairs and cautiously walk to the front and out into the street. We listen for the drone of an engine. We hear none. We have no trouble picking out the building, or what remains of the hospital. It had the red cross painted on the roof, like so many of the helmets in Normandy. The flames guide our steps as we cross the square. The building looks as though a large cake knife has started at the top front and sliced down diagonally to the first-floor rear. The cellar way at the rear is open and the activity is at a feverish pace. We look, wonder what we can do, weigh the danger of another plane attack, and turn to go back to the cellar we call home. The firelight will guide the next bandit with relative ease, if there is one.

After the second step, my conscience brings me to a sudden halt as it takes charge of my first and better judgement. I'M NOT BRAVE, and don't profess to be, but I say to Al and Clyde, "What if we were in there and those who could help turned and walked away because of self-preservation; what would we think and how would we feel about them?"

What can we do? We return and go to the rear to the cellar door that is open and help to pass out the survivors until the wounded have been evacuated.

Recollections from H. Neil Garson, Co. B, 80th Armored Medical Battalion

BEFORE THE ENCIRCLEMENT

I was charged with making sure the bandages were holding, and using the morphine shots before the soldier was put on trucks. I was located southeast of Bastogne, nearly three miles outside. I was close, too close for comfort. I had to first worry about not being captured by the Germans, which almost happened when we selected a gasthouse [gasthaus] for an aid station. I got some sleep after being up for twenty-four hours, and about midnight I heard a banging on the door, a lieutenant from the engineers, and he said, "You have five minutes to get out of here; the Germans are right behind." They were blowing up trees to cover the roads to slow up the attack of the Germans. After that we were about two and a half miles outside of Bastogne. During the siege and before the encirclement there were a group of black soldiers who helped get some of the wounded [out] of Bastogne before the encirclement. We kept in contact with our men who were caught on the inside of Bastogne via radio.

101ST ARRIVE

I was a PFC then, and I was put up on the crossroads to wave the drivers with the ambulances to make a right turn to where the aid station was, outside of Bastogne. I was there when the 101st Paratroopers came marching down the highway toward Bastogne. We gave them stuff we had collected from our ambulance, and blankets. They weren't in their usual woolen uniforms which were warm, and here it was very cold out. Here they came marching in; they dropped off from the trucks about a half-mile from where we were. We tried to give them what we had leftover from the wounded in the ambulances. Before we had time to set up, I was at the crossroads, and here comes a whole company or battery of 105 cannons; they were retreating. Suddenly a colonel in a jeep caught up with them, turned them around. They were also used to keep the Germans from capturing the town. As for our men, they were suffering trench foot. Later on I saw many men suffer so much [from this] that we had to cut off a limb. We had a vehicle, a truck, which was fitted out as a place where the doctors had everything necessary for removing limbs.

TREATING THE WOUNDED, AND SUPPLIES

We had about one hundred wounded that we had to get back to a general hospital. I found myself putting the wounded into an ambulance or a truck, and I gave them drops of morphine. I told the drivers to take the wounded to the nearest general hospital in Paris. That way most of the wounded were evacuated. We only had rations during this time, but later the company got some food from the service cooks. We always had a food canteen. I discovered that the German prisoners had bandages made of paper and that they were very low on supplies when we took care of prisoners. I had my own medical kits, filled with material to keep the soldiers from bleeding to death when wounded.

AFTER THE BREAKTHROUGH

When Bastogne was liberated by Patton's Third Army, we pulled into there and found that their ambulances were a wreck. The center of Bastogne had been bombarded. The battalion aid station was damaged very badly; there were several men who were hit with shrapnel. We met our ambulance drivers and kept on moving wounded men out.

Recollections from Paul Bebout,
501st Parachute Regiment of the 101st Airborne

When I arrived in Bastogne I was in pretty good shape. I didn't need any medical attention right away. The fog was so thick you could hardly see in front of you. At first it rained but then it started snowing, and I think we had about three to four inches. The only place to go was the foxhole. I had my foxhole dug up at the OP [observation post] where I had my phone so I [could] communicate with my mortar crews.

—

After we arrived in Bastogne it started snowing and we only had summer clothes that we'd had since we'd come out of Holland. When the German breakthrough came we went up on trucks from the campsite we were in there in France. It was dark when we arrived in the city of Bastogne, and that's where we unloaded. We were the first truck there. The trip up was kind of scary. I didn't know where we was going or why, and we had to watch for German airplanes; we didn't have no air cover. I had a rifle but half of my section didn't have weapons. But we saw the troops that were holding the line come running through and we had to stop them and take their weapons and they kept on running. They thought the whole German army was after them, and I guess that they really was.

———

I was east of Bastogne and I suspect that I was about a mile from the city. That's where I set up my outpost. The 10th Armored Division came pretty close to my OP. They fired on the tanks with a 37mm "pop gun" and kind of scared them a little bit and made them back up.

———

We all laughed when we heard what McAuliffe had said to the Germans. That was something. They come with a jeep and white flag and a colonel of the 327th met them. They wanted to see the commander. So they brought them in to meet our commander. They wanted to know when we were going to surrender. At first they didn't know what to do. Another executive officer there said it's getting close to Christmas; that's why the boss said "Nuts." That was a good idea. So McAuliffe wrote it on a piece of paper and gave it to them but they didn't understand what "Nuts" meant. We explained that [it] means "Go to hell." McAuliffe had his hands full; he was completely surrounded. I saw him but I never had the pleasure of talking to him.

———

C–47s come in and dropped us some supplies. We had some food and some ammunition then, and we could use what we were holding back. Some of the C–47s got shot down, but we did get some food in. I ran outside the place that was used as a rifle range and watched, I was just so happy to see them.

———

On Chrismas Eve they brought us in a box of candy and some food. As soon as the C–47s had dropped supplies, the crews went and brought the stuff in [and] then they handed it out. That was nice, but I'd seen some of those planes [get] shot down. It was nice to have Christmas. I think we had church services too.

I don't know where Father Sampson was at, but we had a Protestant preacher there. He held a little ceremony and I went to it, in a bombed-out house.

I came down with frozen feet—[frostbite], as you call it. I was treated by a front-line medic. All our medical battalion had been captured. The guy who treated me was a dentist but he looked like a front-line medic. The aid station I was treated in was a rifle range. I met some colored artillery guys from the big guns, 155mms. There was cement blocks; it was a nice long building. Dirt floor, but it had a roof on it, and that's where they stacked us up in there. It was about two hundred yards from the headquarters where McAuliffe was. We had this one guy that I thought was a front-line medic who took our boots off and checked our feet. He just left us lying there; there was nothing he could do. There were quite a few of us there with frozen feet. I was hoping that Patton would put his [foot] to the pedal.

Author's note: The Riding Hall at the Heintz Barracks was also used as a rifle range, and still is to this day.

Patton was the only help we could get. We was attacked by three armored divisions. It got you to thinking, If I'm gonna get out of here, we got to end this. Patton saw us and said he never commanded such a brave bunch of men in his life. He decided to take us, so from then on the 501st Regiment, 101st Airborne, was with Patton.

Recollections from Ralph K. Manley, 501st Parachute Infantry, 101st Airborne Division

Many civilians were in their cellars, and this, that, and the other, and a number of them, of course, it was quite a wonder whether they had home canning, and things of that nature, so they might have [had] canned meat. This was before the days of freezers and that type of thing. They would cook meat and put it into jars and pour lard over it, which would be [melted] fat from hogs, to preserve this, so we could get a jar of meat with them if they might share with us, and scrape the lard off of it, eat the cooked the meat from that. [They had] lots of jellies and apples and things of that nature; even in digging some of the foxholes around, some of them came across gardens that had some potatoes left and things like that—dark black potatoes that had been frozen and so on, but it was something to eat, and one of us even killed a chicken that had about froze to death, I think, and ate the raw chicken in order to have something to eat.

Of course we did not get a resupply of K rations; K rations [were] all we had in the paratroops; we didn't have the C's or the D's or what have you, that troops that had trucks or vehicles [had], because we had no vehicles there. [We didn't have any rations] to supplement the apples or potatoes or whatever, or the canned fruits from the local people, who were scared to death; many of them, of course, had gotten out, but others stayed there, and so they too were subjected to the bombing and shelling that we were.

INTERVIEW WITH MEGHAN SPRINGER, JACK PRIOR'S GRANDDAUGHTER

I moved to Belgium three or four years ago, and when I moved, I never thought I would have any family here or any relationship to the country. But when I went to see Augusta for the first time, it was very surreal, because when I opened the door, there were all these pictures of my family members in her room. My grandfather was a pathologist, and he was a fantastic pathologist. He was known throughout Central New York for his work. He was really admired, and he chose pathology for a very specific reason—there was no suffering. There were no human cries; there were no distressed family members that he would have to deal with.

When he was in the aid station, he had nothing but [what amounted to] a box of Band-Aids, and that, from what I've been told from numerous family members, was such a . . . it left him feeling completely helpless, because he wasn't able to do anything to save the lives of these young men. But it also left him with an extreme aversion to pain and suffering.

I think I'm the only one . . . I'm one of two surviving members of my family that know Augusta. I feel like I'm fulfilling part of Grandpa's wishes in some way. To be able to talk to her and to know her. Unfortunately, she has aged and there is a language barrier, so the relationship between us is not particularly profound. But being able to have a relationship and being able to have seen her multiple times, I feel like I am doing something for my grandpa.

Actually, later on in life, my grandfather had a live-in nurse at his home. This nurse was African-American, and in some ways my grandpa really, really related to her. He wanted her to have a better life. He did a lot of things to try to support her education [so she would] be able to support herself financially. That was really fascinating to members of our family, because of the fact he had finally let somebody into the house. He was so proud, and to have some support . . . and then the fact that the nurse was so . . . she was so tough—from a very tough neighborhood. She had two children in her teenage years and was kind of a typical statistic. And Grandpa tried to help her out and to coach her and support her in making the right decisions for herself and her family, in terms of her education. If you think about it, it's kind of interesting that later on in life he continued to have that kind of influence on people.

My grandfather would never have been that kind of man that would write a letter to [Augusta] and express his affection, because he wasn't capable of doing that. I am quite certain that he cared for her as someone who was a really crucial person in his life. And they shared and they went through the worst times together, so they had an incredible bond. But I don't think that he was ever able to express his appreciation for her in a way that you or I would.

Later on in life we had a neighbor who has a GI truck that is an exact replica of the trucks they used for riding around in Bastogne. It was an open-air jeep, and I arranged for my grandpa to have a ride in this jeep. And he was so excited about that, and it was . . . he really lit up. At the time he was going through some really difficult health problems and his spirits were really low. And for him to go on this ride, you know, it lifted his spirits. And for me, it was a bit confusing, because in my mind, if the war had been so traumatic, why was he so excited about getting on this jeep?

I asked my mom about that, and she said, "I think it's because Grandpa loves soldiering and he loves the institution of the military." So despite the fact that he had gone through so much trauma and pain and suffering, and witnessing so much pain and suffering, because he came out of the war physically unscathed, I think he still had this unusual—well, maybe not unusual, but surprising—amount of affinity for the military, and, of course, he encouraged all of his sons to pursue a career in the military.

When my grandmother gave birth, my grandfather couldn't be anywhere near here. He stayed in a waiting room. Anytime the children became sick, he was extremely distressed. He immediately tried to get help as soon as he could, and he would leverage all of his contacts at the hospital to get [the] kids to see the best doctor right there and then. He was very, very averse to pain, and as a result of that, his own children don't complain very much and they don't express pain. And they aren't particularly affectionate. Grandpa was not the kind of man that would put . . . growing up in my generation, saying "I love you" and expressing my affection for my parents and my loved ones is something I feel totally comfortable doing. But my grandfather didn't have that trait . . . and I would frequently put my arms around him and tell him I loved him, because that is who I am; [that's part of] my culture. And I would do that a lot, especially as he aged. And he could never reciprocate that. He could never tell me, "I love you."

Grandpa grew up really poor in Vermont. He was really poor. He wasn't living on the street, but his family was definitely on the lower end of the economic spectrum. And because of that, he is really kind of the perfect example of the American dream. He sought education and he was extremely dedicated to his career. He pushed as hard as he could and became a great doctor. All of that because of education. And so he had an appreciation for the less fortunate because he knew what it was like to be poor. He was never discriminated against, but he knew what it was like, and to some extent—I remember my mom said to me, He was from Vermont, and being from Vermont was kind of like being from the backwoods. And people would look down on him a little bit for being from that part of that state. And that could have factored into his . . . the way he supported Augusta. But I think in terms of color, I can't tell you that my grandfather was color-blind. I don't think I would see it so much in terms of race; I would see it more in terms of social class.

My grandfather was a very complicated man. He was not an easy man in any way. He was never the kind of grandfather who would give you a big burly bear hug and kiss you when you saw him. He was not particularly affectionate. But that doesn't mean he wasn't caring or cold in his heart or anything. He just had a different sense of his personality. In the context of the war and Augusta, he never expressed his feelings closely or his real sense of affection for her and how deep his relationship was with her, or how important it was to him. He mostly talked in very broad strokes about the war.

I think it impresses me that at the time Grandpa went to war, he assumed there was a woman waiting for him. He was engaged, and I think that in and of itself—in fact, that woman decided not to wait for him. The story of that particular dynamic, that particular relationship of a man going to war, and having an engagement, and having the woman waiting there for him, to kind of keep his spirits and his morale up, is such a common story. And I wonder whether or not when he met Augusta, the fact that they never, as I understand it, had a relationship probably is related to the fact that he was engaged and committed to another woman back home.

But I don't think he had [any] pretentions. He was extremely shy, and I don't think it was so much humanity as it was, he just, you know, he had an appreciation for people who were discriminated against in more social-class terms. [Later on in his career], in the hospital, he was known for really knowing ... he would walk around with my mother and would talk to all the staff. He would talk to the house carpenter at the hospital, he would talk to all the receptionists; he knew all the parking lot [attendants]. He knew all those people by name and he knew what their families were doing and who had recently had a baby. He made a point to pay attention to them, which was interesting, because in the hospital a lot of doctors keep a very firm line there and they don't often make those kinds of efforts. And so my mom was always very impressed that he made that kind of contact.

Interview with Student Nurse Andrée Giroux

During the occupation I remember seeing Augusta and her brother quite often in Bastogne when I was young. They were a little older than me so we weren't really friends, but we did talk sometimes. I don't remember seeing any other Congo people there. I had something in common with Augusta because I was training to be a nurse at the General Hospital in Namur, but I was only in my first year. My father worked for the town hall as a clerk. Augusta's father Mr. Chiwy was a very good veterinarian; he treated our cat once. I was just fifteen when the war began. My older brother Didier was eighteen, and he was taken to Germany to work as forced labor. We didn't see him for four years. He was one of many young men that were taken away from Belgium by the Nazis; many didn't return.

———

I remember our father saying that we had to prepare the cellar because the Germans may be returning. We had a large cellar beneath our house and it had a wood-burning boiler, so it was quite warm. We all worked hard the whole day, moving things we needed down there. I don't remember being frightened at the time. I was a teenager and much more interested in my friends, boys, and music than bombs and wars. One of the girls I went to school with had her head shaved by the Resistance because she practiced "horizontal collaboration" with the Germans, but I didn't know what that meant back in the day. We had all been liberated by the Americans in September, and I didn't get horizontally collaborated once; some of my friends did, though.

———

My mother and father were very worried because I remember them telling me that most of their friends had left Bastogne. As far as I knew, my best friend Blanche [Dombier-Hardy] was also still in town. She was also training to be a nurse. My family didn't own a car back then so there was not much chance of us leaving. The sound of the fighting was getting closer and some bombs even fell on the town. I was just miserable that I couldn't get to see any of my friends. I had a sister who was six years younger than me. Up until we had to stay in the cellar I hadn't had much to do with her, but now I found myself entertaining her to pass the time.

———

We could hear a lot of bombs and guns but the fighting hadn't reached the city yet, because some people were still walking around. I think that I saw the veterinarian Henri Chiwy and a few other people talking on the rue du Sablon. All the shops were closed by now. That was a problem, but my mother was a good cook and she used to make lots of preserves, so we had plenty to eat. I had an old gramophone in the cellar and some records. My favorite singer was Charles Trenet. [**Author's note:** Trenet was also Augusta's favorite singer.] We also had a radio to listen to broadcasts from the BBC. That was *very dangerous during the German occupation, but now the Americans were here it was safe.*

Two American soldiers asked if they could join us in the cellar. My mother was not happy because she said if the Germans found them with us in our home, we would all be shot. My father said that they had traveled a long way to risk their lives for us, so we owed them. I agreed with him. My parents didn't speak any English, but I knew a bit from watching Hollywood movies, so I translated. They taught us some card games and sang songs to us. One of them was very handsome but I can't remember their names. I was very sad because I had heard that my friend Blanche had left town.

A bomb exploded right outside our house, and the street-facing wall in the cellar almost collapsed. There must have been a sewer pipe or something behind the wall, because about twenty rats ran into our cellar. My father and the two soldiers managed to kill most of them. Then they put things against the wall to stop more getting in and to support it from completely collapsing. My younger sister screamed for hours and my mother was terrified, but I was okay. I wasn't afraid of rats. I didn't like them but I wasn't afraid of them either. We shared our food with the soldiers and they shared their food with us. The bombing was getting worse and it was snowing outside, but we were still warm in the cellar, thanks to the stove.

I woke up in the middle of the night with a big rat on my chest, sniffing at my mouth. That must have been one they missed earlier on. One of the soldiers grabbed it off me and beat it until it was flat with his helmet. Then he wrapped it in newspaper and took it outside.

Down in our cellar we were getting low on water. One of the soldiers took a few of our empty pans and returned with them full of snow that we melted on our boiler. The soldiers had coffee with them and I think we drank more coffee than water. I'd had trouble sleeping anyway, but now I was wide awake the whole time. My father talked my mother into letting him go out to see if he could get something fresh to eat. She protested at first but had to admit that she was getting sick from all the tins and jars of food, so she let him go. A few hours passed, and he hadn't returned. We were getting very worried indeed. One of the soldiers offered to go out and look for him. I wish I could remember their names.

———— ‿ ————

This was the most terrible day [**Author's note:** December 22 or 23, 1944; she wasn't sure] *of the war for me. The bombing stopped for a while and a neighbor came to tell us that my father had been crushed beneath a wall in the Latin Quarter. Papa was dead! I couldn't believe it. None of us could. The soldiers did what they could to console us, but I cried all day; we all did. What were we going to do without him? We all loved him so much. Sometimes I still hear his voice in my head and sometimes he still visits my dreams and hugs me like he used to do when I was little. Poor Papa. That evening I heard that my friend Blanche had volunteered to work for the Americans. I told my mother that I wanted to volunteer, too. I couldn't stand being in that cellar anymore.*

———— ‿ ————

I remember Christmas Eve we heard the German airplanes bombing Bastogne. It was terrible. Everything was shaking and my sister wouldn't stop screaming. I desperately wanted to go and join my friend Blanche, but it was too dangerous to leave the cellar. The two soldiers left that evening, though. We never saw them again after that.

———— ‿ ————

It was the most miserable Christmas that I'd ever known. No presents to unwrap, no good food. Just three females trapped in a stinking cellar. I decided there and then that enough was enough, and even though my mama wanted me to stay, I went over to the army barracks. I couldn't believe how many wounded young American men were in the barracks. The best thing I remember was seeing Blanche again. She was covered in blood and she stank, but we hugged and screamed when we saw each other, then we cried when I told her about Papa. She told me that one of her brothers had been killed and three of her cousins. The Americans had good food and cigarettes. I took some home for Mama and my little sister. I just remember praying that it would all soon be over. Bastogne was a ruin.

LETTER FROM ELIZABETH THIENPONT-DUGAILLEZ TO JEFF PRIOR

Elizabeth Thienpont-Dugaillez wrote:

Hi Jeff,

I used to translate some letters from Augusta to your dad. It became hard for me because I had so much trouble with her handwriting. I know one thing: that she was in love with your dad. One of her letters said that "only you and the person translating my letters will know my secret." I feel like I know Augusta a little bit. What a remarkable man your dad was, and I love the fact that his life will be documented and his legacy will go on.

Elizabeth

LETTER FROM MARTIN KING TO JEFF PRIOR

Dear Jeff,

Your narrative gave me a great insight into your father's character. I'd like your permission to use selected passages from this if I may. I had blown up copies made of all the photographs that you sent of your dad for Augusta, and had them framed. I campaigned relentlessly for nearly four years to get her the recognition she deserved. You made some excellent observations about the Belgians, though they can be a cold lot. Augusta's family was very supportive while I was campaigning. Writing is a solitary occupation but ultimately rewarding. The 10th Armored Division's Western Chapter made me a sort of honorary member for all the work I did in arranging for the new plaque to them.

I also believe that your dad was a man of great honesty and integrity, and hopefully this is reflected in my manuscript. There are no stains at all on the man's character in my book; in fact, it's maybe a little over-reverential, but such is my respect and admiration for his memory. None of this would have been possible without your invaluable assistance, for which I am eternally grateful.

Well, back to the grind, Jeff; believe me, this is a labor of love. It has to be, because the publisher doesn't advance anything for this like they did for [my earlier book], Voices of the Bulge. *My wife Freya, whom you met in Albany, is a nurse. With regard to my literary pursuits she's extremely encouraging; she has to be, because I need a lot convincing. I'm not as confident or assertive as I make out. So far I've written and rewritten the whole manuscript three times, and it occasionally drives me to distraction. I'm determined to see this to its conclusion, however, because it isn't about me. It's about those who deserve wider acknowledgment for their deeds. My loyalty to this cause is unremitting and unquestionable; that's what sustains me. Thanks, Jeff*
Warmest regards,
Martin

EXCERPTS FROM JEFFREY PRIOR'S JOURNAL

This journal provides wonderful insight into Jack's character, and about what occurred when he returned to Bastogne with his family to commemorate the fiftieth anniversary of the Battle of the Bulge.

My Memories of the 10th Armored Division Fiftieth Reunion Tour Back to Bastogne, December 1994—by Jeffrey Prior

BASTOGNE DAY

Gigi works for ABC News, and rides along on our bus looking for stories. This changes the atmosphere on the bus completely; everybody is looking for their fifteen minutes of fame. Gigi has all of a sudden made people microphone-crazy. My father and I become nauseous. Some of these stories are becoming rather larger than life. Les delivers loquacious details concerning the background history on the Bulge; Tiny is worried that the ABC gals will spell his last name incorrectly; Lucky claims that he was hit with shrapnel from a Tiger tank in that foxhole. However, I do enjoy Ralph Bret's story about having a Christmas tree in his tank.

Our first bus stop is at the Mardasson memorial center, located just outside of Bastogne. It honors the memory of the 76,000 American soldiers who were killed or wounded during the Battle of the Bulge.

Next stop in Bastogne is at the 10th Armored Division [commemorative plaque]. This is a newly created brick monument with a bronze plaque honoring the 10th Armored Tigers who fought and died here. Les and Don removed an American flag, thus revealing this plaque honoring the 10th Armored Division. Don Olson delivers a speech and ends with a memorable quote: "Greater love hath no man or woman, than they lay down their life for a friend." Next, the mayor has a few words to say in Luxembourgish. Finally, Les says that we have been back to Bastogne eleven times since 1965, and this occasion has a special significance; at this moment he is interrupted by the marching band. End of speech.

Our buses unload at the Bastogne museum. This is where my father meets up with Augusta. She is traveling with her family; it's an impressive entourage: a son who has a PhD in physics, and a daughter who is a doctor. Two cute little grandkids are traveling along also. Augusta and my dad hug and speak through an interpreter. My first impression is how tiny Augusta is. I wish I could speak French because she seems so friendly and compassionate.

At this point we also get the opportunity to meet Renée Lemaire's sister, who has been invited to the celebration. She also seems friendly, but once again we are fighting the language barrier. Her extensive makeup instantly reminds me of the gospel singer, Tammy Faye Bakker. Outside the building there is a dedication ceremony recognizing all the American states that were involved in the battle. Inside the museum, there are documentary movies showing real footage of the battle. My father lays down flowers on behalf of the United States in front of the Unknown Soldier. He then backs up and gives a proud, smart salute. This impressed me, because I could tell how much pride he had for his unit.

Next the mayor lays down flowers on behalf of the town of Bastogne. Finally, Don puts down flowers representing the 10th Armored Division. At the museum my dad gets angry with Don because he seems preoccupied with the ABC News team. My father tells him that the blue bus is making him nauseous, especially Mike Heyman, Lucky, and Les, who stay within arm's reach of ABC anchorwoman, Gigi.

Next an unexpected Belgium marching band leads us to the town square. The people of Bastogne seem excited to greet us in mass numbers; the sidewalks are congested with civilians, and American flags are flying from the windows. It reminded me of the Fourth of July celebration in any American town. Augusta and my father are leading the 10th Armored Division, to his third-story aid station, for the plaque ceremony dedicated in honor of his heroic Belgian nurse, Angel of Bastogne, Renée Lemaire. Next, all the vets gather behind my father, Augusta, and Renée's sister. Speeches are made by Les, Don, and the mayor. My father and Augusta remove the American flag to present the plaque for the first time. The mayor removes his native Belgium flag. Now the Belgium people will have two flags representing this historic monument. My father folds up the American flag and hands it to Augusta. The flag is a tribute to Augusta for her humanitarian volunteer nursing services that helped so many wounded American soldiers. Finally, my dad puts down another wreath in front of the building.

Next, we march to the General McAuliffe monument. He was the division commander of the 101st Airborne Division. Bastogne was completely surrounded by the German troops and he was asked to give up, or be annihilated. McAuliffe's now-famous reply was, "Nuts!" which means "Go to hell." A crowd develops in front of the memorial, so I climb on top of a nearby tank to take photos. My father lays down the first wreath, and Don and Les follow with subsequent wreaths. This was a secondary stop to the aid station memorial, and was not nearly as emotional as the aid station dedication.

Our next visit is to the town hall. The list of speakers in consecutive order would be: the mayor, Les, Don, and my father. Augusta, Renée's sister, and an interpreter are also center stage. Don delivers a condensed speech; he later gives my father the entire draft. My father felt terrible that this man, who worked so hard on his talk, was told to keep it brief. Don claims, "We will never forget the nightmarish month we spent here, but are truly appreciative for your love, courtesy, and respect, given to all vets." Les fires up his pipe during Don's short speech.

My dad hits a home run with an emotional, concise, informative lecture about what happened in Bastogne and Noville to his 20th Armored Infantry Battalion. My father tells the crowd that when he was chased out of Noville to Bastogne, he had 150 patients, many serously wounded, some walking wounded, and others who were experiencing battle fatigue. "My medical staff was not properly trained as nurses," he said. "Most were in fact truck drivers, stretcher bearers, or clerks. On December 23, 1944, I was joined by the angels of mercy, Renée and Augusta; both volunteered in helping me take care of the wounded. I told the mayor that I was returning for this emotional visit, and could you please locate my nurse, Augusta."

Not only did [the mayor] find Augusta, whom he hugs [at this point], but the mayor also located Renée's sister, who is also standing beside him. I am so pleased to be standing next to Augusta, and equally emotional to be in the presence of Renée's sister.

At this time my dad awards the American flag to Augusta that was covering the plaque at the aid station. "Although I have questionable authority to do this, I want to make Renée's sister an honorable member of the 10th Armored Division," and he presents her with a 10th Armored Division pin. He closes by saying that Bastogne will always be hallowed ground.

We toast with peach-flavored champagne and beer. This town hall [event] was very emotional; Dick Malone has tears running down his face next to me, and I have to admit, I did too. Many photos are taken. Eddie has me take a picture of him standing by Augusta. Augusta's family is also in attendance for this event. Thankfully, ABC News corespondents were present to document the euphoric atmosphere. I also noticed that Gigi had a copy of "The Night Before Christmas" in her possession.

A luncheon for the 10th Armored Division takes place at a nearby restaurant in a conference center. My parents, Augusta, and I are at the front table with name tags. Augusta is seated next to Dad. However, we learn later that Augusta's family was not invited to the luncheon, which seems terribly rude. I do not know who was responsible for this oversight. An attractive blonde is coordinating the show by keeping my father on the move and taking care of translating languages. Lunch is excellent: red wine, salad, fancy filled potatoes, asparagus, and a main dish. The mayor gives a pithy speech, with a little brunette translating into English after every paragraph. It amazes me how an interpreter can remember so much, without losing the content of what is being said.

After lunch, the town awards the guests at the front table with a few presents. Augusta receives a book on the Battle of Bastogne; my parents receive crystal glasses with a Bastogne logo; and Renée's sister is given a present too (sorry, I do not recall what it was). Following lunch, a local historian gives a lecture in front of a blackboard, outlining the course of the battle. The talk *is a little dry, and after a while, I notice that the town mayor cuts him off by coughing extensively. Finally we break into two bus tours. The women take a shorter tour around Bastogne. Meanwhile, the vets and I get the extended tour of battle sites around Bastogne, with the lunch historian providing details. All the vets seem very interested in hearing where certain divisions were located; it reminds me of our bus tour around Waterloo.*

My father and the mayor lay two wreaths in front of the aid station. My father is being interviewed by ABC News, and he points out where the wounded were located, the church, and the backyard. We also get the opportunity to enter the basement. Bloodstains are still visible on the basement floor, and my dad points out to Gigi where the tavern owners (old woman and her husband) were saying rosaries for two days. Also I learn at this time that the mayor's father and six civilians were later shot in Noville by the Nazis, under the assumption that they were aiding American soldiers.

THE DEPARTURE

My parents and I say our good-byes to Augusta and her family. We kiss her good-bye, and wish her well. Augusta makes such a kind gesture; she invites us over to her house on Wednesday to spend the day. It's unfortunate that my father never deviates from a plan; he was never known for his spontaneity. He thanks her for the generous offer, but claims we must be in Paris with the travel group on that day. Dad has a few more kind words; it's obvious how much he appreciates her help years ago, and how much he respects what she accomplished later in life.

As people board the buses to return to the hotel, my father has a reflective moment. We walk a short distance, and he says to me "I want to look around this street once more, because it's the last time I'm ever going to be here." He then asks me a pondering question: "I wonder if my grandchildren will ever remember the sacrifices that we made in this small town years ago?"

Irving Naftulin was a dental officer that was assisting my father at his aid station in Bastogne. He was wounded after a bomb blast and had scrapes and blood on his face. He was shell-shocked, which resulted in short-term blindness. He was no longer helpful, and my dad was able to send him home. When mentioning Irving Naftulin, my father always had nothing but kind words to describe the man. In fact, after the war, Irving was traveling through New York, and he stopped by our home for a visit.

Author's note: I really can't thank Jeff Prior enough for his patience, his humanity, and his invaluable assistance in bringing this story to the public.

Interview with Augusta (2013)

I had a lot of character. During my second meeting with Jack Prior, I explained to him that I am small because three of my vertebrae were crushed [during the explosion]. As for the color of my skin, in August I'm the color of the sun; when we worked together in Bastogne, I was the same color as the snow.

E-mail from Craig, Webmaster, 10thArmored.com

Dear Martin,
Thanks again for your work on [Augusta's] behalf, and on the 10th Armored plaque. A newsletter was mailed to Augusta as well, and I expect someone will translate it for her. Both are wonderful accomplishments that honor very deserving souls.
Best regards,
Craig

ABOUT THE AUTHOR

Martin King is a well-qualified British military historian, author, and lecturer who's had the honor of reintroducing many US, British, and German veterans to the World War II battlefields where they fought. He lives in Belgium, near Antwerp, where he spends his time writing, lecturing, working with veterans' organizations, and visiting European battlefields.

Widely regarded as a leading authority on European military history, Gen. Graham Hollands referred to King as the "greatest living expert on the Battle of the Bulge." Stephen Ambrose called him "our expert in the Ardennes." Fellow writer and notable historian, professor Carlton Joyce, said, "[King] really is the best on the Ardennes."

King's campaigning work for World War II veterans recently came to the attention of some leading military personnel at the Pentagon, who cordially invited him to present his latest work, *The Tigers of Bastogne*. He has been awarded Service to Education certificates by the USAF and NATO. In 2015 King's documentary feature, *Searching for Augusta: The Forgotten Angel of Bastogne*, received no less than seven Emmy Awards for Best Historical Documentary.